I0795873

Behold an Animal

FLASHPOINTS

The FlashPoints series is devoted to books that consider literature beyond strictly national and disciplinary frameworks and that are distinguished both by their historical grounding and by their theoretical and conceptual strength. Our books engage theory without losing touch with history and work historically without falling into uncritical positivism. FlashPoints aims for a broad audience within the humanities and the social sciences concerned with moments of cultural emergence and transformation. In a Benjaminian mode, FlashPoints is interested in how literature contributes to forming new constellations of culture and history and in how such formations function critically and politically in the present. Series titles are available online at http://escholarship.org/uc/flashpoints.

A complete list of titles begins on p. 254.

Behold an Animal

Four Exorbitant Readings

Thangam Ravindranathan

NORTHWESTERN UNIVERSITY PRESS | EVANSTON, ILLINOIS

Northwestern University Press
www.nupress.northwestern.edu

Printed in the United States of America

10 9 8 7 6 5 4 3 2 1

Library of Congress Cataloging-in-Publication Data

Names: Ravindranathan, Thangam, author.
Title: Behold an animal : four exorbitant readings / Thangam Ravindranathan.
Other titles: FlashPoints (Evanston, Ill.)
Description: Evanston, Illinois : Northwestern University Press, 2020. | Series: Flashpoints | Includes bibliographical references and index.
Identifiers: LCCN 2019046422 | ISBN 9780810140714 (paperback) | ISBN 9780810140721 (cloth) | ISBN 9780810140738 (ebook)
Subjects: LCSH: French fiction—21st century—History and criticism. | Animals in literature.
Classification: LCC PQ683 .R38 2020 | DDC 843.9209362—dc23
LC record available at https://lccn.loc.gov/2019046422

For Ravishing Devi and Devilish Ravi,
my mother and father

In my childhood I was a fervent worshiper of the tiger . . . . I used to linger endlessly before one of the cages at the zoo; I judged vast encyclopedias and books of natural history by the splendor of their tigers. . . . Childhood passed away, and the tigers and my passion for them grew old, but still they are in my dreams. At that submerged or chaotic level they keep prevailing. And so, as I sleep, some dream beguiles me, and suddenly I know I am dreaming. Then I think: this is a dream, a pure diversion of my will; and now that I have unlimited power, I am going to cause a tiger.

Oh, incompetence! Never can my dreams engender the wild beast I long for. The tiger indeed appears, but stuffed or flimsy, or with impure variations of shape, or of an implausible size, or all too fleeting, or with a touch of the dog or the bird.

—Jorge Luis Borges

Contents

Acknowledgments

In fact a kind of joy sustained me through the writing of this book. The garden by night brimmed and my soles wore thin. Many conversations and friendships through these years knowingly (and sometimes unknowingly) made place for dogs and bits of hedgehog. Animals led me ultimately down the longest and most affecting road I could find through literature and philosophy; and the night unexpectedly endeared me to the day.

My inexpressible appreciation goes first to Timothy Bewes, wondrous companion and fearsome reader; and to my playmates and chief co-conspirators in the night: Michelle Clayton, Virginia Krause, Jess Regelson, Antoine Traisnel, Tina Tryforos, David Wills, Vazira Zamindar. What follows emerges in so many ways from these deep imaginative affinities and immense solidarities.

I am sincerely grateful to Dick Terdiman, Susan Gilman, Gianna Mosser, Christi Stanforth, Nathan MacBrien, Steven Moore, and the wonderful Anne Gendler at Northwestern University Press, for their support and hard work on this book. An especially warm thank you to Warren Motte and Stephanie Posthumus, whose close, thoughtful reading of the manuscript was a great help, and a real honor.

For reading/hearing and believing in this work at various points, I wish to thank ever so warmly Elizabeth Weed, Denise Davies, and the *differences* team at Brown; the Cogut Institute for the Humanities; Jonathan Strauss and the faculty and students of French at Miami University, Ohio; Derek Schilling, Jacques Neefs, and the faculty and students of French at Johns Hopkins; Suzanne Guerlac, Jacques Khalip, Elissa Marder, Alain Romestaing, Pierre Saint-Amand, Allan Stoekl, and Alain Trouvé. A special thanks to my friends in French Studies at Brown, including Stéphanie Ravillon, Gretchen Schultz, Lewis Seifert, and Annie Wiart. Without such a community of intelligence and sympathy, I might not have continued.

I have been inspired and accompanied throughout by writers, teachers, colleagues, and friends. But also by my students: I'd like to mention here especially St. Clair Detrick-Jules, Christine Dreyer, Liana Ogden, Antonia Shann, Christian Suarez, Sonja Stojanovic—sometimes, when my thoughts made little sense to me, they picked them up and put them together again.

Warm thanks to my *amis d'enfance*—Nathalie Dupont, Éric Trudel, Gaspard Turin—and to my sister, Sadhana Ravindranathan, for believing in me; to the *animalistas* Connie Crawford, Nancy Jacobs, Thalia Field, Iris Montero, Ada Smailbegovic, for generative, inspiring exchanges; to kindred beings whose paths have run closely alongside mine and to whom I knew my questions mattered deeply: Branka Arsić, Ariella Azoulay, Réda Bensmaïa, Stuart Burrows, Hannah Freed-Thall, Cary Hollinshead-Strick, Joanna Howard, Maurizia Natali, Adi Ophir, Jessica Severens.

For vital spaces real and unreal over the last many years in which to write, think, speak, not speak, dwell, and grow quietly, I am indebted to my dear friends Clotilde Baret, Arundhati and Neel Chattopadhyaya, Beatrice Jauregui, and Prakash Megha. Thank you, finally, to my amma and bubu, for being my strength and inspiration.

An earlier version of chapter 2, "Unequal Metrics: Animals Passing in La Fontaine, Poe, and Chevillard," was originally published in *differences* 24:3, 1–35. I am grateful to be able to republish it here by permission of the copyright holder and the present publisher, Duke University Press.

Behold an Animal

Prologue

In the old days I had too much respect for nature. I put myself in front of things and landscapes and let them alone.

No more of that, now I will *intervene.*

I was then at Honfleur and was getting bored. So I resolutely brought in some camel. [*Alors résolument j'y mis du chameau.*]

—Henri Michaux

There was a time not so long ago when the presence of animals in a story made its world appear more compelling and complete, more like our own. There were the bullock-carts and horse-drawn carriages, the cattle and fowl, the hunting dogs and running prey, the horses that shared men's fate in battle, the ominous or auspicious bird, the occasional ferocious beast. Such authenticating references to a known world would have worked rather like what Roland Barthes memorably called the *reality effect*: so whole and uncontroversial that those places in the text seemed to draw their substance from reality itself, as if dispensing with the operations of language or "meaning." "*We are the real*," such elements seemed to say; in them a certain danger (of what derives its certitude precisely by excepting itself from analysis) vied with a certain laziness.[1] At these points, the text claimed to be connecting with—even directly borrowing from—the very flesh of the world, apparently without need (and therefore beyond suspicion) of mediation or construction. True, Barthes was writing about how Flaubert's and Balzac's prose registered the material texture of, say, Western, urban, bourgeois life, then served it up as sheer (or mere) reality. But the assumption and confidence he described—namely, that words in a text can point directly at real things and lives—encapsulate more fundamentally the wager of literary realism itself. "The 'real' is supposed to be self-sufficient," wrote

Barthes, it is thus "brandished like a weapon *against* meaning, as if, by some statutory exclusion, *what is alive cannot signify, and vice-versa*" (146; my emphasis).

This book was born of the unnerving sense that, today, animals—or "what is alive"—are no longer the self-evident assurances of a story's realism but, rather, riddled entities, "vague" places where literature most self-consciously admits the weirdness of its commerce with the world. Time and again I noticed this in recent French novels (these being the books I most often read and teach). Almost invariably, when an animal appeared, rather than attesting to the referential "well-meaningness" of a text—rather than *montrer patte blanche* (showing its hand), as a good animal should[2]—it tended to be hard to read or clearly "see." An undecidedness blurred the text in these places, so that it was not easy to say where the animal started or ended; what in its ostensible vicinity was in relation with it; how, once it was there, its presence could be distinguished from its absence; or what precisely was at stake in supposing it to be a bit of life or a bit of meaning. Weren't animals supposed to be vouched for by "real life"? Here they posed rather, as if by an inverse logic, the enigma of what literature itself was in relation to world. Somewhere along the way they had turned into the tokens of literature's *un*realness—far from being transparent, self-standing indices of the world, they were a reminder that literature's objects had never been entirely, or only, or properly, those of earthly reality.

The reality effect is a trompe l'oeil, of course—this had been Barthes's whole point, and there is no better testament to the power of the "referential illusion" he was describing than the fact that we persist in reading (or in remembering) his 1968 essay as saying the opposite: that this *was*, essentially, how literature's realism worked. Rather, Barthes singled out "useless details" such as the barometer mentioned in Flaubert's "Un cœur simple" because he deemed "realist" *only* such details, while insisting that literature itself was "fundamentally, constitutively unrealistic." Indeed, he would write: "Literature is unreality itself, or more exactly, far from being an analogical copy of reality, *literature is on the contrary the very consciousness of the unreality of language*: the 'truest' literature is the one which knows itself as the most unreal, to the degree that it knows itself as essentially language; is that search for an intermediary state between things and words; is that tension of a consciousness which is at once carried and limited by the words, which wields through them a power both absolute and improbable."[3] Regarding realist narrative in particular, he would clarify: "Realistic literature is narrative, of course, but that is because its realism is fragmentary, erratic, confined to 'details,' and because *the most realistic narrative imaginable develops along unrealistic lines*" (*The Rustle*, 147–48; my emphasis).

If this book's focus is not on realism or unrealism (so that this opening is itself a trompe l'oeil . . .), one of its earliest and deepest intuitions does concern that distribution, and where it has tended to leave animals. My working hypothesis, long before I could articulate it in such terms, has been that animals only *seem* to be literature's real*est* "details." In fact, when one looks more closely, tentatively resisting the assumption that "*[they] are the real*," they turn out on the contrary to describe rather the *unrealistic lines* (to stay with Barthes's term) along which a narrative's thinking may be developing. This is not to say the creatures considered here are fantastical or allegorical, far from it—they are of identifiable species, their presence is easily explained, they move on the same plane as the human characters; indeed, in each case this contact is what brings them into the story. Yet "the animal" in these novels is never a simple, positive, or accountable entity. In each case, it is as if it were at the same time something *over*determined—shaped and preceded and overlaid by everything we think we know about that animal, its natural and unnatural history, its various inscriptions (its "bio-graphy") in literature and philosophy—and something continually *under*determined—for what on earth (let alone in a text), in the end, is an animal? Both forms of lack/excess consign it to a potentially interminable reading, arrested typically by the assumption that the animal is being cast, precisely (or rather *im*precisely), *as that* animal, that it is in that capacity somehow self-identical and self-evident, and that therefore what it *is* is not at issue. In fact, it may well owe the gist of its legibility to this way it has of preceding itself. Recall Nietzsche on this: "If I create the definition of a mammal and then, having inspected a camel, declare, 'Behold, a mammal,' then a truth has certainly been brought to light, but it is of limited value, by which I mean that it is anthropomorphic through and through and contains not a single point which could be said to be 'true in itself,' really, and in a generally valid sense, regardless of mankind."[4]

What do (we think) we see when (we think) we see an animal in a text? Is it innocence, affection, anxiety, or melancholy that leads us to believe—or pretend to believe—that we *recognize* it from prior knowledge or from the "real world"? *Behold, an animal.* In these moments we readily suppose that literature is drawing its life and truth from the real. Or perhaps we are comforted to conclude *from* literature that animals still share lived space with us. (So that there must have been a moment, not easy to locate, when the burden of proof shifted, and literature started vouching *for* the world.) Considerations of vulnerability, suffering, empathy, justice, interspecies relation and difference brought to bear on literature's animals entail especially earnest versions of this naturalist assumption. Here lies a quandary: with each ethical reading we reinstate and renaturalize "the animal" even as, in our lives, animals assume increasingly unnatural and mediated forms, from endangered or artificially preserved populations to the multi-million-dollar pet industry, to the colossal, largely invisible, daily "rendering" of flesh into meat and ("innocent") sign that Nicole Shukin investigates with devastating clarity in *Animal Capital*.[5] With each realist reading we ourselves unwittingly supply animals' missing limbs, presence, perspective, blood, breath, so that their *un*wholeness, their *un*worldliness, made systematically unthinkable in our world, also goes unprocessed in our stories. A kind of retinal persistence—what in the brain-eye collaboration leads us to see things in the gaps—becomes the hallucinatory principle for reading animal life (endlessly back) into literature.

An altogether more unsettling experience of reading opens up when we resist the naturalist temptation and defer "recognition." What we then face when we "behold an animal" is a place in a text where two mirrors face each other (the creature and the figure, life and literature, flesh and intertext). And as would happen when two mirrors face each other, there is an endless multiplication of the image. The reflection is so infinite that, technically speaking, we could continue to see the image long after the thing itself has vanished. (In this way, the animal is not altogether unlike a star.)

Animals are vehicles of literature's signifying and figurational powers, writes critic and essayist Tiphaine Samoyault, noting that "the catalog of figures and forms of meaning attached to a given animal can strip it of all literality—not to say of all existence, to situate the statement on another plane."[6] Intrigued by literality's (or existence's) way of *missing* in such instances, Samoyault considers how the sheer meaningfulness of the animal may be blocking, precisely, any encounter with its "impossible" realness. This she demonstrates by means of a reading of rats in literature (Shakespeare, Hofmannsthal, Freud, Montale, Bataille): the repulsion the rodent elicits animates its work as a figure; at the same time the figure when pressed may reawaken the rat's intolerable fleshliness. In the case of Hofmannsthal's *Letter of Lord Chandos*, where Chandos experiences a crisis of meaning—and specifically of writing—by imagining the agony of the rats in his cellar where he has laid poison, Samoyault notes that, in the throes of death, the rat offers an unbearable—*dis-figured*—image of the human. Thus we are faced with a curious chiasmus, for if "literally, the rat's life is untenable, figuratively, its death too is untenable" (236).

Meditating on the enigma of Hofmannsthal's *Letter*, namely, on what the mortal agony of rats might mean *for writing*, Samoyault ventures that the rat, repeatedly cast as "a limit case" in literature, is the "place of a conflict between the letter and the figure" (237). Written in response to the question "Why the animal?," this short essay, in treating the rat as a sort of boundary condition, in fact makes legible a truth about literature's animals, a truth hidden in plain sight, and only further dramatized by contemporary literature's generation of vanishing (or faint or flickering) creatures. This truth concerns, in the end, the irreducible *literariness* of animals, the way an animal pulls discreetly yet insistently at the line "between literality and figurality" (231)—or between what deconstructive analysis would call the thematic level of the text (what it says) and its rhetorical level (what it does). Perhaps it is simply that the animal configures—or reveals—these two as intimately, chiasmatically connected, where one keeps turning into the other or, more trickily, concealing or passing for the other. Beyond a point, presumably, the "literal" (thematic, referential, and by extension material, historical, narrative, affective, ethical) animal is too literal to bear—beyond predator, prey, food, captive, commodity, curiosity, or vermin, it mirrors our automotor and heteroaffective life, including its "flesh and finitude,"[7] its drama, its insignificance. The animal as animal is experienced as burdensome or unbearably light. It vied with our ancestors for habitat and resources—humans responded by destroying the forest. It still vies with us, arguably, in the ultimate frame, for meaning (Who and what survived? Under what conditions? What mattered in the end?). We flee from unseemly promiscuities (or vague disquiet) to a more figural realm, where the animal, gathered in new configurations, merges with the forms of our thought, detaches itself from the breathing body, yields more abstractable meanings. But neither is this a "clean" operation. The figure never uses the whole of the animal, so that something is left unsubsumed and protrudes—an extra limb, incongruous flesh, an unseemly gait. A repressed literality remains, to compromise the figure, reconnect it to the world, or betray the costs of its severance from the world. It is not a conflict between the literal (or material) and the figural that in the end fascinates me in literature's animals, but the continual communication between the two, and what it means for an entity to be irreducibly, and from the very beginning, both—that is, the most real thing and the least real. In its extreme unreality, as we shall see, the animal can reveal also how fabulous (in the sense of *fable*) the relations and transactions forming reality are, in its thinking, its making, its unmaking, how unworldly the world.

That the animal marks a place in stories where meaning chases its own tail (or the human *its* tail), I can only suggest in somewhat elusive, metaphorical terms here, but will proceed to demonstrate in the detail of slow, exorbitant readings. My teachers through this reflection have been a poet, a novelist, and a philosopher—Francis Ponge, Éric Chevillard, and Jacques Derrida—all writers for whom the animal is inseparably and originarily (as Derrida would say) word *and* thing, the live joint between the two realms. All three model a radical exposedness—which is at the same time essential insight and embarrassment—when it comes to writing's relation to (or mode of contact with) animals. Each admits in some way that, where it seriously approaches the animal, writing—not to say thinking—may be difficult to mark off from "the animal's own" movements and forms. In these places, it is just possible to imagine that the animal is eluding capture, objectification or, indeed, falsification, by "itself" supplying the forms and writing its way. Such a fiction operates not on a thematic level; it is a radical meta-fable by which writing and thinking allegorize their own essential estrangement. As Cary Wolfe writes, in a striking formulation of deconstruction's fundamental insight, "what we too hastily think of as 'our' concepts, our readings, our histories, [are] in an important sense not ours at all."[8]

An animal may appear at first glance to be the discrete object of a ("our") sentence or story; in fact its "presence"—its "work"—is more thoroughly described in the exorbitance with which it affects the entirety of a text's meanings. A thickness—the vast archive of our sightings and citings over time, the intricate network of neural and intertextual pathways by which *we* have thought *it and* by which *it* has entered (imprinted, oriented, opposed, obsessed, riddled, merged with, ex-orbited) *our* thinking—comes to separate a story from (and tie it interminably to) itself. What Ponge—with whose work Derrida's and Chevillard's share a deep affinity—called the "parti pris des choses" (the commitment to things)—inspiring Jean-Christophe Bailly's "parti pris des *animaux*"[9]—names an attentiveness to that which, paradoxically, lends itself *perfectly* to language, calls for ever more elaborate, exacting acts of language—but precisely because words reach it through thickness and homonymy (writing's "biomimicry," one could say). Writing gets closer to the thing not through transparency or referential clarity but by producing more of itself; it feels the contours and texture of the thing through its own concretions. Thus, with Ponge, at the same time as the text described the object, as the poet and critic Gérard Farasse put it once so insightfully, *the object described the text*.[10] Similarly, in the pages that follow, I consider the animal insofar as it may describe the text, that is to say, for what it might teach us about meaning's ways of working in our texts. Rather than supposing the creatures beheld—a horse, an orangutan/wolf, dogs, (bits of) hedgehogs—to be flesh-and-blood emissaries from the earthly real, or, conversely, explicable, interpretable motifs or themes, I approach them as totems of the unending co-implicatedness of flesh and thought. In doing so, I have been inspired by writerly insights and theoretical propositions alive to the uncanny *unequality*—the nonpositive, nonaccountable, non-self-identical character—of the animal in our texts and minds. These include John Berger's observation of the fact that an animal in a zoo is always visually disappointing, out of focus; Derrida's insistence on reflexives, double negations, chiasmuses, catachreses when discussing the animal; Thomas Keenan's hypothesis that every fable is about a "passing" (toward "human" subjecthood); Jean Rolin's suggestion, as he rereads nineteenth-century travel writings, that there are places where a stray dog should have been present but is missing. I have been drawn to subplots and incongruous scenes themselves seemingly out of focus within novels, where an animal appeared to be present but was in effect being intercepted on the verge of appearance or disappearance, and through whose flickering something important found expression (but also, precisely, was spared expression, compressed) which otherwise, by properly narrative, thematic or conceptual means, might have been ungraspable, or taken an inordinate amount of time or conceptual work to unfold.

Telltales of a tricky sort, these animals may yet be taken for coherent, meaningful fictional avatars or "emanations" of "real" animals. An experimental homonymy—that is, resisting realism as "truth" while welcoming it as alibi—may even be the key to these "exorbitant readings": the condition of such tellings (mine, here) being that the animal narrated be indistinguishable from its "real" counterpart, or at least, be sufficiently like it to look/sound like a plausible being of the world. This persistent likelihood of (mere) homonymy does not exactly disrupt a thinking that would carry ontological or ethical dimensions—on the contrary. This book's vital assumption is that literature, when it thinks (through the names, forms, alibis of) animals, is always also rehearsing decisions and confessing quandaries to do with allotments of flesh, place, thought, with what it means to mean, to be embodied, to die, and that to this extent it is in its animals—locations of deep riddles and ironies—that literature is most philosophical. We know this from powerful readings of fables (Louis Marin, Paul de Man, Marc Escola, Keenan) and from the provocations to reading that philosophers have consistently found in literature's animals (Deleuze, Blanchot, Kofman, Derrida, de Fontenay, Bailly). To consider animals in contemporary novels as bits of fable is to remember that animals have always been complicated places of passings and turnings and borrowings. In classical fables they spoke despite muteness, lived on borrowed human properties (yet died as animals). Contemporary animals may be disinclined to speak and generally less anthropomorphized; complicated conversions and paradoxes are nonetheless at work in them. One of these has loomed through the time I have spent writing this book: that of animals vanishing—an unthinkable horizon hanging over world and thought. Arguably, when it happens, given our "fabulous" thinking—animals are a fabulous complication, no less than the human—we might not bear it, or not believe it.

The defeated predicament of animals in our world today lends a gravity to every step of my reflection here. Yet it seems to me that, if we are to continue to believe it is possible to think, and to ensure that there is a place from which to think, we must learn again what we have forgotten about poetico-philosophical thinking: that where it is *catachrestic*, or borrows from other realms (Derrida's argument since the beginning about philosophical concepts, wherein he anticipated the animal long before naming it), it is hardly inconsistent or lacking rigor. Rather, that is where it is most reflexive and vigilant in admitting that certain things be named improperly so as not to be left altogether unnamed or unthought. It is as if, in animals, thinking were compelled to be most attentive to its own tangled scene.

I have made every effort through this book to refuse, or at least to continually defer, playfully but also gravely, any presumed divergence between "deconstructionist" and materialist/"biopolitical"/"ethics"-based approaches.[11] In doing so, I have been moved by the personal conviction that a kind of uneasy collaboration between these perspectives was demanded by the particular object that is the animal. Hence my practice of periodically feeding back into a philosophico-literary reflection a "scientific-realist" fact about the animal under consideration. I have intended this as an ongoing experimentation, a deliberate impurity and restlessness in method, a challenge to myself to continually keep each method's "represseds" in play, to see how far this could be taken and what insights it might yield. It is this wager—and the very real question of how I might bring my mind closest to thinking what an animal is, while contending honestly with the reality of having "lived with" animals most intensely through reading—that has formed the sustained challenge of this book.

CHAPTER 1

Melancholy of Horsepower

Jean-Philippe Toussaint, with Eadweard Muybridge

Just as every photographic instant has taken place
in an eternity from which it must be detached in order to be,
every instant of every flight [. . .]
takes place a little further away in an open that is still
opening and that is more than time.
—Jean-Christophe Bailly, *The Animal Side*

Art was born in [man's] attempt to delineate an animal in
motion.
—Eadweard Muybridge, *Animals in Motion*

THE SOUND OF HOOVES

In an untitled novella by Patrick Modiano, the third of a triptych published in 1999 under the title *Des inconnues*, a nineteen-year-old female narrator, having lost her job in London, accepts an acquaintance's offer to stay in his studio near the Porte de Vanves, in Paris's fourteenth arrondissement, only to wake in the early hours of the morning to the sound of marching hooves. "Certainly I have forgotten a lot of the details," reads the opening sentence, "but when I think back to that time I can still hear the sound of those hooves."[1] Crystallizing anxieties of her own, the sound of the hooves gnaws at her consciousness. With the eerie persistence of a mirage at the city's frontier, it seems to expose an unspeakable secret about the world. In the course of her wanderings she comes upon the sound's source: on the rue Brancion is the horse abattoir of Vaugirard. Rising early one morning she catches a procession of horses being led in the dark: "I saw them emerge from the night and walk down the deserted boulevard Lefebvre. The same sound of hooves, at the same cadence, that I usually heard in my half-sleep, but lighter. There were only ten or so of them. This time, I could see them. On one side, almost leading the line, a man was pulling one of the horses by the halter" (126–27). These particular horses, she learns, were from Neuilly ("Horses that had known pretty neighborhoods and rich people"), fairground horses being disposed of ("This would happen from time to time"). But on most mornings, horses arrived "by truck, by train, and the sound of hooves one heard in the morning was also the animals being led out from the stables of the *quartier*. Those stables where the horses waited, they were out there, all around. The traffic started as early as four o'clock in the morning" (130–31). These matinal marches to the slaughterhouse are not given any explicit sentimental or ethical tenor in the story. We do learn in passing that while growing up the protagonist had had a weakness for dogs and horses. But in the way that the narrative is set up, its objective is simply "to understand what the sound of the hooves meant" (155), and this is achieved a few pages in. What remains and continues to haunt the (otherwise centerless, and somewhat unfinished-seeming) story is the fact itself in its irreducibility. Looking at a house facing the street, the narrator wonders: "From that lit window, the sound had to be heard even more distinctly, and one would see the horses pass. For years, the person who lived there and all the others whose windows faced the boulevard had seen, as I did now, the horses at dawn. I would have liked them to tell me what they thought about it. We were only a few to know it, from the millions of people who lived in this city" (129–30). What might others have said? What sort of feeling expressed by them might have echoed her own? What sort of knowledge precisely is being designated by the indefinite "it" of "know it [*le savoir*]"? One person the narrator meets does say something, notably void of any judgment or sentiment: "Well, for a hundred years they've been taking care of [*s'occupe de*] horses here" (145). "Always that calm voice," thinks the narrator, "And even a smile as if the thing spoke for itself: taking care of horses." A little further on she muses: "For a hundred years, he had said. So it had been hundreds and hundreds of thousands of horses that had passed through the boulevard and the rue Brancion." (At this point her interlocutor finds her pale.)

If this story seems largely unmoored from historical circumstance, it is a well-known fact, emphasized in his 2014 Nobel Prize citation, that most of Modiano's writings are directly or indirectly about occupied

France and the Holocaust.[2] We may remember here by way of precedent Georges Franju's disturbing film *Sang des bêtes* (1949), which, documenting the graphic slaughter of animals within the interiors of abattoirs—located, as they have been historically, at the "portes de Paris," the old city gates—also inscribed the vastness and hiddenness of a violence which, with the unfolding of the century, would come to be seen as constitutive of the modern. The horror of hundreds of thousands of horses being walked to their deaths is indeed compounded for Modiano's unnamed protagonist by that of being the only person to really *think* it, of being the only consciousness in which it assumes its full proportions. Reluctant to stay on in the neighborhood, she hardly knows where to go, realizing simply that there is no escape: "In any case, even if I lived in a different neighborhood, far from here, that wouldn't change anything. There would still/always [*toujours*] be in my head a line of horses walking on in the night, and turning at the corner, and that guy in cowboy pants, pulling one of them by its halter—a black horse. It didn't want to walk and would certainly have fled, if it could" (128). Only in this recalling of the scene, at a good page's distance from the actual sighting of the horses, does one get a glimpse of the first horse being led by "that guy in cowboy pants." In this replay of the procession in the narrator's mind ("in my head"), this black horse singled out from the others that follow it—and the hundreds of thousands that precede it—in being ascribed the individual (if hopeless) will to escape its deathly fate, fleetingly breaks their numberlessness and facelessness, rescales their impending fate as that, industrially multiplied, of a single, sentient, captive creature.

Francis Bacon, painter of crucifixions and carcasses, had confessed in an interview to being "moved" by "extraordinary photographs which have been done of animals [. . .] before they were slaughtered," where it seems clear "that they're so aware of what is going to happen to them, they do everything to attempt to escape."[3] As it happens, the reference to photography is appropriate here (and part of a larger point to which I will return), as this scene—the replay of the procession "in my head"—also seals the somehow *hypnotic* space-time that the horses' march toward their slaughter opens and keeps open within that of the narrative. They walk in an endless time ("toujours"; still or always), in an indeterminate space ("dans ma tête"; in my head / "dans la nuit"; in the night). Even when directly witnessed, the horses "sort[aient] de la nuit" (emerged from the night) (126); the narrator imagines other inhabitants of the *quartier* who would have seen, like her, "the horses at dawn" (130). The point is that the horses pass as if interminably on the boulevard Lefebvre in the night (strictly at dawn), walking to the corner where they turn into the rue Brancion, street of the abattoir. Then it is the sound of the hooves that, ghostlike, outlives awhile the sight of the animals: "I could no longer see them but I could still hear the sound of the[ir] hooves and stood still, waiting for the moment when I would no longer hear them" (127). The marching horses, heard nightly in the uncertainty of a "half-sleep," in this liminal zone that is the "portes de Paris," seem to walk the very edge of the real, toward an end that lies outside the story's field of view and sound. In this sense, it is as if the stomping hooves in the night marked the outer border of the story, where it meets its own insomnia, its untranquil night. "We live, it is said, like sleepwalkers," the narrator reads later, in a pamphlet she types up for a group committed to "work on the self." "WE WERE LIVING IN OUR SLEEP [. . .]. We therefore had to come out of this state and this could be done only by the 'remembrance of self.' But even though I kept stopping to type to reread each sentence, I couldn't understand very well what this exercise involved" (154).

What the narrator professes not to understand, the narrative itself does, consummately, in the way it smuggles into its space these sequences of cadenced movement in the night, where agency (walking) and passivity (being led) conspire incomprehensibly, in a temporality somehow mythical, fatal, as if the horses were being endlessly sleepwalked to their deaths. And why? The absence of any allusion to a horse meat industry or to another reason for the disposing of the horses, the reference to the trucks and trains that transport them, to the neighborhood stables where they stand waiting to be taken to the boulevard, suggest a scene of reasonless, systematic slaughter, as if that border of the story and of the city were being sinisterly maintained by the continual extermination of horses. Leaving no carcasses, only sawdust, traces of blood, and wads of money in the hands of massive men the narrator assumes to be horse traders (126), the horses march from the hiddenness of stables and unnamed places far away to the hiddenness of the slaughterhouse, ghostly not least because they are momentarily drawn from this night ("I saw them emerge from the night") into the somnambulic march toward their vanishing.

But then the ghostliness of the horses also tells of a real and historical disappearance of horses from the streets of France, and from the urbanized world at large.[4] At one point, in a quiet street lined with low houses, the narrator thinks: "One could have imagined this were a small garrison town where every morning one hears the sound of hooves, but it is a squadron passing and the horses are not going to the abattoir" (152). The mythical despair of this story is in the unvarying direction of the horses' march, in the ineluctable singularity of their destination. The only resolution that can be wished for in this symbolic space so wrought is that the hooves could sound a path *not* toward the slaughterhouse. But this, precisely, cannot happen in the space of the story, whose inscription is inseparable from the *frayage*, the path traced and retraced by the horses toward the "abattoirs de Vaugirard." If we do learn that years later "the abattoirs have disappeared" (164), we must imagine this matched by the obverse fact that from the waking, diurnal, everyday life of humans, horses too have largely disappeared.

EXODUS

"Frankly, three hundred grams per person per year," wrote Jean-Louis Aragon in a supplement to *Le Monde* in 2010, "that is, less than one gram per day, that is really nothing to make a big fuss about [*il n'y a vraiment pas de quoi fouetter un chat*]."[5] He was alluding to contemporary French consumption of horsemeat, a dying taste if one is to believe Yannick Dubois, one of eight hundred remaining butchers still trading in it, and who, interviewed by Aragon, admitted to eating horsemeat twice a week himself, essentially to support the trade. "We are the victims of much disinformation with these campaigns against hippophagia," laments Dubois, "but I have to say there is a lack of culture, people are not accustomed to eating horse." At the time at which he was speaking, France was importing 80 percent of its horsemeat, exporting (mainly to Italy) most of its own young horsemeat, a "unique genetic heritage in the world," as Aragon points out, derived from "nine species of draft horses." For the French prefer not to eat their own horses: "Serving [foal meat] here, I tell you, one would be killed, even the *habitués* don't want it," says Dubois. Most of his own meat comes from horses "living in semi-freedom in the United States" and slaughtered in Mexico or Canada. The meat is then transported by air, for consumption within a week after slaughter. His produce is thus fresher, Dubois assures *Le Monde*, than Argentinian horsemeat that might be imported as sea freight.

The dramatic decline of *hippophagie* is balanced out, in *Le Monde*'s supplement, by the "return of the horse" in urban space, through collectively owned stables, a renewed enthusiasm for competitive equestrian sports, and even an initiative by the city council of Saint-Prix, Val-d'Oise to henceforth collect biodegradable waste from residential neighborhoods in a vehicle drawn by "Leone," a Comtois mare. A council spokesperson confirmed that the shift from motorized transport to the "ancestral solutions" of horse-drawn locomotion had saved the city seventy euros per ton of green waste (iv–v). If all of this amounts to an ambiguous picture of the horse's place in today's France (and beyond), it moves me to reflect on the historical vanishing from which it so supplementally returns. In an article written in 1956 Étienne Souriau had pointed out that "the sixty years"—now more than a hundred—"of development of cinema coincide[d] with a technological fact of extreme importance in the history of humanity [. . . ,] the sudden and almost total cessation of the use of the horse as a motor force, as a practical mode of locomotion and as a means of combat."[6] John Berger, in his oft-quoted essay "Why Look at Animals?," wrote more broadly of the marginalization of animals as a result of numerous inventions of the nineteenth and twentieth centuries, including the "railway, electricity, the conveyor belt, the canning industry, the motor car, chemical fertilisers."[7] If draft animals were disappearing from streets and factories, the technologies that were replacing them also symbolically or phantomatically *incorporated* them, as Akira Lippit has for his part persuasively shown:

> When horse-drawn carriages gave way to steam engines, plaster horses were mounted on tramcar fronts in an effort to simulate continuity with the older, animal-driven vehicles. Once considered a metonymy of nature, animals came to be seen as emblems of the new, industrial environment. Animals appeared to merge with the new technological bodies replacing them. The idioms and histories of numerous technological innovations from the steam engine to quantum mechanics bear the traces of an incorporated animality. James Watt and later Henry Ford, Thomas Edison, Alexander Graham Bell, Walt Disney, and Erwin Schrödinger, among other key figures in the industrial and esthetic shifts of the late nineteenth and early twentieth centuries, found uses for animal spirits in developing their respective machines, creating in the process a series of fantastic hybrids. Cinema, communication, transportation and electricity drew from the actual and fantasmatic resources of dead animals. Technology, and more

> precisely the technological instruments and media of that time, began to serve as virtual shelters for displaced animals. In this manner, technology and ultimately the cinema came to determine a vast mausoleum for animal being.[8]

Indeed, fascinating endnotes detailing the complicity of this period's key inventors in the exploitation of "actual and fantasmatic resources of dead animals" recall, for instance, the countless public animal electrocutions by which, in 1887, Thomas Edison and his assistant persistently attempted to demonstrate the dangers of alternating current, thereby threatening the canine and feline pets of the West Orange neighborhood with decimation, as noted by Edison's biographer. The famously filmed 1904 electrocution of Topsy, an elephant that Coney Island's Luna Park had decided to put down after an untoward incident, would have early "cinema" symptomatically coincide with an instance of literal electrical animation—of animals "fuel[ing] the phantom thermodynamic engines" of modernity—to which Lippit devotes the last page of his book (187; 248n73). Another note describes the curious quantum experiment of Austrian physicist Erwin Schrödinger in 1925, consisting in placing a cat in a black box "along with a decaying radioactive nucleus, a trigger mechanism and a cyanide capsule." The question "Is the cat dead or alive?" accrued increasing uncertainty past the first minute (at which point there was a 50 percent chance that the nucleus had decayed and the device was automatically switched off). Till the box was opened and the answer to the question could be empirically ascertained, the cat was both dead and alive (or "kept alive so as to be left for dead" to quote Derrida on the crypt, a topology privileged here by Lippit [189]), in "suspended animation," thus "allow[ing] for the conceptualization of alternative, parallel worlds" (249 n75) but also aptly emblematizing animals' fate in modernity, that is, in Lippit's terms, as the "undead" (1).

To return to our horses, the most interesting of Lippit's notes recalls how new means of power at the dawn of the Industrial Revolution were gauged and represented in precisely the terms of the capacities of the henceforth supplanted animal. Thus "a French 'cheval-vapeur' was estimated at the ability of a horse to lift seventy-five kilograms one meter in one second" (248). In England, "horsepower" referred no less literally to the units of a horse's physical endurance. Lippit quotes Richard Lewinsohn, the author of *Animals, Men, and Myths*, in relating how James Watt, having built the first steam engine, had conducted experiments to compare its output with what a horse could lift in a minute. The figure arrived at for the horse—22,000 foot-pounds—was subsequently "arbitrarily increased to 33,000 foot-pounds per minute and called a horsepower" (quoted in Lippit, *Electric Animal*, 248 n72). The arbitrariness of the increase is in itself interesting, of course, as, even while phantomatically incorporating the horse as its standard, as its originary unit of measure, steam technology inscribed within it a difference (a lie), and an oddly counterproductive one at that (since not increasing the figure would have assured the steam engine a more impressive output), whose main consequence was to even more effectively displace the horse from the very place that it was being commemoratively reserved. This honorary place in the new regime would be graced with its name, while the horse itself as it were would lag eleven thousand foot-pounds behind. "Horsepower," then, gauges the power of a superhorse, an impossible horse, a horse already transfigured, transcended, technologically prosthetized (whence Lippit's term "fantastic hybrids"), treacherously hypostasized to signify henceforth its own obliteration, by the always already superior strength of mechanical force over the muscular. It is in such a context, where actual horses had become discarded shells, their strength drawn from them and inflated to run the new machines, that the "plaster horses" on the tramways assume their poignancy as monuments to a massive vanishing.

"Modernity," writes Lippit, "can be defined by the disappearance of wildlife from humanity's habitat and by the reappearance of the same in humanity's reflections on itself: in philosophy, psychoanalysis and technological media" (2–3). The lucidity of Lippit's demonstration lies, however, in the crucial insight that "animals never entirely vanish." "Rather," as he writes in the opening lines of the work, "they exist in a state of perpetual vanishing" (1). Indeed, it is the endlessness of such a present continuous that haunts Modiano's novella, where the marching horses confined to the night and to that stretch of boulevard, in their "perpetual vanishing," come to figure the flickering edge of consciousness, the outer (or is it the inner?) limit of the phenomenal world. In this sense, they continually reinscribe the exilic movement of animals toward the periphery of human experience and perception. Berger accounts in just such terms for "the unprofessional, unexpressed" disappointment one cannot help feeling when watching animals in a zoo: "In the zoo the view is always wrong," he writes, "like an image out of focus" (23). This is because "*you are looking at something that has been rendered absolutely marginal;* and all the concentration you can muster will never be enough to centralise it" (24). The utter marginalization of animals, their removal from the space of the world, from their instincts, from interactions, from movement, from the vitality of habitat and natural survival, results in "their tendency to bundle towards the edge of [their cage]. (Beyond its edges there may be real space.)" (25). The same may be said, in its essential implications, for the place the animal has increasingly come to occupy in the world—that is to say, "bundle[d] towards [its] edge," disquietingly "out of focus." This would account for why, whenever and wherever animals appear, they seem to occasion an unsettling of phenomenality itself, as the ghostly survivors of a world which, for something like modern time and space to occur, had to be written over. "It was as though the world itself were growing less substantial," writes Rebecca Solnit about the last decades of the nineteenth century, when places, proximity, wilderness, landscape, materiality, bodily experience were lost and regained as "information and images."[9] In Lippit's account, animals entered around this time "a new economy of being [. . .] no longer sacrificial in the traditional sense of the term but [. . .] *spectral*" (1). The analogy he draws between the animal and the unconscious—and modern technological media—as struck-through supplemental dimensions to the phenomenal world is both remarkably productive and in places too neat.[10] I must remind myself to be careful, and take my cue from Berger ("all the concentration you can muster will never be enough to centralise it") as I prepare to follow horses in the night.

SPLIT SECOND

An impressive study by Raymond Bellour traces photography back to a "principle of invisibility" shared by the guillotine.[11] Integrating the Foucauldian thesis of modernity as entailing an altered relationship between the visible and the invisible, and thereby also a new proximity between life and death, Bellour points out that in the same year—1791—were invented in England the panopticon and the panorama, both constructed around the idealized all-seeing position of the spectator (24–25). A year later, however, something different would occur with the invention of the guillotine in revolutionary France. "The executioner," writes Bellour, "released from [*soustrait à*] the old logic of torture [*des supplices*], becomes a mere executor, even a sort of projectionist—it is indeed an *image*, but the difference with the older spectacles is that [now] the public sees nothing, the blade moves too quickly for one to grasp its effect otherwise than by pure subtraction." In these conditions, he writes, "the invisible is what is to be seen [*ce qu'il faut voir*]," and further, quoting a contemporary: "The instant of the guillotine produces a real temporal divergence where the unity of the subject breaks [*éclate*]" (26). Indeed, the event of death, by guillotine, was located in the progression from a visible presence (that is, to be blunt, of a head) to a sudden absence, with no visible transition. In this sense, "the instant of the guillotine" was not an instant in a positive, perceptible sense, but rather a missing instant, a robbed, infinitesimal slice of time, in which life instantaneously turned to death. The event of death itself, then, could only be negatively perceived, in other words, as what could not be perceived, as an active production of invisibility at the heart of the spectacle. For Bellour, the evolution of society and visual culture at this time was thus premised on "a contrast internal to visibility: on the one hand a sort of omni-visibility is shared by the panopticon, the panorama and fantasmagoria; bursts forth on the other hand the invisibility of the pure instant of the guillotine, through which a hyper-consciousness of material vision is shot through with the effect of a sort of machinic unconscious [. . .] as if the machine took away in one sense what it provided in others" (28–29).

The constitutive tension in the modern regime of the visible found its most natural form in the instantaneous snapshot, capturing moments of stillness subtracted from movement, such that, in the words of Michel Frizot (quoted by Bellour), "any moving object, whatever its own speed, appears in total and rigid stillness." "Seized faster and faster from life," writes Bellour, "these instants produce a serial image by which time divides up onto itself" (34). The slicing up of time that the guillotine had occasioned (and somehow made irreducible, irreversible) was extended by photography to affect the social and subjective body at large. The fascination with this newly revealed discontinuity in the world of appearances would be confirmed by the obsessive work done years later on the *photo spirite*, in which the fastness of exposure coincided with the evanescence of ghosts both to supplement absence and to further dispossess the human eye of its command over the visible. Through the coming to light of what Walter Benjamin would call the "optical unconscious," that is, the evidence of a layer of the visible that showed itself not to the human eye but only to that of the machine, the world of appearances had become, one could say, *intermittent*. Photography and later cinema would both work on the basis of this "interruption of movement," capturing life, writes Bellour, by producing death. Of course, cinema restores seeming continuity to movement, thus effecting a denial of "the interruptions on which it is founded"; nonetheless, Bellour insists (contra Deleuze), the still, the "arrêt sur image" (freeze frame) continues to be "its secret core, always waiting to reveal itself" (40–41). Cinema is haunted by an immobility—the stillness of the "cadaver or [the] sculpture"—exposed in the materiality of the still ("photogramme") to be its hidden mechanical truth (43).

Nowhere perhaps is this haunting by stillness, this immobility at the heart of movement more patent than in the horse photographs Eadweard Muybridge took in the 1870s (with which, inexplicably, both Lippit and Bellour deal only in passing). As fascinating as the pictures is the story behind the series of experiments that led to the publication, in 1887, of *Animals in Motion.* Here is how Muybridge himself, in an original preface to the 1898 edition, summarized the polemic that he had resolved to settle through this work:

> In the spring of the year 1872, while the author was directing the photographic surveys of the United States Government on the Pacific Coast, there was revived in the city of San Francisco a controversy in regard to animal locomotion, which we may infer, on the authority of Plato, was warmly argued by the ancient Egyptians, and which probably had its origin in the studio of the primitive artist when he submitted to a group of critical friends his first etching of a mammoth crushing through the forest, or of a reindeer grazing on the plains.
>
> In this modern instance, the principal subject of dispute was the possibility of a horse, while trotting—even at the height of his speed—having all four of his feet, at any portion of his stride, simultaneously free from contact with the ground.
>
> The attention of the author was directed to this controversy, and he immediately resolved to attempt its settlement.[12]

The debate to which Muybridge here lends vast historical perspective formed, by some accounts, the substance of a $25,000 bet with Central Pacific Railroad mogul and horse breeder and trainer Leland Stanford (who had served as governor of California in 1862–63). In any case it was Stanford who funded Muybridge's experiments, which would be pursued in their second stage at his stock farm at Palo Alto (later the site of the university), and which would feature some of the horse breeder's own "first-class trotting horses" (14). The "controversy," itself quickly resolved, became the pretext, for Muybridge, for conducting a series of detailed photographic studies of horses—and later, of various animals at the Philadelphia zoo, and finally of humans (athletes and faculty) at the University of Pennsylvania—while engaged in various forms and speeds of movement. To this purpose, at Palo Alto, Muybridge had devised a system that involved positioning a series of twenty-four stereoscopic cameras parallel to the horse's progressive movement, with exposures automatically regulated by the use of a motor-clock that made and broke an electric circuit at determined time and distance intervals as the horse advanced. The result was plates of successive stills of the horse taken at what for this time were impressively short time intervals—that is, from a 0.126-second interval (or an eighth of a second) for a walking horse ("Elberon with rider," plate 14) to a 0.023-second interval (approximately a fiftieth of second) for a galloping horse ("Annie G. with jockey," plate 72), and even 0.019 seconds (a hundredth of a second) for a trotting horse ("Lizzie M. with Sulky," plate 50).[13] The distance interval for a galloping horse could be, for instance, 13.75 inches between one "phase" of movement and the next, as seen in illustration 14 ("The Gallop") (see fig. 1.1).

Eighty-five photographic plates break down in this manner various types of horse movements organized under the categories "The Walk," "The Amble," "The Trot," "The Rack (or Pace)," "The Canter," "The Gallop," "The Ricochet," "The Leap," "The Buck and Kick," and "Change of Gait," to each of which Muybridge devotes a few pages of text. The "Analyses" are interesting in their hybridity of purpose, being as much about the mechanics of equestrian movement as they are about a history of representation—lexical, locomotional, artistic—of the horse. Most noteworthy in this regard is the chapter on "the gallop," a term "now almost universally employed to designate the most rapid of all quadruped movements," and "adopted by nearly all animals, in one or the other of its methods, when, from caprice, persuasion, or necessity, they exercise their utmost power for the attainment of their greatest speed" (49). In these pages Muybridge comments on the controversial "period of unsupported transit" (13), indeed shown in illustration 14 of a galloping horse to start at the point at which its right foot leaves the ground in the second of the frames (phase 2): "In this stride, the spring is effected from [the right foot], and we soon find the horse with all his legs more or less flexed under the body, affording no support thereto until a period that occurs between 6 and 7; the exact phase of

Figure 1.1. Eadweard Muybridge, "The Gallop," illustration 14 from *Animal Locomotion* (1887).

first contact did not happen to be photographed" (49). Nevertheless, the illustration clearly demonstrates that for "about seventy-eight inches" and "a little more than the tenth of a second" the horse galloped, as it were, with all four of its feet off the ground (51).

The proof is not the main point of the chapter on "The Gallop," however, presumably because by the time the book was published Muybridge's first photographs taken on the Sacramento racetrack in 1872 of the "celebrated horse named Occident" (13) were already known, and the debate thereby resolved. More than half the chapter is devoted, rather, to a discussion of the "history of the artistic delineation of the gallop," sketched in three stages (53). The first he names "the Primitive; suggested to the artist by keen observation, and expressed by him with entire freedom from conventionality" and which, depicting the galloping horse with all legs in flexure and "more or less under the body, with one or both the hind feet free from contact with the ground," neatly corresponds to phases recorded through photography. The second classification, covering the Egyptian, Assyrian, Grecian, Roman, and Byzantine conventions, is called "the Ancient[, i]n which the support is rendered by the two hind feet, the anterior legs are more or less flexed [. . .] at various elevations above the ground" and which also finds corresponding substantiation in Muybridge's own illustrations. As for the third, termed "the Modern," it "exhibits an entire absence of careful observation, unprejudiced impression, or serious reasoning," portraying "a body, neck and head, all of abnormal length, and arranged in a nearly horizontal line" with the anterior legs ending far in advance of the head and the hind legs similarly "thrust far to the rear, with their shoes turned upwards," resembling, writes Muybridge, less any verifiable phase in the gallop of a horse than "the leap of a cat." Proceeding to survey an impressive range of iconographic and sculptural treatments of the horse through the ages and in different parts of the world, he then writes:

> About a hundred a years ago, the artists of Europe, apparently with one accord, came to the conclusion that the rising body, with the bent, uplifted anteriors, and the contact of the hind feet with the ground, as indulged in by the ancient sculptors, was inconsistent with the correct interpretation of speed, and, as if by preconcerted agreement, there suddenly appeared from their various schools the conventional phase which attained the zenith of its absurdity in a well-known picture, by a celebrated animal painter, representing ten horses, each a replica of the other, with limbs extended fore-and-aft, and gliding through the air, distinguishable from each other only by the colours of their riders. (56–57)

Muybridge's utter disapproval of the horizontally extended and spread-eagled limbs in the work of the unnamed painter moves him to emphatically defend the fleshly referent over the arbitrary sign:[14]

> "And yet," it is sometimes remarked, "the phase gives one an impression of rapid motion." Possibly, but in precisely the same way as a printed word unconsciously suggests, through long usage, the sound or the substance of that which it represents.
>
> If it is impressed upon our minds in infancy that a certain arbitrary symbol indicates an existing fact; if this same association of emblem and reality is reiterated at the preparatory school, insisted upon at college, and pronounced correct at the university; symbol and fact—or supposed fact—becomes so intimately blended that it is extremely difficult to dissociate them, even when reason and personal observation teaches us they have no true relationship.
>
> So it is with the conventional galloping horse [. . .]
>
> During the past few years the artist has become convinced that this definition of the horse's gallop does not harmonize

> with his own unbiased impression, and he is making rapid progress in his efforts to sweep away prejudice, and effect the complete reform that is gradually but surely coming. (57)

At no point in the volume does Muybridge wax as passionate as when pledging to "sweep away [the] prejudice" that leaves the horse suspended in a posture unnatural to it. The belabored semiotic analogy is striking, premised as it is on the conviction that while symbolic language might content itself with an arbitrary, constructed system of correspondences to the real, pictorial representation is not simply bound by the conventions of realism, but somehow almost ontologically obligated to accurately register worldly movements and forms. If Muybridge, on painting, appears here to align himself with an age-old school of thought on mimesis, and against fiction, his position, in being significantly mediated by photography, in fact effects a crucial epistemological shift, displacing the truth of the horse from the Platonic realm of ideas onto the "wet collodion plate" (13) on which the traces of the moving body of a real horse are chemically captured. Intending photography to correct popular misrepresentations of the galloping horse, Muybridge in his reverence for collodion truth prefigures what writers like André Bazin or Roland Barthes would some decades later sense about the ontology of the photographic image: that is, that unlike other media, "[it] always carries its referent with itself, both affected by the same amorous or funereal immobility, at the very heart of the moving world."[15] The photograph, in preserving the material, bodily contours of a being standing (or, as it were, galloping) in the light, "is literally an emanation of the referent," would write Barthes. "From a real body, which was there, proceed radiations which ultimately touch me, who am here" (80–81). The pains taken by Muybridge to critically review numerous depictions of horses through the ages, and the vehemence with which he decries the "absurdity" of "the conventional phase" may appear excessive, until one considers that, unwittingly extending the ontology of the photographic image to that of all images, the studious photographer now saw in the "limbs extended fore-and-aft" a form of representational violence. What he called "the Modern," and ascribed to deplorable observation and an abandonment of reason, was a painful contortion inflicted on the very being of the horse.

Thereby emerges a definition of modernity as good as any, it would seem, and more oddly poignant than most. The Modern error, while historical, measures a lost proximity from the empirical reality of the horse that, if one is to believe Muybridge, catches up (ontogeny repeating phylogeny, etc.) with each human as he or she leaves the Primitive and Ancient and enters the age of "conventional representation." Thus, after noting the correct depiction of horses with "all their legs flexed under their bodies" in sculptures and engravings of the Hittite, prehistoric Scandinavian, Mycenaean, and contemporary Alaskan and North American Indian traditions, he evokes "an intelligent child, known to the author, who, having a talent for drawing, and, happily, not familiar with the conventional representation of the gallop, [when] asked to sketch her idea of a runaway horse, which she had seen, produced a similar phase [i.e., legs correctly flexed under body] as her impression of the action" (54). With a similar wistfulness, only inspired by the primitive drawing of a human, poet Henri Michaux had eloquently lamented the loss, in normativized adult perception, of archaic wisdom:

> Louis XIII, at eight years, does a drawing similar to that of the son of a New Caledonian cannibal. At eight years, he is of the age of humanity, he is at least two hundred and fifty thousand years old. A few years later, he has lost this, he is now merely thirty one, he has become an individual, he is merely a king of France, an impasse from which he would never get out. What is worse than to be finished/complete [*achevé*]?[16]

A TIME WITHOUT HUMANS

While not acknowledged as such, a rarefied intactness, a certain *purity of form* is preserved in that tenth of a second during which, in the study already referred to and others, "the [horse's] body was hurled through the air" (51). One wonders whether Muybridge's intolerance of liberties taken in representing the horse in this "period of unsupported transit" was not a displaced anxiety concerning, more essentially, the fragility of that split second, its exposure to a corruption not merely symbolic but real. For as it happens, for "the attraction of gravity [not] to have much effect," as specified in the "Prelude to Analyses," requires "very rapid motion by a *good* horse" (27; emphasis added). While "good" easily describes Stanford's "first-class" thoroughbred trotting and racehorses (whose speed could not be emulated by, say, the "powerful, heavily built mastiff" of plate 118, whose "weight[. . .] is against him" [52]), behind this qualitative distinction the epithet more consequentially marks a divide between animals endowed with the freedom of maximal movement (because required to be so by their use, or because living in a natural habit where "caprice, persuasion or necessity" could afford to come into play) and those living in artificial confinement. So it is that plate 151 (fig. 1.2), which "leaves much to be desired," recording "the stride of a fallow-deer in captivity, followed by its frightened fawn," illustrates a *missing* period of unsupported transit: "Had not long confinement in a small park impaired the elasticity which the deer would have exhibited in its natural state, a phase *would have occurred* between those of [frames] 6 and 7, in which all the feet would have been off the ground" (52; emphasis added). Stanford's racehorses, it turned out, were dream-worthy subjects. With most other animals studied, Muybridge's photographic work inevitably came up against a sort of doubly constitutive limit: constitutive in the first instance because, since they called for elaborate arrangements—a series of cameras set up in a row anticipating the direction of the animal's movement—he had to seek controlled spaces in which to conduct his experiments, namely the Sacramento racecourse, the farm in Palo Alto, and the Philadelphia zoo, thus restricting himself to the alternative of racehorses or confined animals; and doubly constitutive because photography was a medium born of an age of industrialization and technology that was concomitantly—that is, consequently—characterized by the receding of wild animals. In a final chapter, titled "Records of Movements from Observation," Muybridge thus admits that "it would have been desirable [. . .] to have photographed many of the animals while they were enjoying more freedom of movement than that afforded by the gardens of a Zoological Society, but the difficulties attending a satisfactory investigation under their natural conditions of life were, at the time, too great to be surmounted" (67). One can understand why Bazin confessed admiration for the filmmaker who would not succeed in returning safely from the encounter with that which he had gone out to film (see Bellour, *Le corps du cinéma*, 539). Photography and cinema, when it came to their fascination with the animal, placed themselves in the paradoxical position of pursuing an object which, when it was not in captivity (thereby removed from its full capacities) and not fleeing *from* the photographer (for what better and worse situation can one imagine in which to catch an animal galloping in the wild?), could always run *toward* him, thereby marking the point of no return, the point of its own annulment with which, perhaps, the camera always flirts, phantasmatically and/or disingenuously.[17]

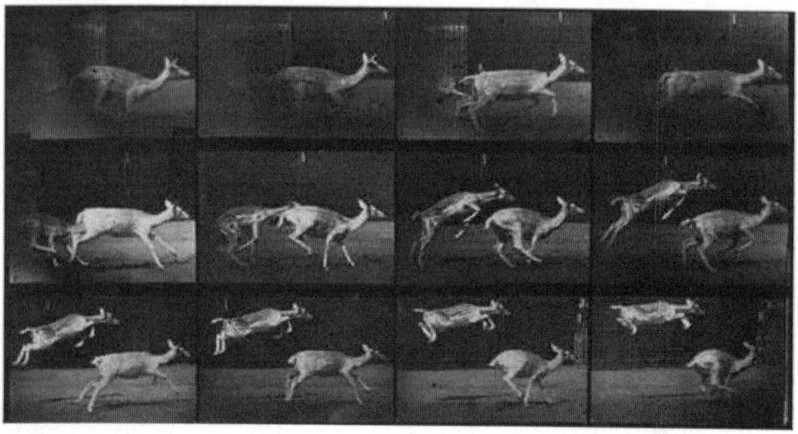

Figure 1.2. Eadweard Muybridge, "Doe Galloping and Fawn Jumping," plate 151 from *Animal Locomotion* (1887).

All this to suggest that Muybridge's instant of "unsupported transit" carries a content somehow otherworldly, literally a slice of time of an *other world*, in which animals would run freely—while a camera's eye would capture their freedom from constraints and from gravity. The terrible contradiction of photography, in this sense, is that the "optical unconscious" reveals a prehistoric time, that is, a time without humans. This is all too evident, negatively as it were, in Muybridge's eighty-five plates of horses engaged in various motions. Only four of these (plates 12, 28, 32, and 33) depict a horse walking or trotting "free," that is, without a rider and without a specific task. Sixty-six of them show a horse with a rider or jockey, or pulling a sulky. This leaves fifteen plates, eleven of which (plates 1 to 11) feature horses "hauling a heavy weight," and in one of them, a man is "pulling at [the horse's] head" (plate 11). These plates portraying horses as industrial beasts, significantly, open the series, as if to illustrate, in all-too-human, mechanical terms, the speed of "horsepower." The four remaining plates portray horses engaged in a range of extraordinary acts: plate 29 shows a horse carrying a bucket in its mouth, plate 30 a horse rolling a box, and plate 84 first a horse rocking on a teeterboard and then a different horse rolling a barrel; plate 85 shows different horses, one with a rider, "rearing, pivoting, etc."[18] There could not be a more apt reminder of how "domesticated" the (photographed, photographable) horse is at this point of human history; indeed, the next section is titled "Other Domesticated Animals" (comprising a mule, an ass, an ox, a sow, a goat, a camel, a guanaco [galloping!], an elephant, a dog, and a cat). Perhaps the first half of plate 84 is the most interesting series of them all, featuring as it does a horse named Hornet, who, teetering good-humoredly on said teeterboard, succeeds in perfectly resembling, in "life size" (but this hardly matters in a photograph without a human to indicate what the scale of "life" is), a *rocking horse* (fig. 1.3). For Berger, we might recall, this object exemplified a "new demand for verisimilitude" in children's toys, in contrast with the "traditional hobby horse": "The first was merely a stick with a rudimentary head which children rode like a broom handle: the second was an elaborate 'reproduction' of a horse, painted realistically, with real reins of leather, a real mane of hair, and designed movement to resemble that of a horse galloping. The rocking horse was a 19th century invention" ("Why Look at Animals?," 22). It is remarkable that the penultimate of Muybridge's horse plates should feature a real horse *simulating* a rocking horse, in a reversal of the direction of resemblance that offers a telling picture of the fate of animals in the folds of humans' "modernity."

ZAHIR THE INVISIBLE

It is time to move to another story and to another horse (if only to better return, later, to Muybridge's). Jean-Philippe Toussaint's *La vérité sur Marie*, published in 2009 (ten years after Modiano's novella), is the third of a tetralogy of novels relating, over sixteen months or so, the strained

Figure 1.3. Eadweard Muybridge, "'Hornet' Rocking; 'Eagle' Rolling a Barrel," plate 649 from *Animal Locomotion* (1887).

love between an unnamed narrator and the classy, moody, dreamy "Marie." The four books enroll a quadrangle of spatial coordinates—Tokyo/Kyoto in *Faire l'amour* (2002; *Making Love*); Shanghai/Beijing, Paris, and Elba in *Fuir* (2005; *Running Away*); Tokyo, Paris, and Elba in *La vérité sur Marie* (*The Truth about Marie*); Paris and Elba (with a short Tokyo flashback) in *Nue* (2013; *Naked*)—to write the uneven, hypnotic temporality, the ruptures and rapprochements, of a fraught intimacy. We might quickly recall here the chronology of the main events in the overall plotline: in January, the narrator accompanies Marie to Tokyo for the opening of an exhibition of some of her fashion design pieces. *Making Love* recounts the insomnia and estrangement of the time spent together in Tokyo, interrupted by the narrator's decision to exile himself in Kyoto, from which he returns at the end of the novel. In *Running Away* we are taken back a few months to the preceding summer, where the narrator, in China, supposedly on a business trip, learns from Marie in Paris of the death of her father. The news leaves the narrator reeling through a senseless journey into the impenetrable opacity of Beijing. In the third section he joins Marie in Elba, the home of her deceased father, with ambiguous results. As to the third novel, *The Truth about Marie*, the one that will occupy me here—and whose title, suspect in its (characteristically Toussaint-ian) grandiloquence, might give us equally spurious grounds to expect the truth, the *key* to the series—it chronologically both prolongs the other two and interleaves them, set as it is, in its first section, in the early summer of the second year (where a night that Marie spends with a certain Jean-Christophe de G. ends in his unexpected death by cardiac arrest and the narrator's arrival on the scene), to then swing back to January of that year (when, in the days of the narrator's disappearance from Tokyo, Marie had started to spend more time with Jean-Christophe) to finally, in its last section, unite the two again in Elba, in the late summer, a year after the death of Marie's father. The last novel, *Naked*, picks the story up at the end of the summer after the couple's return to Paris from Elba, and includes a section that writes the narrator back into important Tokyo days (of the preceding January) from which we might otherwise have assumed him to be missing. After a two-month separation the narrator learns something significant from Marie and accompanies her to yet another funeral in Elba.

Chronology matters, in this story where things—entire scenes, events—are regularly withheld from knowledge or "view" to be pieced together only much later (and with a dark, stylized intensity, an intimate extravagance—not unlike a slow-motion scene in a Wong Kar

Wai romance—that seems to also lay bare the narrative's hallucinatory heart). The long middle section of *The Truth about Marie* is the sequence that ventures furthest in this regard, filling in a gap in narrative knowledge discreetly preserved in *Making Love*, when the story had followed the narrator through his wanderings (leading him eventually to Kyoto and back), during which time Marie's experience was left unwritten, that is, lying outside the frame. Reconstructed here from what the narrator has since learned from Marie and extended through tender and vivid imagination, this sequence thus inscribes a space of supplementarity within the architecture of the completed story. Now, what better figure to phantasmatically ride this supplementarity but a horse? In the space of the narrator's vanishing, Marie had grown closer to Jean-Christophe de G., the owner of a magnificent thoroughbred named Zahir who, after being disqualified from a prestigious race in Tokyo, had to be quickly escorted back to France on a plane. Jean-Christophe invites Marie to accompany himself and the horse on a dark and rainy evening. Such are the premises of what follows, earning Bernard Pivot's admiring review in *Le Journal du Dimanche*: "One-fifth of this novel—from page 84 to page 138—is occupied by an anthology-worthy scene that no reader will be able to forget. The embarkation, at Tokyo's Narita airport, aboard a Lufthansa Boeing 747 cargo, of a thoroughbred. [. . .] Epic and exhilarating. [. . .] There is ancient fatality in this literature so modern in its writing and in its resources. [. . .] Yes, Jean-Philippe Toussaint is a god of the Olympus who, with benevolence or with fury, manipulates a few well-chosen creatures and projects them into planetary adventures under the auspices of Eros and Lufthansa."[19]

The epic and exhilarating horse is first alluded to more than sixty pages into the novel, where he gives his name to the scandal ("the Zahir Affair," referring to his disgrace due to suspicions that he had been administered a performance-enhancing drug) that cost him his future on the racecourse and his owner much anxiety—not to say, perhaps, a few months later, his life.[20] But Zahir's first bodily appearance is dramatically delayed, insinuating itself in the text through metonymies and displacements by which he slowly assumes flesh. This is permitted by a narration loosely anchored in Marie's point of view, extended sometimes in her absence by her companion's, so that the first appearance of Zahir is of what Jean-Christophe sees (or could see) as he awaits her at the hotel: "The horse trailer was parked at the hotel's entrance, its long and still silhouette could be seen through the lobby's bay windows, its aluminum body just the same as a rock star's trailer, with two concealed and barred windows on each side, the whole grooved mass gleaming under the golden lights of the hotel's entrance. The trailer's back door was open and its ramp lowered to air out the rear and let the thoroughbred breathe" (84/67; translation slightly modified). In this first appearance that is not one, the horse's presence can only be inferred from contiguous elements: the trailer, its barred windows, the imagined exhalations by which an invisible body comes into material contact with the surrounding air. The descriptive detail concerning the panoply of the van and the uniforms and accessories of the three Japanese men attending to it, which continues in the following pages (84–85/67), further displaces and diffuses the presence of the horse. Indeed, as the travelers and van set out on the road, ambiguous syntax makes the van seem to prosthetically stand in, in its difficult progression, for what it transports: "The imposing aluminum horse trailer [. . .] struggled around the bends and made wide turns with infinite precaution" (87/69). If the insistence of adjectives like "long," "still," and "imposing" in these pages seems a little suspect, in that they might apply equally, or more pertinently, to what is concealed, a passage further on confirms the subtle logic by which, in effect, epithets describing the van tantalizingly seem to drill through the aluminum and trace a lexical path toward the immobilized body contained within it:

> Through the foggy rear window, Marie saw [*apercevait*] the aluminum trailer's *monumental* silhouette, its *powerful* headlights on in the rain by the day's waning light—the trailer at a near stop, *majestic, rocking slightly* [*chancelant*] on the wet pavement, its tires and axles creaking. Marie looked at [*regardait*] the trailer *immobile* behind her in the rain, this *immense* and *incongruous* vehicle, dark and mysterious, run aground in the Tokyo traffic, with its two barred windows on each side, behind which one sensed the living, quivering, hot presence of an invisible thoroughbred. (88/70; my emphasis; translation slightly modified)

Several formal strategies now easily identified as the signature gestures of Toussaint's prose find their ideal object, through this passage, in the ciphered motif of the horse in transit. They include the dislocating work of hypallage (*hippo*lage?) by which the qualities of the invisible horse appear to seep through its encasing; the dominance of the imperfect tense and the recurrence of the name ("Marie apercevait," "Marie regardait") serving to repeatedly restart time, ordering as a procession of perpetual presents a temporality of fascination; and the reinscription of certain details already known (the aluminum trailer, the small barred windows, previously mentioned word for word on 84/67) which, generally in keeping with Toussaint's anxious, cinematic treatment of time—wherein the repetition of details seems almost necessary for the recomposing of each successive frame—here earns diegetic justification in the sealedness of the van, which obstructs vision, forcing it to mark and re-mark the contours of what it cannot penetrate. The breach, when it is made at the end of the passage, is a breach in the rational bodywork of appearances, as description slips into a sort of hypnosis, an out-of-body projection toward what is hidden from view. The invisible beast, divined in its aliveness, its warmth and trembling, can only be phantasmatically imagined into the sealed space of the van, there being no other path into it *but* the supplemental. Here too, coalescing around the present-absent figure of the horse, we may recognize an obsession that has long haunted Toussaint's prose, namely the problem of Schrödinger's cat. Is the cat alive or dead inside the black box? Can we even be sure that it is *there*? Years ago such questions had preoccupied the eccentric protagonist of *Monsieur* (1986). In their fascination with closed spaces (bathrooms, telephone cabins, automatic photo booths—*L'appareil-photo* [1989; *The Camera*] was replete with them) and the death-driving possibility that in them time itself might come to a standstill, Toussaint's characters have, in a sense, not ceased to themselves be drawn toward the "struck-through" place marked by Schrödinger's cat, as that far side of the visible, of the known, as that which cannot be absorbed into the continuum of a recordable real. Here a horse occupies and emblematizes that space, to which after an interval it will again retreat when it is placed in the hold of the cargo plane. In the meantime, the aluminum trailer carrying it on the road toward the airport carves out a moving block of sealed opacity in the space of Tokyo. This animal that is diegetically quite real—the reason for the journey, for its urgency and difficulty, and for the decline of Jean-Christophe de G.—is thus also a highly abstract body, a body subtracted from the visible, to which the term *le pur-sang* ("the thoroughbred," literally "the pure-blood"), used throughout to refer to it, only adds further quasi-mythological ethereality. The thoroughbred has yet to be seen, it has yet, in the space of the narrative, in this transit supported by aluminum and wheels, to touch the ground with its feet.

As the cavalcade (to use a thoroughly inappropriate term) approaches Narita airport, there is much concern that they might arrive too late to fulfill customs requirements:

> Jean-Christophe de G. knew the customs office at the cargo zone at Narita closed at seven and there would be no possibility of extending their hours (theirs were inflexible hours, Japanese hours), arriving late wasn't an option, the slightest dispensation was out of question. In other words, either they get the horse to the airport before seven and board the plane, or they arrive late and the horse remains stuck in customs in the cargo zone of Narita Airport with all the attendant consequences.
>
> Jean-Christophe de G. knew the horse's papers were in order, its vaccinations records updated, its permission for transport validated, but he feared a final complication with customs, some required document of which he was perhaps unaware. (89/70–71; translation slightly modified)

The passage, with its many references to regulations and protocols, conveys the incongruity of the administrative procedures incumbent on an animal which, left to its own resources, would have had no use for national borders and customs (and would presumably not have considered crossing the Pacific). But the anxiety building up around the horse's passage could be equally seen to formulate, as if through an elaborate play on words, the uncertainty of another, ancient enigma, by which administrative and technological possibility spill into the mythological: *Can the horse fly?*

We are thus momentarily led back to the very question that had perhaps, secretly, driven Muybridge's experimentations. Recall that they were provoked by a query from Leland Stanford, a wealthy owner of thoroughbreds (a plausible model, incidentally, for Toussaint's "Jean-Christophe de G."). While accounts vary of the precise circumstances of the challenge put to Muybridge, the question as to "the possibility of a horse, while trotting—even at the height of his speed—having all four of his feet, at any portion of his stride, simultaneously free from contact with the ground" (Muybridge, *Animals in Motion*, 13) seems less than completely pertinent to the interests of a horse breeder and trainer.[21] What would he gain from knowing that a horse could have all four of its feet off the ground? Or that it could not? Muybridge's allusion in his preface to the "primitive artist" depicting a "mammoth crushing through the forest" at any rate casts the question in its grandest world-historical scope and as primarily relevant to artists. How should one understand, then, the fact that the question came from someone like Stanford, and with significant financial support in tow? Whatever explanation might be hidden from view here for this curious circumstance, one might be justified, given the revelatory character that photography had at this time, in opting for a hypothesis no more fanciful than the truth revealed through the series of stills. For to show the period of a horse's "unsupported transit" Muybridge had to still movement, fragment it, divide it into infinitesimal intervals, extract from the moving real its chrono-micro-scopic unconscious. Thereby it transpired that the joints of the visible, as it were, escape us: the human eye cannot—was not destined to?—see with certainty, at certain instants of a horse's gallop, that its progressive motion is shot through with split-second moments of flight. The points of "unsupported transit" appeared as so many loose stitches in the real, moments which, if they were to stand on their own, would be unthinkable, defying reason, and which can only exist because movement is inscribed in time, whence the paradox: immobilized and exposed to light, those tenths of a second are minuscule shards of myth imperceptibly sewn into the texture of the real—Pegasus. A supplement to the *Boston Daily Globe* on October 21, 1882, had understood this perhaps, to report as it did Muybridge's findings under the competing headlines: "Animals in Motion—Science Upsetting the Theories of Observation—Instantaneous Photography Finds Horses in the Air." Rebecca Solnit more recently described it in equally vivid terms: on a racetrack in 1877, she writes, and from the owner's and trainer's point of view, the horse was striving "to defeat the limits that nature places on the movement of bodies, to dissolve the weight of matter and the binding force of gravity, to fly, to become instantaneous, to annihilate time and space" (179).

IN THE NIGHT

When Zahir at last makes a visible entry in Toussaint's text, after more synecdoches have played at prying open his "black box" (98–100), he forms a gigantic, inconsolable mass of nervous, "brute force" against the darkness of Narita's cargo clearance zone:

Alors, lentement, apparut la croupe du pur-sang—sa croupe noire, luisante, rebondie—, à reculons, les sabots arrière cherchant leurs appuis sur le pont, battant bruyamment sur le métal et trépignant sur place, très nerveux, faisant un écart sur le côté, et repartant en avant. Il ne portait pour tout harnachement qu'un licol et une longe, une courte couverture en luxueux velours pourpre sur le dos, et les membres finement enveloppés de bandages protecteurs et de guêtres de transport fermées par des velcros, les glomes et les tendons momifiés de bandelettes pour éviter les coups ou les blessures. C'était cinq cents kilos de nervosité, d'irritabilité et de fureur qui venaient d'apparaître dans la nuit. Le pelage noir et lustré, la musculature apparente, il descendait à reculons, les deux Japonais en blazer bleu marine collés contre son corps à la hauteur de l'épaule pour essayer de le contenir, s'agrippant à la longe, le tirant et le retenant. Le cheval ne se laissait pas faire, rétif, tournait la tête pour se dégager, s'ébrouait, se débattait, des frémissements spontanés couraient le long de sa crinière comme des ondes visibles de tension et de nervosité. Sa puissance physique était impressionnante, il émanait de lui une énergie animale électrique. Les deux Japonais semblaient dépassés par les événements, ils perdaient pied, leurs blazers défaits et les cravates en bataille, ils lançaient de vaines injonctions dans le vide pour qu'on leur vînt en aide, on sentait leur émotivité, leurs mains et leurs visages tremblaient. Immobile sur le pont, le pur-sang ne bougeait plus, n'avançait plus, ne reculait plus . . . personne ne bougeait plus, ni le cheval, arrêté à mi-pont—immobile, furieux, impérial—ni les spectateurs, fascinés par la force brute de cet étalon immobile, ses muscles, longs et puissants, saillants, tendus, qui contrastaient avec le tracé gracieux des pattes, la finesse des paturons, minces, étroits, délicats comme des poignets de femme. (100–101)

Then, slowly, the thoroughbred's croup emerged—its black croup, smooth and shiny—as it stepped backward, its back hooves seeking holds on the ramp, loudly clinking on the metal and stamping in place, wildly nervous, shying to the side before being brought back on track. [. . .] Eleven hundred pounds of fury, of strained nerves, and of excitement had

> just appeared in the night. Its coat black with a fine sheen, its muscles pronounced, it was descending the ramp backward, the two Japanese men in navy-blue blazers pushing all their weight into its shoulders lest it slip, holding on to the lead, tugging it and keeping it taut. The horse wasn't cooperating, the stubborn beast, turning its head in an attempt to break loose, snorting, fighting, shivers spontaneously shaking its mane like visible waves of tension and excitement. Its physical strength was astonishing, a beastly electric energy emanated from its body. The two Japanese men [. . .] grunted and groaned out stifled and vain calls for help, their hands and faces trembling, their emotions on edge. Immobile on the ramp, the thoroughbred stood stock still, stepping neither forward nor backward in spite of the men's efforts, who continued to pull on the lead to no avail. Lufthansa's station manager, walkie-talkie in hand, walked up to the trailer and no one moved, not the horse, stationed in mid-ramp—immobile, furious, imperial—nor the onlookers, entranced by the sheer force of this unflinching stallion, its long and powerful muscles, tense, bulging, and the contrast marked by the graceful step of its legs, the finesse of its pasterns, skinny and narrow, delicate like a woman's wrists. (79–80)

It is a magnificent piece of writing, the very flesh of the horse made prose. A stealthy infiltration of terms occurring nowhere before or after in the text graphically transcribes the anatomy and "electric animal energy" of a body silhouetted against the night ("croupe," "battant bruyamment," "trépignant," "glomes," "tendons," "pelage," "musculature," "s'ébrouait," "se débattait," "frémissements," "criniere," "muscles, longs et puissants, saillants, tendus," "pattes," "paturons, minces, étroits, délicats"). Through repetitions and derivatives (*noire/noir; nerveux/nervosité/nervosité; fureur/furieux; puissance/puissants; immobile/immobile/immobile; musculature/muscles; tendons/tension/tendus*), the lexical field thickens around the patent evidence of a tense "nervous system,"[22] a live foreign presence that has *occupied* language. Dismembered and recomposed, caught in the fascinated time of the imperfect, the horse draws its immense, throbbing, hallucinatory silhouette into the frame of the text.

It is a short-lived emergence into full visibility. A few pages further, as a brewing storm bodes an extraordinary event that will break the natural order, the thoroughbred suddenly breaks loose. The hypnotic spell of the imperfect, the near-exclusive tense of the novel, is at this point ruptured by a string of five verbs in a rare *passé simple* (the tense of the event, of history and the epic)—"se raidit," "se braqua," "pivota," "recula," "s'emballa" ("tensed up," "bucked," "pivoted," "jumped back," "took off")—that register the sudden, irrepressible movements of a body become somehow alien to the prose, whose strength and intent the narrative cannot sedate nor foresee. Neighing furiously and "baring its teeth in the night," the horse rather than the storm ("thunder rumbled in the distance, lightning slashed the sky" [103–4/81–82]) metaphorically tears the night. This novel, evidently different in its thrust and affect from Modiano's story, yet shares something of the phenomenology of the latter, something that is crystallized in the repeated occurrence, in both texts, when they evoke their horse(s), of the phrase *dans la nuit* (in/into the night). In a summary count, I found a good twelve instances of this phrase in forty pages of Toussaint's novel, there were probably more. Zahir's first emergence ("Eleven hundred pounds of fury, of strained nerves, and of excitement had just appeared *in the night*" [100/79]), his anger ("its mouth open as if ready to bite, baring its teeth *in the night*" [104/82]), his escape ("The thoroughbred had escaped, had vanished *into the night*" [104/82]), his gallop ("Zahir galloped off *into the night*, already disappearing in the distance" [104–5/83]), his pursuit ("three vehicles had already sped off *in the night* in pursuit of the horse" [105/83]; "for a more patient pursuit *in the night*" [107/85]) all occur against the referentially elusive backdrop of the night. Elementary French grammar would call "dans la nuit" a *complément circonstanciel de temps/espace*, or an adverbial locution denoting time/space. But it is increasingly clear in the novel, with each occurrence, that "la nuit" does not describe only a milieu or a time. Rather, through its repeated mentions the night accrues a mythic depth, of space itself returned to darkness, to its unbounded "outside," with which the horse comes to merge, significantly reassuming its name as it is swallowed: "There wasn't the slightest trace of Zahir in the lot, he'd dissolved *into the night*, he'd evaporated, melted, black on black, into the shadows. The darkness of the night was impenetrable, as though the thoroughbred had managed to slip into its very substance, and the night had swallowed the horse up and consumed it immediately" (106/84). Likewise, when the horse materializes again, it is as if tearing back its flesh from the very night: "Suddenly, charging out of nowhere, with the same unexpectedness as when he'd disappeared, Zahir's black and powerful body materialized in the beam of the headlights, at once galloping and at rest, mad, his eyes gleaming with terror, his coat black and wet, as if suddenly defined against the night into which he had, just moments before, dissolved" (108/85–86). The passage is fascinating in its implications. Where was the horse during this time, concealed "in the night" when there was no place, amid this vast flatness, in which to hide? In this mysterious time interval, in which the animal had vanished from rational space, could it have been in that *other* world outside the frame, the "real space" "beyond its edges" (Berger)? Representation has but a loose hold on this creature, it would seem, which has the ability to "evaporate," to vanish into thin air. Another way of saying that it was flying, with all of its feet off the ground (of representation, of phenomena), unlocatable because "unsupported" by rational ground, ungrounded. Its irreconcilable posture when it reappears, "at once galloping and at rest," can oddly be made sense of only in photographic terms: stilled *in his gallop*, in the immobility that is at the heart of movement. Indeed, the chase culminates in an extraordinary scene, shortly before it is finally captured, where the horse is seen galloping "as though ready to leave the ground, to take flight into the sky, a winged Pegasus vanishing into the darkness to join the thunder and lightning" (110/87).

"Zahir," the novel tells us, in Arabic means *visible*—"the name comes from Borges, and even further back, from the myths of the Orient, in which legend has it that Allah created the first thoroughbreds with a fistful of wind. And, in Borges' eponymous story, Zahir is a being who, once perceived, cannot be forgotten, nor can he rid himself of this terrible virtue" (106/84). The narrator of the cited Borges story descends into madness after having come into contact with a coin called the zahir.[23] The word, as he discovers to his horror in an old manuscript, "means visible, manifest, evident; in that sense it is one of the ninety-nine names of God; in Muslim countries, the masses use the word for 'beings or things which have the terrible power to be unforgettable, and whose image eventually drives people mad'" (246). While in its sense of "visible" "Zahir" might seem an ironic appellation for a being so prone to vanishing, it does dramatize the border zone at which Toussaint's thoroughbred stands, negotiating as it does a back-and-forth commerce between the visible world and the invisible. Zahir *is* that passage, evaporating and rematerializing as he crosses the border. He alone finds the seams in the real, wherein to "dissolve into the night." But he is also "evident" and "unforgettable"—because, even in his concealedness, in his visual intermittence, it is his erased body that orders the disposition of the gaze and thereby of the visible. His is a trace, a *frayage* "in the night" of the text and of the human world. Toussaint's, Modiano's, and Muybridge's horses indeed all share the quality of being both invisible and hypervisible. In this sense they are the volatile figures of the divergence at the heart of seeing that Bellour recorded as being the deep truth to modernity.

HORSE IN THE AIR

"To preserve artificially bodily appearance is to snatch it from the flow of time, to stow it away neatly, so to speak, in the hold of life," wrote Bazin. "If the plastic arts were put under psychoanalysis, the practice of embalming the dead might turn out to be a fundamental factor in their creation."[24] If Muybridge was undoubtedly one of the pioneer contributors to the development of cinema, it was because he had a keen sense of the ghost in the horse. The cameras used in the Palo Alto studies, we remember, were stereoscopic, which meant they photographed the horses from both sides. In his first protocinematographic experiment, after selecting a sufficient number of stereographs to compose a full stride, Muybridge had "placed the appropriate halves of each, respectively, in one of the scientific toys called the zoetrope, or the wheel of life—an instrument originated by the Belgian physicist Plateau, to demonstrate the persistency of vision." With the two zoetropes operating at the same time and at identical speed (and with said stride complete so as to form an endless loop), "the respective halves of the stereographs were made simultaneously visible, by means of mirrors [. . .] with the result of a very satisfactory reproduction of an apparently solid miniature horse trotting, and another galloping" (14). Several incarnations later, and with some improvements credited to contemporaries Étienne-Jules Marey and Thomas Edison, the device had become the *zoöpraxiscope*, thus baptized by Muybridge, and described by him as "the first apparatus ever used, or constructed, for synthetically demonstrating movements analytically photographed from life" (15)—that is, reconstituting (*praxis*) life (*zoon*) from recorded vision (*skopein*). "Professor Muybridge and His Queer Zoopraxiscope" is how the *Boston Daily Globe* supplement put it (October 21, 1882). Here was an early technology of animation, which, working with Bellour's "principle of invisibility" (the necessarily missing instants) repaired by the phenomenological principle of the "persistence of vision," created a nearer-to-life-size illusion of continuous movement from a quickly rotating succession of stills. Muybridge anticipated a day when the zoöpraxiscope could integrate sound to produce an even more complete simulation of life:

> In the—perhaps not far distant—future, instruments will be constructed that will not only reproduce visible actions simultaneously with audible words, but an entire opera, with the gestures, facial expressions, and songs of the performers, with all the accompanying music, will be recorded and reproduced by an apparatus, combining the principles of the zoöpraxiscope and the phonograph, for the instruction or entertainment of an audience long after the original participants shall have passed away; and if the photographs shall have been made stereoscopically, and projections from each series be independently and synchronously projected on a screen, a perfectly realistic imitation of the original performance will be seen, in the apparent "round," by the use of properly constructed binocular glasses. (16)

The hallucinatory reanimation ("long after the original participants shall have passed away") of the "entire opera" that Muybridge imagines thus projected "in the apparent 'round'" (no doubt prefiguring VR 3D animation of the sort one can view today) gives elaborate form to the ghost that, by these early experimentations in recording technologies, was at this time entering the real. Photography and phonography had made possible the continued presence of beings in reality absent in time and/or in space. But then the ghostliness is also a function of the retinal "persistence of vision" that fills the invisible instants and thus sutures discontinued life as if from the outside—that is, from the side of the spectator (of seeing) rather than that of the recorded subject (of being). The slippage is perhaps imperceptible in its effects, and would become increasingly so with the shortening of exposure times and reduction of time intervals; still, to not lose an instant, to evacuate the "principle of invisibility" and thus restore being in its ontological wholeness would, strictly speaking, require dividing the second into an infinite number of intervals, an inconceivable task, or one that would, paradoxically, take an infinite amount of time. In the moving image, a version of Zeno's paradox (another of Toussaint's long-standing obsessions)[25] is ineluctably at work, guaranteeing that however minutely one reconstructs the optical unconscious, however laboriously one slices each time interval composing a sequence of life, the truth of the moving body will always lie in a receding phenomenal beyond, at the end of an unending line of vanishing—or what in pictorial perspective is called *a line of flight.*

Immortally captured in those eighty-five plates of decomposed movements that seal the beginnings of chronophotography, the horse stands exposed at the place of production of modern visuality, as if immemorially galloping "in the round" behind every moving picture, "flying" on the secret horizons of the visible—as if turning the very wheels of life (zoe-trope). No wonder, then, that a story about a horse can become a story about seeing, about that trembling horizon between the seen and the unseen, between light and dark, what is recordable and what is not. Zahir will fly, but standing and tethered (and likely sedated) in the dark hold of the Lufthansa cargo plane. As Toussaint's prose continues to seek consummation in the continually receding picture of a horse in flight (in this novel written like a film which in turn phantasmatically wants to "freeze" on its disavowed "photogramme"), Jean-Christophe de G. and Marie climb the stairs to the plane to see, at eye level, "the horse's travel stall floating weightlessly in the air [*en apesanteur dans les airs*], with the living thoroughbred inside, slowly rising in the night [*dans la nuit*] up to the fuselage of the Boeing 747 cargo plane. Reaching the cargo hold, the lift, after a brutal jolt, shook the stall violently, was pushed horizontally into the dark opening of the hold, and then the stall disappeared into the bowels of the plane" (122–23/96–97). By elaborate mechanical and electrical means the defiance of gravity is here achieved (blessed by the ceremonial "in the night"), but at the cost of the horse's visibility, as it moves toward further erasure in the gaping darkness of the plane's entrails. The living horse must settle for levitation between the dashes (lost in English: "—avec le pur-sang vivant à l'intérieur—"/ "with the living thoroughbred inside") of its prosthetic conveyance. The plane's takeoff only confirms the triumph of metal technology over mythological weightlessness in the "clinking and straining of chains and straps, hooks, hoop irons, bungee cords, and clasps" (127/100). In the ensuing "[zone of] turbulence" (131/103)—aptly named, given the veritable turbulence of forms, not to say of being—the horse, growing nervous, attempts action through a disempowered *passé simple* and a renewed flash of white in the dark: "The horse wanted [*voulut*] to turn around, and it reared up [*se cabra*] in the stall, stood [*se redressa*] on its hind legs, and began neighing [*se mit à hennir*], its long mouth open, suddenly baring its teeth and gums in the dark" (132/104) to then, in its agitated stomping, crush the flashlight Jean-Christophe de G. had left at his side in an aborted effort to calm it. "The stall was impenetrably dark [*plongé dans les ténèbres*] now, hiding the horse's black figure, its shifting [*mobile*], invisible body, raging noisily in its narrow compartment, locked in on all sides" (133/105). All the tense threads carrying the horse through the narrative converge in this saturated black "box" (as the stall is designated in the French), filled by Zahir's silhouette. Simultaneously "invisible" and "mobile," in its mobility *unseen*, this horse is the optical *opposite* of Muybridge's subjects frozen in motion and in stereoscopic light, their dark other, re-equated with the night. Zahir fills out a space lost to human vision, a loss dramatized as Jean-Christophe de G. and Marie disorientedly stumble through the hold of the buffeted aircraft. Reaching the door, they intuit with a sense of terror that "no more than ten, twenty centimeters, the mere width of the plane's hull, separated them from the definitive night [*on entrait de plain-pied dans la nuit définitive*]" (134/106; translation modified). But could this really be the night that was being referred to all along, the "real space" "beyond [the] edges"? Is the definitive night, counterintuitively, the native or ultimate space of the animal? Modernist writings like Apollinaire's "Zone" had of course testified to the analogy likening planes, as they first entered human skies, to large birds. But the empyrion sensed outside the hold, too high, too cold, too dark for a bird, is no easily signifying space. Mythical, prehistoric (that is, preceding the human, and/or indifferent to it), or technological (technology's concomitant *production* of a dark inhuman night), it easily conflates with its contrary, a space marking the outer limit of technology and the inner limit of myth. No Pegasus can fly its rider through this night. By the same thrust, the lie of "horsepower" stands definitively undone in the melancholic tableau of this racehorse encapsulated within the narrow cargo hold of the airborne plane, not its engine and its dynamic force but its frightened, deadweight load.[26] It is at this place of *dis*empowerment that the novel pierces through for the first time to something like *the horse's point of view*:

> Zahir was aware of nothing but the certainty of being then and there, he had that certainty shared by all animals, silent, tacit, infallible. What lay outside his stall remained unknown to him, the sky, the night, the universe. The power of his imagination stretched no farther than the space in which he stood, his mind was stopped at the walls of his stall and could only return to the confusion of his own hazy consciousness. It was as if mental blinders prevented Zahir

> from imagining the world beyond his field of vision, cut off in every direction, dark, sightless, metallic. He was incapable of conceiving anything beyond the material limits of his stall, of mentally moving into the night [*dans la nuit*] through which the plane was flying, he didn't feel any irrepressible urge [*ce désir immémorial*] to stretch these limits or go beyond them, and, supposing he were able to accomplish this, supposing he could cross the walls of the plane in thought—leaving his skin [*sa peau rivetée*], passing through the fuselage—he would have leaped blindly into the sky, four horseshoes splayed in the air, Icarus burning his wings in an attempt to wake from a dream of his own making. (136–37/107–8)

Can one call this a point of view? It draws, rather, a relation of coterminousness, located in Zahir, between the real and imaginary worlds. For "him" (the French *lui* not distinguishing between human and horse) there is no elsewhere, only a here and now, the plane's dark hold and his confinement in it is all there is. His feet can leave the ground ("four horseshoes splayed in the air") only at the cost of tragedy or farce, where Pegasus trades his fate for Icarus's, and in a transport of imagination clearly not his own. Marking a heterogeneous space in this section of the novel otherwise entirely (and phantasmatically) composed around the impenetrable spaces successively occupied by Zahir (the van, the night, the conveyance stall, the hold), the passage gives voice to the view from inside the black box, abandoned by fantasy, a space without remainder, as it were. Is this Toussaint's conclusion regarding Schrödinger's cat? We have arrived in any case at the other pole of the narrative, that "animal" space thus far barred to it, where imagination reaches the place it must end. If it finds a way out nonetheless, it is through an elaborate subterfuge:

> For Zahir was as much in the real world as he was in an imaginary one, as much in this plane as in the haze of consciousness, or a dream, unknown, dark, troubled, where the turbulence of the sky mirrors the intensity [*sont les fulgurances*] of our language, and, if in reality horses never vomit, are unable to vomit (it's physically impossible for them to vomit, their physiognomy won't allow it, even when they're nauseated, even when their stomachs are full of toxic sub-

> stances), Zahir, on this night, spent, stumbling in his stall, falling on his knees in the hay, his mane stuck to his head, matted with dirt and dried sweat, his jaws slack, his tongue pasty, chewing air, a bitter drool dribbling from his mouth, sweating, feeling horrible, trying to stand up in his stall, [. . .] his stomach heavy, bloated from fermentation, feeling food rise up his stomach, now breaking into a cold sweat and suddenly feeling the concrete, physical nearness of death, that sensation you feel when about to vomit, the sour saliva that fills your mouth and forecasts the vomiting to come [*annonce l'imminence des vomissements*], when your intestines contract and food shoots up your throat and enters your mouth, Zahir, on this night, irrespective of [*indifférent à*] his own nature, betraying [*traître à*] his species, began to vomit in the sky in the hold of a Boeing 747 cargo plane flying in the night [*dans la nuit*]. (137–38/108–9; translation modified)

In a single sentence (truncated here) exceeding the length of a page, the most "metadiegetic" moment in Toussaint's oeuvre thus gathers around the unseemly allegory of a vomiting horse. What was given as the horse's consciousness starting in the preceding paragraph and continuing here (its animal certainty of being there, its imagination hugging the confines of its box, its nausea, its sense of proximity with death) turns out to be but a screen for the now-unmasked narrator ("les turbulences du ciel *sont des fulgurances de la langue*": the turbulence of the sky mirrors—but also *is*, *expresses*, *issues forth from*—the intensity of our language). It is a complicated allegory, exposing the artifice of fiction by means of the pure fictionality of the horse. As if to suggest that fiction too, like steam engines and cinema, ran on horsepower, were secretly fueled by *a horse in the night*, which to occupy this position must violate the physiology of its species ("betraying his species"), transcending its nature ("irrespective of—or indifferent to—his own nature") through the inscription of a supplemental difference—the eleven thousand fictional foot-pounds, the tenth of a second of flight, and, here, the pure fiction of a vomiting.

But *vomiting*? Why sacrifice zoological realism at this late stage only to make a horse vomit (and when there is so much more beauty in flying)? The riddle is somewhat resolved in three stages. For one, the framing of the scene is supported by a consistent spatio-symbolic configuration. Zahir does not simply vomit, he vomits "*in* the sky *in* the hold of the Boeing 747 cargo flying *in* the night." The mediations forming concentric circles in the night place the horse at the remotest point from any fantasy of its flight. There is nothing "natural" in the horse's overdetermined location—it has been multiply *incorporated* in the night, the "outside" turned into so many "insides," calling for an action from it equally "unnatural" that might turn the world, to the wretchedly limited extent that it could, *inside out*. Recall the baggage hold of the plane likened to entrails (123) and, further back, the night in which Zahir had been swallowed and digested ("englouti et digéré" / "swallowed and digested" [106/84]), and the concentricity makes an obscure sort of sense. What seems to happen—and this is the second stage—is that the vomiting occurs as the exact negative image of flying, as per a chiasmic correspondence between on the one hand the inside of the world and a body's outside (flight, the weightless absorption of the body into the surrounding night), and, on the other, the body's inside and the world's outside (vomiting, the expulsion of inner matter outward).[27] The mirroring is further assured by the fact that neither flying nor vomiting are acts of which a horse is anatomically capable; they form, rather, two polar gravity-defying impossibilities, the two pessimal thresholds of its being (i.e., thresholds at which it ceases to be)—one its outer horizon, one its inner.

But then there is a third orbit of meaning to the unraveling of the riddle of the vomiting horse (I too can be concentric), whose clues are in the numerous words the passage writes off to Zahir's gastroenterological turbulence—*nauseated . . . stomach [. . .] full of toxic substances . . . his tongue pasty, chewing air, a bitter drool dribbling from his mouth . . . his stomach heavy, bloated from fermentation, feeling food rise up . . . the sour saliva that fills your mouth and forecasts the vomiting to come, when your intestines contract and food shoots up your throat and enters your mouth*. In this remarkable ebullience of words describing the "imminent" antigravitational reflux of nausea one word is glaringly omitted, yet with every other word hollowly signified, as if the passage were but a long periphrasis. This word is "bile," in Greek *cholia*, which, united with the blackness of the night, gives *melancholia*. There is perhaps no term that better writes the fate of animals as they recede in the world (Lippit, *Electric Animal*, 18–19). Another theme that haunts Toussaint's prose, from the melancholy of *The Bathroom* to "the Saturnine influences" moving Zidane, here it is literalized by means of the invisible, unforgettable horse, in "an overflow of black bile into the solitary night."[28]

ICARUS

Technology has surely always, whether knowingly or subconsciously, given expression to humans' secret wish to transcend their grounded fate and fly. Succeeding through the millennia in taking two of their feet off the ground,[29] yet humans could not surrender the terra firma beneath the remaining two, their bipedalism a frozen station on the way to flight. While the innovations of aeronautics (literally "sailing through the air") and space travel have offered numerous prostheses and supplements to human winglessness, photography and cinema recorded in their beginnings a more archaic fascination with flight. Muybridge's *Animals in Motion*, opening with its "flying" horses, closed with a chapter called "The Flight of Birds" (66), with corresponding plates titled "Pigeon[s] in Flight," "Cockatoo[s] in Flight," a "Hawk in Flight," "Vulture[s] in Flight," and an "Eagle in Flight," followed by "Eagle[s] in Flight near the Ground," an "Adjutant," and an "Ostrich" respectively "Walking" and then "in a Flying Run" (plates 169–83). The work of Étienne-Jules Marey, carried out at the Station Physiologique of the Bois de Boulogne and featuring numerous horses, likewise significantly privileged flying creatures, which we see in short strips of black-and-white film (his [chrono]photographic gun taking twelve images per second, later his films up to sixty images per second): so ancient and silent they now seem in their eight-second flickering, in the silent paths the birds draw across the frame, that we wonder if we are seeing traced out on the screen someone's buried dream.[30] Even a stingray, pinned so that it could only wave its fins, seems to have been filmed in imitation of a bird in flight.[31] The tenacity of the fascination with flight no doubt found its match in the constitutive difficulty the subject posed to the camera. "The subjects of flight and soaring," wrote Muybridge in his analysis titled "The Flight of Birds" (the briefest of the "Analyses") "present so many intricate problems that the author is reluctantly compelled to relinquish his attempt to elucidate them" (66). He didn't need to state the nature of these "problems": an airborne creature is difficult to see for the human eye naturally positioned "near the ground"; and what sort of device could make a camera—that mechanical, chemical, phantasmatic extension of the human eye—soar so far up as to catch the detail of birds' flight? The extent of the difficulty is illustrated in the elaborateness of a way found around it, in 2001, by Jacques Perrin and Jacques Cluzaud, the unseen cameramen of *Winged Migration* (*Le peuple migrateur*). For it was not enough to have devised tall tripods and mobile cameras, nor to have positioned oneself in trees or on mountaintops. To watch birds *as they flew*, to record visually the flapping and span of their wings, the muscular craning of their necks—a kind of vertical unconscious to the human real, if you like, what unfolds so far above us that it is lost to view[32]—the only way was to somehow make Icarus's wager work, and to *fly with them*. The wings were not the problem: modern man knew materials less vulnerable than wax. The difficulty would lie, rather, in the fact that birds are not likely to want to fly with a human. A limit is thereby reached that photography and cinema could not and cannot solve technologically, because its nature is morphological, not to say ontological, that of a threshold constitutive of the difference between species. What was needed was for an eye to fly without a human (which was possible, no doubt, by attaching a minuscule camera to a bird, but this would mean relinquishing all control on the frame, and finally, perhaps, the loss of the captured footage)[33] or to surrender humanity and become a bird. The astonishing solution Perrin and Cluzaud opted for was of the second order, a *becoming-bird*. In a process called "imprinting" which took several years and was carried out simultaneously by teams stationed in different places, flocks of various bird species were habituated from an early age to the continual company of humans, and particularly of one human who would, in a flying contraption worthy of Leonardo da Vinci, "learn to fly" with them. It was a Deleuzian wager to the letter, premised both on the humans' *becoming bird* and on the birds' *becoming human* (in seeing in the human a mirror of themselves), with no actual *term* to either becoming but a projected zone of indistinction. Amazingly, the birds were persuaded that this huge human-with-flying-machine(-plus-camera) was simply another bird, an overgrown sibling perhaps, who, when the time came to migrate hundreds of miles to the other end of the earth, would naturally be flying with them. So the human infiltrated the ranks of the birds to film hours of their silent soaring weightlessness. *Winged Migration*, whose unsuspectable secret is in its blind spot (the editing-out of the "bird" that "sees"), is made of breathtaking footage, capturing birds as never before seen (that is, tautologically, *by humans*), unbelievable, otherworldly, like sculptures in movement. The implications cannot be overstated; it is as if photographic sight had broken free of its human coordinates and were recording momentous journeys in an empyrion before or after, in any case *without*, man. The truth is ultimately more startling, in that it is the human himself who has broken free of his last fetters to literally fly—that is, we now understand, broken through to his own vast unconscious, his limitless in-humanity, his night.

Not so with Toussaint's horses, alas. The last section of *The Truth about Marie*, set in Elba, mourns its share of flightless horses, when a fire breaks out near Marie's father's property. Destroying much of the horse club nearby where Marie had left her father's own horses following his death, it does not miss the stables, where tortured animal shadows and cries, both seemingly human and terribly inhuman, are all we will ever perceive of the dying horses (who perhaps thus die for the eternally marching horses of Modiano): "Screams could be heard here and there, there was great confusion around the stables, locked, inaccessible, where the silhouettes of animals stamped and writhed, whinnying hoarsely and desperately, human in their intonation and inhuman to the ear" (191–92/150; translation modified). A few pages further, Marie and the narrator return to the site to find "three makeshift shrouds covering forms whose dimensions were unclear in the silent gray light of dawn, not human forms but clearly dead bodies of some sort, charred carcasses of animals" (202/158). Too close to the fire, the three horses, wings melting, could not fly. The trembling of the line, once again, between human and nonhuman ("not human forms but clearly dead bodies [*cadavres*]") here only confirms that the animals have been robbed in death of their mythical ancestry. They die the deaths of *fallen humans*: as Julia Kristeva recalls in *Powers of Horror*, the word "cadaver" comes from *cadere*, that is, "to fall."[34]

A fourth horse survives the fire but has sustained such grave burns that they would "probably have to put her down" (203/159). The horse in question is Marie's favorite, a "mare with beautiful eyes" named Nocciola, whom she had first ridden on the day of her father's burial, escorting the hearse to the cemetery (160/126–27). In her time in Elba before the fire, Marie had often mounted Nocciola, as we learn in a passage that brings us back in its own way to Muybridge: "It wasn't long before Marie needed no help in riding Nocciola, she saddled the mare herself when she arrived at the club, leading her by the bridle, mounting the saddle, and riding around the paddock at a slow pace [*au pas*], then, firmly kicking the horse's sides, riding at a trot [*au trot*], and, after a week, at a gallop [*au galop*]" (161/127–28). In hindsight, when it transpires that Nocciola is destined for slaughter, her progression through the various phases (the walk, the trot, the gallop) of horse motion is invested with all the more ill-fated poignancy—for, having reached the gallop, should she not have known to fly?[35]

If the "sound of hooves" was the sound of sentenced footfalls, of feet that could leave the ground only in death, Toussaint's novel, read from the struck-through place of the horse, assuredly seals a *fall from flight.* One should not be surprised, perhaps, to count so many horses fatally impeded in their flight. A failed attempt by paramedics to revive Jean-Christophe de G. in the first pages of the novel had in a sense already suggested that electric (re)animation of the dead body (zoopraxiscopy?) had lost its magical powers. Receiving a "brutal electric shock, causing [its] chest to shake on the floor," the body had fallen lifelessly to the ground, appearing then to Marie's eyes as "white inanimate flesh dotted with electrodes, skin like a fish, cod or flounder, [. . .] this objectified, medicalized body, this shaved, intravenoused, ventilated body—this body reduced to its bare substance" (33–34/27; translation modified). This human body turned into the inanimate white flesh of fish pierced with electrodes cannot but bring to mind Marey's stingray, immobilized, with only its fins free to move in a pathetic tableau vivant of a bird flapping its wings but covering no distance: the fate, one might imagine, of the Elba horses.

So, at the convergence of technology and myth, a long *dream* of flying horses seems to come to an end, or to be "troubled" if one remembers how Zahir is last seen—vomiting *in* the hold *in* the plane *in* the night but also *in* the narrator's "*dream*, unknown, dark, *troubled* [*rêve*, inconnu, sombre, *agité*]" (137/108–9; my emphasis). Fortuitously perhaps, we find in this *rêve agité* (troubled dream) two words that had notably figured in the opening sentence of Kafka's *Metamorphosis.*[36] It was from a "troubled dream" that Gregor had woken to find himself transformed (from human to overturned animal); here from a "troubled dream" the horse tries to exit—impossibly, as in so doing it can only burn its wings and fall (turning from animal to falling human: "Icarus burning his wings in an attempt to wake from a dream of his own making" [137/108]). As it happens, *The Metamorphosis* too featured lost wings, through an enigma that should allow me here to conclude, suggesting simply and obviously that human stories are lined with a trail of flightless, falling animals. The quote is from Marina Warner's *Fantastic Metamorphoses*: "Vladimir Nabokov, uniquely both distinguished lepidopterist and fabulist, wanted to establish exactly which species of insect Kafka [was] evoking [in *The Metamorphosis* . . . He] concludes that the bug is simply 'a big beetle,' indeed, as he can reach the door knob with his feelers, one that is three feet high. Nabokov points out that Gregor should have realized that as a beetle he had a pair of wings hidden under 'the hard covering of his back,' which could have carried him for miles and miles in a blundering flight."[37]

CHAPTER 2

Man of the Forest

Éric Chevillard, with La Fontaine and Poe

Literature was born on the day when a boy came crying wolf, wolf and there was no wolf behind him. That the poor little fellow because he lied too often was finally eaten up by a real beast is quite incidental . . . Between the wolf in the tall grass and the wolf in the tall story there is a shimmering go-between. That go-between, that prism, is the art of literature.
—Vladimir Nabokov

"They are no longer anywhere, everywhere they are not, even if while living they did not occupy all points in space; one could go some time without meeting one, look up from one's task and not see any around, this would occur and was not shocking, [but] now they are missing in every place and in every instant." Éric Chevillard's *Sans l'orang-outan* (2007; *Without the Orangutan*) imagines a dire predicament.[1] The last two orangutans have died, and with them has perished a species now realized, too late, to have been the subtle cog in the very wheels (*le subtil rouage*) of the human world (21). Without the orangutan the world now collapses, all meanings reel between extremes, and Chevillard's riotous novel, espousing these reelings as its very form, places the animal, in its extinction, everywhere where it is not to offer a sort of paradoxical and irreverent orangutan-machine, a 187-page account of the world exhaustively abandoned—and proportionally haunted—by the orangutan. Causality, identity, difference have all broken down: people and things no longer reach their destinations, the sun has fatally receded from the earth, humans have started to resemble each other, and space and distance themselves have ceased to be differentiated, causing collisions and incest. What is more, "the length of the meter has changed"—it has increased, for this length had naturally been set by the millennially brachiating limbs of the orangutan as it had swung from trees.[2] Chevillard has ostensibly done in this book what he does in all his fiction: approaching the real as a deserted stage, he introduces a particular and thoroughly unaccountable entity in all its empty places, as if to see what might happen.[3] Such exercises in thought and style are in Chevillard's hands so many experiments in possible worlds. Even so, in *Sans l'orang-outan*, the imagined extinction of a species arguably provides the most provocative, not to say the ideal material for such experiments, for reasons that, like (or carried away with) the orangutan, escape the boundaries of the text. "The orangutan carries away also the name orangutan," writes Chevillard, "and our language is orphaned in turn, for the sign [*signe*] will not long survive the ape [*singe*]" (53). The novel reads, in its entirety, as an exploitation of this lag between *singe* and *signe*, between the animal body and its name. To consider seriously the stakes of such a lag, to recover their legibility beyond the evident terms of some sort of postmodern wager (language as absence, as free play of the signifier, as generalized pastiche or irony, the receding of the referent, etc.) is to return to a long tradition of animals enrolled in narrative. What long made possible, or at least invisible, a contract—between language and animal bodies—which, now, on the death of the last orangutans, should lie so exposed and undone? And, for that matter, why, with the vanishing of the orangutan, in its severance from its name, should the meter, and indeed all measure, all assurances of distance and positionings, be also lost?

WOLF TRAP

A "double fable" first appearing in the 1668 original collection of Jean de La Fontaine's *Fables* had the wolf twice positioned outside a door, and twice tricked. The first fable within the fable ("Le loup, la chèvre et le chevreau" / "The Wolf, the Goat and the Kid") saw the wolf using the mother sheep's password to deceive a lamb into opening the door. The strategy fails, as the lamb, "twice prudent," not content with the password, and looking through a tiny crack in the door, asks the wolf to show "patte blanche" (a white paw, and thus, symbolically, its "hand," i.e., its good faith/intentions). The wolf walks away, defeated. In the second fable ("Le loup, la mère et l'enfant" / "The Wolf, the Mother, and Her Child"), the wolf, standing outside a village house, overhears to its delighted surprise a mother telling her wailing infant that if it does not quieten down she will offer it up as food to the wolf. When the child (understandably) continues to wail, the mother changes her line to assure it that if the wolf appears it will be killed. Hearing this, the eavesdropper is indignant: "Dire d'un, puis d'un autre? Me prend-on pour un sot?" The line is translated in 1841 by Elizur Wright (the first to translate the entire fables into English) as: "'Humph!' cried the veteran mutton-eater / 'Now this, now that! Now hot, now cool! / Is this the way they change their metre? / And do they take me for a fool?'" The wolf promptly cries out its resolve to eat the child the next time it finds it collecting nuts in the woods. Whereupon people exiting the house find the eavesdropper, capture it, and, hearing its story (in line 26, "Aussitôt il conta l'affaire" / line 40, "He told it all"), decide to kill and quarter it. The dismembered parts of the wolf are exhibited on the village headman's door, along with a placard warning wolves not to heed tales spun by mothers to their children.

LE LOUP, LA MÈRE ET L'ENFANT

Ce loup me remet en mémoire
Un de ses compagnons qui fut encor mieux pris:
Il y périt. Voici l'histoire:
Un villageois avait à l'écart son logis.
Messer Loup attendait chape-chute à la porte;
Il avait vu sortir gibier de toute sorte,
Veaux de lait, agneaux et brebis
Régiments de dindons, enfin bonne provende.
Le larron commençait pourtant à s'ennuyer.
Il entend un enfant crier:
La mère aussitôt le gourmande,
Le menace, s'il ne se tait,
De le donner au loup. L'animal se tient prêt,
Remerciant les dieux d'une telle aventure,
Quand la mère, apaisant sa chère géniture,
Lui dit: "Ne criez point, s'il vient, nous le tuerons.
—Qu'est ceci? s'écria le mangeur de moutons:
Dire d'un, puis d'un autre! Est-ce ainsi que l'on traite
Les gens faits comme moi? me prend-on pour un sot?
Que quelque jour ce beau marmot
Vienne au bois cueillir la noisette!"
Comme il disait ces mots, on sort de la maison:
Un chien de cour l'arrête; épieux et fourche-fières

L'ajustent de toutes manières.
"Que veniez-vous chercher en ce lieu?" lui dit-on.
Aussitôt il conta l'affaire.
"Merci de moi! lui dit la mère;
Tu mangeras mon fils! l'ai-je fait à dessein
Qu'il assouvisse un jour ta faim?"
On assomma la pauvre bête.
Un manant lui coupa le pied droit et la tête:
Le seigneur du village à sa porte les mit;
Et ce dicton picard à l'entour fut écrit:
"Biaux chires leups, n'écoutez mie
Mère tenchent chen fieux qui crie."

THE WOLF, THE MOTHER, AND HER CHILD
(translated by Elizur Wright)

This wolf another brings to mind,
Who found dame Fortune more unkind,
In that the greedy, pirate sinner,
Was balk'd of life as well as dinner.
As saith our tale, a villager
Dwelt in a by, unguarded place;
There, hungry, watch'd our pillager
For luck and chance to mend his case.
For there his thievish eyes had seen
All sorts of game go out and in—
Nice sucking calves, and lambs and sheep;
And turkeys by the regiment,
With steps so proud, and necks so bent,
They'd make a daintier glutton weep.
The thief at length began to tire
Of being gnaw'd by vain desire.
Just then a child set up a cry:
"Be still," the mother said, "or I
Will throw you to the wolf, you brat!"
"Ha, ha!" thought he, "what talk is that!
The gods be thank'd for luck so good!"
And ready at the door he stood,
When soothingly the mother said,
"Now cry no more, my little dear;

That naughty wolf, if he comes here,
Your dear papa shall kill him dead."
"Humph!" cried the veteran mutton-eater.
"Now this, now that! Now hot, now cool!
Is this the way they change their metre?
And do they take me for a fool?
Some day, a nutting in the wood,
That young one yet shall be my food."
But little time has he to dote
On such a feast; the dogs rush out
And seize the caitiff by the throat;
And country ditchers, thick and stout,
With rustic spears and forks of iron,
The hapless animal environ.
"What brought you here, old head?" cried one.
He told it all, as I have done.
"Why, bless my soul!" the frantic mother said,—
"You, villain, eat my little son!
And did I nurse the darling boy,
Your fiendish appetite to cloy?"
With that they knock'd him on the head.
His feet and scalp they bore to town,
To grace the seigneur's hall,
Where, pinn'd against the wall,
This verse completed his renown:—
"Ye honest wolves, believe not all
That mothers say, when children squall!"

The seventeenth-century French scholar Marc Escola, in his wonderful book *Lupus in fabula*, playfully analyzes both the internal structural-moral coherence of these fables and certain elements of unaccountability within them that appear to arbitrarily block certain other equally possible unfoldings.[4] For instance, why does the lamb in the first fable go further in its caution than even its mother had advised? If not for this excessive caution, indeed, the wolf's strategy was set to succeed (as his acts of deception and disguise do in certain other well-known fables—recall the "wolf in sheep's clothing"). And, in the second, what makes people exit the house at precisely the moment at which the wolf is plotting to kill the child one day in the woods, when the inverse scenario was equally possible—in other words, that the wolf enter the house at this moment and eat the child, fulfilling the mother's first promise? The fable's outcome consists instead, critically, in a realization of the *second* promise (that the wolf, on appearing, be killed).

Escola's concern, in analyzing these fables, is to demonstrate how it is always possible to activate supplemental textual potential within a given text by recovering the traces of what he calls an "erratic structure," bared in surface "dysfunctionings" or places of "disequilibrium" where narrative logic, hesitating, then making a decision which instantly becomes its constraint, is seen to move from one "local coherence" to another. The method allows him to show, with great finesse, how the two seemingly irreconcilable parts of La Fontaine's double fable can be recombined to produce a tale bearing an uncanny resemblance to Charles Perrault's *Le petit chaperon rouge* (*Little Red Riding Hood*). As for me, my interest lies particularly in the second fable and in the fate of the wolf, and in the structure of duplicity to which the fable resorts, both in content and in form, in order to *trap* it. As Escola notes, the wolf's error, in "The Wolf, the Mother, and Her Child," is in failing to distinguish between the literal and the figurative—or, we could say, between "reality" and fiction. Indeed, what the wolf takes literally (the promise of the child as food) was only intended figuratively—and this is its *error*. However, and conversely (and here, I will suggest, lies a murkier realm), its *crime*, for which it must die, is not a real act (for it has not killed the child) but for having *imagined* it—and this is presumably what it confesses to in the abyssal line 26/40 ("Your dear papa" through "He told it all": *abyssal* because in this recounting and its eliding is also a *mise en abyme* within the fable, from the wolf's vantage point, of the whole of the fable). Now, within the logic of the fable, it is a temporal conceit (or rather deceit) that makes sense of such a *conversion*: the wolf, harboring such designs, would have killed the child at the next opportunity, it was only a matter of *time*, itself encapsulated within line 26. But since the fable cannot tolerate within its diegesis this extension of time (wherein the wolf would commit the deed and thus in reality earn its retribution), it resorts to a canny short-circuiting, and incorporating the extension as unbearable future yet (crucially) *not* as permissible unfolding of time, performs a forced symbolic reparation of the logical contradiction that had so perplexed the wolf: "Dire d'un, puis d'un autre?" ("Now this, now that! Now hot, now cool!"). Temporality and morality are here chiasmically at odds: following a de Manian reading, one might say that a discontinuity of structure *passes for* a temporal continuity and vice versa[5]—and that the dismembered body of the wolf stands at the site of this two-way conversion. In preempting the crime, the fable effectively annuls it; yet in folding in the annulled time/crime in which the wolf can realize its always already guilty lupine destiny, it maintains the authority to punish the wolf for it.

Another place from which to approach the fable's deceitful structure is found at its close, in that placard on which the village chief inscribes in Picard, beside the trophied head and leg of the wolf, a warning to wolves not to heed what a mother may tell her crying child. An exquisite twist, this. That the message should be addressed to wolves (with the added *effet de réel* of the Picard dialect) is remarkable enough, marking a place of overdetermined, saturated liminality in which the frontispiece (the writer/reader "interface") of the fable and the human/wolf border appear to coincide, and the fable's moral coherence is suggested as being organized around and in respect of the wolf's interpretive agency—a suggestion itself preciously paradoxical given that what the wolf is shown as incapable of understanding is precisely the fictional mode, in other words fables, and thereby this fable . . . Then there is the unconcealed amorality of the inscribed message, affirming the untruth quotient in human-speak. Or clarifying that untruth to the one entity at the expense of which it circulates, the only interpreter, perhaps, who can—if only it could—recognize it *as* untruth. As if the wolf stood at (and for) the exposed side of human meaning, the unprotected side, where it lay bare and inconsistent, words and things stitched together loosely, irresponsibly, fit to persuade only crying babies and idiots ("me prend-on pour un sot?" / "And do they take me for a fool?").

Something like a fourth-wall *dispositif* was of course at work from the very outset of the fable, as the wolf positioning himself outside the villager's dwelling *overheard* the mother speaking to the child. This would be a classic instance of irony arising from an unequal distribution of knowledge within a space, or, more precisely, from a differential in symbolic competence (in telling apart the literal from the figurative, the false promise from the serious), but for the added factor of a *homonymic* pull, shall we say, whereby Messer Loup believes himself to be the referent of the mother's utterances, and identifying immediately with every occurrence of the word "loup," must then, in the face of the irreconcilable, be literally dismembered (if the *logos* itself, here challenged by the wolf, is to be repaired)—it is, here again, a mere matter of time. The most powerful event of "The Wolf, the Mother, and Her Child," then, is in the threat posed to the functioning of language itself, as the wolf with its stubborn presence, with its very body, attempts to close the gap (between the world of things and the world of words, or between the referent and the signified) constitutive of symbolic possibility. In this sense, the fable is, in its broadest terms, shall we say, about what happens to signification when an animal enters the scene. For if the wolf cannot bear to hear its name spoken in vain, if the wolf cannot tolerate metaphorical language, nor can metaphor in the end really suffer the wolf. As Susan McHugh lucidly notes, "The aesthetic structures of metaphor, though precariously supporting the human subject, seem unable to bear animal agency."[6] Metaphor would rather work its "substitutive logics" (489) at a safe imaginative distance from the real wolf, as unperturbed by its realness as it is by its quickness to spot contradictions. What a naive literalist, the wolf. The Picard sign points the way to the more sophisticated world of humans, where words do not have to mean what they say. This in itself cannot be a systematic principle, however, as the fable itself duplicitously demonstrates. The mother may not have meant that she would give her child to the wolf, but, manifestly, she did mean that if the wolf appeared it would be killed. How was a wolf to know?

THE PASSING (OR "I AM A WOLF")

The fold noted in La Fontaine's fable is no doubt not as curious as all that; rather, such folds may well be constitutive points of torsion in all fables. For Thomas Keenan, author of *Fables of Responsibility*, indeed, a fable is always a story about subject accountability, in other words, what fables recount over and over again is, precisely, the paradoxical advent of something like an "I."[7] Keenan devotes a chapter of his book to Aesop's fable "The Eagle and the Raven," in which a raven, thinking it is an eagle, swoops down on a sheep, only to find its claws stuck in the sheep's thick wool and to thus learn at its own cost that it is not the bird of prey it thought it was. The failed eagle ends its days with clipped wings as a pet for the shepherd's child, acknowledging now, at the end of the fable, that it *is* in fact *a raven*. Keenan writes: "The fable tells the story [. . .] of a non-symmetrical movement from nameless bird to birdless name, the generation of the pure name that is the precondition for the invention of the 'I.' This I is just as disfigured as the so-called raven, a plaything for children, just as empty and robbed of its properties, and this doubled blank provides the equivalence that makes the utterance 'I am a raven' possible. With difficulty, and at the price of its intelligibility" (65). The chiasmus ("from nameless bird to birdless name") could just as well apply to La Fontaine's wolf, whose plight also carries it from being a body failing to decisively occupy its name (*dire d'un, puis d'un autre?*) to a body quartered, restored in its destruction to its name. Invoking the "dehiscence 'within' the bird" in Aesop's fable, Keenan recalls the substitutive or supplementary lag that, for thinkers like Levinas, Blanchot, and Derrida, marks the arrival of the subject, caught between an "already there" and a "not yet": "Like us, caught in the structural delay or the crippling lag of reading, the raven 'is' this *morcellement du 'sujet,'* passing without return across the trope or the pseudonym—the error—that marks its only possibility: there are borrowed names, or no names at all" (69).

The "passing *without return* across the trope" gives me pause here, for Keenan's own lucid parsing of the fable leads, rather, to the insight that there *is* a return in this commerce between names and bodies. A continual return, precisely, in that specter of a nameless body which every naming on one side of the trope produces on the other side as if retroactively, that is, as per a "structural delay" or a "crippling lag" whereby (ironic) structure is grasped *as* (temporal) event *and* vice versa. In other words, that as soon as there is a turn (a *trope*, i.e., representation) there is also, as its shadow, a return, and that this alone, the fable *as* return, if you will, can make available to thought—(at the price of being thought of) as what lies *on the other side* of naming—a habitat for nameless, unaccountable ravens and wolves. Naturally, Keenan's account of the "passing" evinces a directional prejudice consistent with his concern with responsibility as a problematics of human subjecthood. Indeed, it is in this capacity that his analyses are taken up by both Judith Butler in *Giving an Account of Oneself*[8] and David Wills in *Dorsality: Thinking Back through Technology and Politics*.[9] Keenan's postulate of an "across" nonetheless locates a sort of threshold that makes equally possible the thinking of its "passing" *from the other side*, as it were, so that his very insights are productively, for our purposes, reversed. Just as every fable attempts to account for a "passing" into accountable (humanlike) subjecthood, and precisely because this passing implies (folds in) a place that works as a trope, or a ("nonsymmetrical") chiasmus, where structure works like narrative, and narrative like structure, what we may well find (looking back) *on the other side*—in turn irreducibly indistinguishable from a *before, and vice versa*—is a prehistoric ahuman subject, that is, *the animal*.

If for Aesop's raven, repairing the subject-predicate declaration of self-identity ("I am a raven") was at the price of its freedom and properties (its wings clipped, its life now that of imprisoned pethood), for La Fontaine's wolf, saying "I am a wolf" could only be at the cost of its life. In these fables offering, then, if that is what they are doing, an allegory of a coming-into-responsibility, the animal body whose "errancy consists precisely in wandering away from its name" (Keenan, *Fables*, 62) is not so easily subsumed or "sublated" in the telling. But nor is it so easily "recovered," in this fabulist theater of passings, counterfeitings, maskings, and unmaskings (which may yet only be remaskings). In *Limited Inc.*, Jacques Derrida, writing about how theories of subject unity and responsibility entail a certain policing to exclude the "parasitism" and errancy that he names the unconscious or undecidability, had told his own fable: "It is sufficient to introduce, into the fold [*la bergerie*] of speech acts, a few wolves of the type 'undecidability' . . . or of the type 'unconscious' . . . for the shepherd to lose track of his sheep [*pour que le pasteur ne puisse plus compter ses moutons*]" (quoted in Keenan, *Fables*, 48–49). A little earlier he wrote of the effects of a "structural unconscious" that would "make appear (and [. . .] leap) the security barrier which, *at the interior of the system*, . . . condemns the unconscious as one condemns or bars access to a forbidden place." Keenan, recalling the intertextual network linking Derrida's wolf fable to earlier fables (particularly the one in which the wolf in sheep's clothing succeeds in obtaining plentiful access to its prey, but also a variant, in which, accordingly mistaken for a sheep, the wolf is killed one day for meat), notes beautifully here that, in Derrida's recasting of the parts, "the wolf of undecidability imitates [. . .] not only the sheep but also the earlier wolves, and so the fable itself plays the part of the wolf in fable's clothing" (50). If the morality of Derrida's fable is, in Keenan's words, that there is "no responsibility without undecidability, without the unconscious and its parasites, and no fable, no example, without the risk of a certain simulation" (51), one could perhaps also say that there is no morality, no allegory without a "return" of/to a forgotten "literality"—which Derrida/Keenan's preoccupation with subjecthood here must occlude, but which some of Derrida's later seminars such as *The Animal That Therefore I Am* or *The Beast and the Sovereign* (so interested in La Fontaine's *Fables*) make clearly (*as if* retroactively) perceptible. In a certain and absolutely nonincidental sense, the *destinerrance* or adestination that came to be the condition of subjecthood and signification through all of Derrida's work—the originary possibility of forgery in the signature, the fact that a letter *can always not arrive* and therefore, in a certain sense, *never arrives*, or the premisedness of the *oikos*, the home or (any) economy, on the possibility of transgression of its borders, to recall some of the best-known of these "supplementarities"—carves out nothing less than a place for the animal. For in inscribing within the possibility of identity, of intent, of meaning, the possibility, always and since the beginning, or even before the beginning ("depuis le temps" / "*since* time"), of an indirection, of an interception, an expropriation, had the philosopher not allowed, before the beginning, the possibility that while a mother wove innocent/guilty lupine fictions for the instruction/amusement of her child, a wolf stood *eavesdropping* at the door?[10]

CHAPE-CHUTE

The word La Fontaine uses to describe the wolf at the door, *chape-chute*, draws on an erstwhile literality largely lost to modern French. The medieval compound, from *chape*, the older word for "cape" (or woman's/nun's veil), and *chute*, the still-used word for *fall*, would have meant, at the time La Fontaine wrote, literally, a "cape-fall," or "cape loss," and accordingly, figuratively, an unsought chance to profit from the negligence or misfortune of another (*Littré*). The word *chape* itself in the meantime had evolved both as a term in certain specialized vocabularies (maritime, architectural, technological) and more generally to mean a lid, a cover. There may be a limit to how far one can go in untangling the literal and metaphorical, and in regulating scale, in the case of this word, which very quickly seems to name both the "lid" of the very firmament (*chape du ciel*), and, as it turns out, a layer of waterproof cement reinforcing vaults or roofs, no doubt to prevent rainwater from dripping (so that we are not far from the scene of eaves, the edges of a roof, dripping, which is in turn the "forgotten literality" of the English *eavesdropping*)—but also, just perhaps, to stop words uttered within four walls from es*cap*ing? *Échapper* (to escape), also from *chape*, suggests the *Littré*, would have derived its meaning from the act of throwing off one's cape or robe, or, perhaps, of fleeing while leaving one's cape or robe in the hands of one's pursuer.

Standing outside the door, happening to profit from the villagers' negligence in not properly shutting the door or in not cementing gaps in the walls, La Fontaine's wolf is the witness, not to say the very "function," of a slip—a slip of a cover, or a slip in attention—that opens the inside to the outside, and verbal meaning to its exorbitance. The wolf, *chape-chute*, is, in a sense, *both inside and outside*, its overhearing, whatever its competence, exposing the boundaries of language, reminding it of the bodies in which it trades, of the intimacy of its transaction with the outside and the nonhuman. This is a good place to recall that the house, for Levinas in *Totality and Infinity*, is a "primary appropriation" of interiority, so much so that the process of subjective individuation asks to be understood *first* in the terms of the construction of a house: "The domicile, condition for all property, renders the inner life possible. The I is at home with itself. Through the home our relationship with space as distance is substituted for the simple 'bathing in the element.' But the adequate relation with the element is precisely bathing."[11] David Wills, commenting on the "*demeure*" (domicile) in Levinas, makes clear its place as primary and paradoxical *dispositif*, as it were, in "allowing the I to be precisely by being defined as an I that is housed within itself. From that point of view, the I does not exist without the conception of the house; the house exists and is constructed, as it were, prior to the formation of the I" (54–55). Levinas's insistence, nonetheless, on an "adequate relation with the element" (which the house would seem to already interrupt), leads him to concede to the originariness of the house only on the condition that its "door to the outside must . . . be at the same time open and closed" (148). *Chape-chute*?

A side note here: for one, there is little reason to believe, as some did in the past, that La Fontaine was a minute observer of fauna. He was not, for his animals came much more from a vast bestiary of fables and tales than from any attention to nature.[12] Likewise, it is well known that Levinas was reluctant, in his thinking on subjecthood and ethics, to extend it to the realm of animals (with the notable exception of "Nom d'un chien ou le droit naturel").[13] Derrida enjoyed quoting that occasion on which, asked in an interview whether his ethics might apply to the animal other, Levinas had retorted with the counterquestion "Does the serpent have a face?"[14] *It remains* that in La Fontaine's positioning of the wolf at the porous edge of a house, and in Levinas's description of the house as the permeable closing off of a finite interiority from an interiority without limit ("the element," which Rilke and then Heidegger and Agamben would call "the Open"), we recognize in (differently) dramatized form that important if imperfectible boundary drawn between, on the one hand, human space as enclosure, separation, *inside*, and, on the other, an *outside* which we know, historically, immemorially, ecologically, ethologically, if now precariously, to be the space of the animal.[15] There is reason to expect and suspect, then, that any entry of the animal *into* human space will concern this border, and that if this border is *duplicitous* (that is, constructed on a double fold, of the Baroque sort, whereby the inside is folded on itself, and the outside folded out),[16] that this entry, or any ensuing exit, will, in complicating it, shed further light on what, following Keenan, I have been calling the "passing."

THE UNEQUAL ANIMAL

The exemplary text here is, of course, Edgar Allan Poe's "The Murders in The Rue Morgue" (1841), which, if it famously inaugurated the genre of detective fiction, did so equally famously through the supreme twist of ultimately tracing the gruesome murder of two women in a Paris apartment to an animal recently arrived from Borneo. The lengthy discussion, opening the story, of the differences between the respective skills needed for playing draughts and chess, serves to set up the method by which self-appointed sleuth Auguste Dupin will finally arrive at the orang-utan. This method is based on a twofold refusal of given parameters. On the one hand, analytic skill involves a further, deeper penetration *into* thought than "ordinary understanding" might obtain: "The analyst throws himself into the spirit of the opponent, identifies himself therewith, and not unfrequently sees thus, at a glance, the sole methods (sometimes indeed absurdly simple ones) by which he may seduce into error or hurry into miscalculation."[17] It is a method relying, in this sense, on *chercher chape-chute*, on waiting for the slightest slip whence advantage might be gained. The analyst must accordingly have "a comprehension of *all* the sources whence legitimate advantage may be derived"; these, in turn, "lie frequently among recesses of thought altogether inaccessible to the ordinary understanding." On the other hand, skillful analysis involves extending thought *beyond* the apparent boundaries of the very game: "It is in matters beyond the limits of mere rule that the skill of the analyst is evinced"; "our player confines himself not at all; nor, because the game is the object, does he reject deductions from things external to the game" (240). In modern terms, what is being argued for here is a thinking outside the box—verily, the sealed apartment on rue Morgue cuts a compelling box—but which presents itself at the same time as an *intensive* movement probing into the "recesses" of the box.

It is the *extensive* direction of this thinking that will proceed to be most explicitly applied in the investigation that follows. Yet it is useful to note the dialectical character of the analyst's skill as presented in the prologue, something to which I will return. Let me briefly recall the circumstances of the case. The apartment, whose doors are locked from the inside, and windows all tightly closed, is found in a state of great disorder; possessions are strewn about though a large quantity of gold coins had apparently not been taken by the intruder; the body of Mme L'Espanaye is found in the rear yard, with its throat "so entirely cut that, upon an attempt to raise her, the head f[alls] off"; the corpse of her daughter, equally mutilated, is found partially shoved up a chimney; neighbors and passersby, when interrogated by the police, all concur that they had heard two voices as they ascended the stairs to the apartment, but in each case the person interrogated said the first voice, male, spoke in French, while ascribing to the other voice—described as "unequal" (249), "uneven[]" (250), "unusual" (256)—a foreign language the witness himself did not understand. Amateur detective Auguste Dupin in his analysis will proceed partly from this fact, noting that, when it came to the second voice, "no words—no sounds resembling words—were by any witness mentioned as distinguishable" (256). The "no" phrase, the decisive negation of human traits, this forced expulsion of the intruder *out* of the field of possible human subjects, will trace, by means of a series, as we shall see, the path toward the orangutan.

The "clew" thanks to which the mystery unravels is come upon as Dupin stubbornly focuses his thinking on modes of "ingress" and "egress." All paths connecting inside and outside seeming to be sealed (and there being "*no* secret issues" [257]), they must be eliminated. Dupin persists: "The doers of the deed were material, and escaped materially. Then how?" (257).[18] The solution is found in a difference masquerading as identity. Two windows, identically sealed shut, with a spring mechanism and a nail, lead the very "perceptions" of the police to be "hermetically sealed against the possibility of the windows having ever been opened at all" (262). The *hypallage* here (yet another one), by which the terms describing the apartment ("hermetically sealed") are displaced onto the police's "perceptions" is fitting, as when Dupin discovers that one nail only *appears* intact, but that this is so only because it is so perfectly cracked that its "resemblance to a perfect nail [is] complete" (259), it is both the sealedness of the domicile and that of the police investigation that comes undone. From this point it is only a *matter of time* before the riddle is solved: "the almost *praeternatural* character" ("praeternatural" meaning, precisely, *outside* or *beyond* the "natural") of the strength a body would have needed to have swung itself into and out of the fourth floor apartment by means of the shutter and then the window, the adding up of the "ideas of an agility astounding, a strength super-human, a ferocity brutal, a butchery without motive, a *grotesquerie* in horror absolutely alien from humanity, and a voice foreign in tone to the ears of men of many nations, and devoid of all distinct or intelligible syllabification" (263), in short, the "something *excessively outré* [from the French *outre*, or "beyond"]—something altogether irreconcilable with our common notions of human action" (262), must lead to a criminal *outside* the field of the human. The final clues are in some ways redundant (and in others, sufficiently decisive, so that one can wonder why such a careful "analysis" was even necessary): an undescribed "little tuft" of "most unusual" hair found on the scene of the crime is deemed "no *human* hair" (263), the "deep indentations" found on the throat of Mademoiselle L'Espanaye,[19] in turn, form "the mark of no human hand" (263).

But there is another "clew," subtler still, that had led here. Let me return to an earlier stage of the investigation, already alluded to. Neighbors and passersby, when questioned by the police, had all concurred that as they had ascended the stairs to the apartment, they had heard terrible female shrieks, followed by a brief exchange between two voices, but in each case the person questioned was certain that the first voice, male and gruff, spoke in French, while ascribing to the other voice, more shrill or more harsh, uncertain gender and indistinguishable words pronounced in a foreign language. Thus, an Italian witness thinks the second voice was that of a Russian, a Spaniard judges it to be that of an Englishman, the English witness is sure that the shrill voice was that of a German, and two French witnesses ascribe it respectively to a Spaniard and an Italian, while a Dutchman is sure the voice was that of a Frenchman, remarking that the words, impossible to distinguish, were "loud and quick—*unequal*." Of all the adjectives used to describe the voice, shrill, harsh, strange, unusual, uneven, it is this "unequal" that Dupin will recall a few pages later as he builds the chain of deductions that will ultimately lead to the orangutan. Incidentally Dupin will say that *two* witnesses used the words "quick and *unequal*" (the last word italicized in the original) when in fact only one had used the word. A second witness had said that the voice had spoken "quick and unevenly"—it is presumably this "unevenly" which Dupin apparently considers to be synonymous with unequal. And why not, after all? It remains that in rereading this story so exacting in its accounting of all facts pertaining to the case, one's attention catches on this unnecessary doubling and italicization of "unequal," with which Dupin proceeds, it turns out, to do nothing. There are arguably several threads that are not quite followed up in Dupin's demonstration, but simply woven together more and more tightly till somehow the animal is ensnared in them as in a net. Even so, a few pages further on, the word "unequal" recurs as Dupin recapitulates his observations: "My immediate purpose is to lead you to place in juxtaposition, that *very unusual* activity of which I have just spoken, with that *very peculiar* shrill (or harsh) and *unequal* voice, upon whose nationality no two persons could be found to agree, and in whose utterance no syllabification could be detected" (260). Hearing this, the narrator says: "At these words a vague and half-formed conception of the meaning of Dupin flitted over my mind. I seemed to be upon the verge of comprehension, without power to comprehend—as men, at times, find themselves upon the brink of remembrance, without being able, in the end, to remember" (260–61).

In the frisson, the *unheimliche* of this moment, the story itself seems to be poised on the verge of comprehension, on the brink of remembrance. On the brink of *recognition*, almost, of the animal that it will only be able to *cognize* a few pages later when, after lining up several other elements that will retroactively support his thesis, Dupin supplies, by means of an excerpt from Georges Cuvier's *Le règne animal* (1817; *The Animal Kingdom*), the textual portrait of the murderer as "the large fulvous Ourang-Outang of the East Indian islands," of "gigantic stature," "prodigious strength," and "imitative propensities." To remain with this moment, though, where the place of the murderer has been strained of human properties but has not yet received the name of *animal*, it is the word "unequal" that seems to suture the impossible remembrance, this word "unequal" itself already in excess of itself. For if it is a word actually pronounced in the testimony of a witness to qualify the second voice he had heard, something like *unequal from within*, because the words pronounced by it were not in themselves or among themselves distinguishable, in Dupin's use of it apposed to what follows, it seems to equally describe the fact that no two testimonies agreed on its nationality or language, so that that in this clashing of irreconcilable languages this voice was in effect *unequal from without*. But what does the word "unequal" even mean, when there is no other term to which the thing it describes is being compared? When used to describe a single entity, according to the *Oxford English Dictionary*, the word could mean, starting from the sixteenth century, unfair, uneven, as in undulating, or insufficient, inadequate, as in *to* a task, but also, starting in the eighteenth century, excessive, disproportionate, as in an "unequal task" or an "unequal weight." A strange word, then—a strange unequal word.

But its emphasis in Poe's story must lead me to wonder whether by a kind of dislocation the adjective is not being summoned to describe not so much the animal's voice, as the animal *as* unequal to itself, as an unequal *place in* the text, as if marking the very seams of the text, a place where the text itself is somehow, unequal.

The Cuvier passage, read by the narrator but not quoted in the text, is the only "glimpse" we are allowed of the "large fulvous Ourang-Outang" in Poe's story, which ends with the confession of its "master," a Maltese sailor who, having captured the animal in Borneo during one of his voyages, had been keeping it "carefully secluded" in his house, till it recovered from a wound in its foot and he could sell it. It was during this time that, unbeknownst to the sailor, the animal had observed him shaving "through the keyhole of the closet," which, given the "imitative propensities" of orangutans, would lead directly, on the day it escaped, to its brutal use of the razor in the L'Espinaye apartment, which he (the sailor) himself would witness while standing outside the window (whereupon he would exclaim in horror, and the animal would respond in confusion, these supposedly being the two voices heard by passersby) (268–70). Some time after the murders, the orangutan is found by its master, "who obtain[s] for it a very large sum at the *Jardin des Plantes*" (the Paris zoo).

The movement that takes the orangutan from being "at *large*" (264), as it is for some days following the murders, to being recaptured and sold for "a very *large* sum" (270) is that of an *inequality* converted into a "passing." And if the first "passing" is that which by means of "ingress" and "egress" saw it momentarily and disastrously enter the Paris apartment, constituting a *crime*, this movement forms, in a sense, only the shadowy "return" of a second, the real, "passing," whose intention (it was only a matter of time) preceded the crime, that is, the transaction by which the orangutan, from the forests of Borneo, *is entered*, as it were, on the French *market*. This movement, of course, is the *economic*, the irony of whose derivation from *oikos*, or house, will not be missed here. If the crime forms the shadow of the economic passing, it is because if, on one side of the transaction we now have an animal conferred a name and (exchange) value in exchange for bodily freedom and natural habitat (become, at the Jardin des Plantes, no more than a "plaything for children, just as empty and robbed of its properties" as Aesop's raven [Keenan, *Fables*, 65]), on the other side stands a nameless body, unrestrained, unscripted in its movements, unaccountable in its actions. Indeed, the serial path of the "no"s had carved out a place for the orangutan that was at most the unnameable, hollowed out, *outside* the human: "No words—no sounds resembling words," "no human hair," "no human hand" . . . The "imitative propensities" of the orang-utan place it, at the same time (and this is where we must return to the twofold direction of the analyst's skill both outside and inside the box, a tension in the story not entirely reconciled), at a difference of degree from the human. If in imitating the human it is symbolically less than it, and can thus be sold on the market for a price,[20] in its "superhuman strength," its "almost praeternatural character," it is physically *more* than human. Or, to put it in tighter spatial terms, if in imitating the human it is *inside* it,[21] in exceeding it ("excessively *outré*") it is continually *outside* it. It should not come as a surprise, given the insistence of such a chiasmus, that the shadow scene in which the crime is committed is both a time lag in which the rules of accountability (economics, or the theory of the subject) are faced with (and must fail before) their own struck-through prehistory (for the criminal is a pre-economic, not to say an-economic, even *anti*economic being, its "value," as yet unestimated, is none or infinite—*unequal*), and a space that folds in/out to connect both the inside to an outside (revealing suddenly a path linking the Paris apartment to the forests of Borneo) and, conversely, an outside to an inside (revealing, as if within the human, the "recesses of thought altogether inaccessible," where an altogether unaccountable "Orang-Outang"—in Malay, the word means "man of the forest"—persists in its "wild ferocity"). No doubt it is because the animal in Poe's story is so inextricably entangled with this very *fold*, indeed, because it *is* this very fold, that Dupin must, in his preface to his demonstration, call for a flexibility, a *folding out*, of perception itself to recover sight of it: "To look at a star by glances—to view it in a side-long way, by turning toward it the exterior portions of the *retina* (more susceptible of feeble impressions of light than the interior), is to behold the star distinctly—is to have the best appreciation of its lustre—a lustre which grows dim just in proportion as we turn our vision *fully* upon it. [. . .] By undue profundity we perplex and enfeeble thought; and it is possible to make even Venus herself vanish from the firmament by a scrutiny too sustained, too concentrated, or too direct" (252–53).

WHAT SONG THE SIRENS SANG

"The Murders in the Rue Morgue" carries as epigraph a quote from Thomas Browne: "What song the Sirens sang, or what name Achilles assumed when he hid himself among women, although puzzling questions, are not beyond *all* conjecture" (238). The second of the "puzzling questions" refers to the episode related in post-Homeric texts wherein Achilles's mother Thetis, learning that her son would be killed if he went to war with Troy, had him sent to the island of Scyros, where the king Lycomedes hid him among his daughters in maidens' clothes. Achilles is discovered through the cunning of Ulysses, who, after placing a shield and spear among maidens' gifts in the king's courtyard, simulates an enemy approach. Believing it, Achilles tears off his female clothing (*chapechute*), picks up said shield and spear, and is thus identified and enlisted. While Statius's *Achilleid* does indicate that the name by which he was called by his "sisters" during this time was Pyrrha (from *pyrrhon*—"flame colored"!), this is perhaps a finer point. More likely pertinent to Poe's purposes in this intertext is the motif of mistaken or concealed identity, subsequently unmasked (and, in this light, *pyrrhon* as concealed "clew" *is* interesting, as it happens, describing aptly the color of orangutans). Following this logic, we might say that the trap laid for Achilles, whose hiding in Scyros is, to borrow Keenan's words on the raven, a "wandering away from [his] name" (62), provides a model for the ruse (an advertisement in a newspaper regarding a found orangutan) by which Dupin lures the Maltese sailor to his doorstep, whereupon, having committed this slip, the latter is forced into a confession, and identity as accountability (if split, complicated) can be ascribed. We find here the expected "fold": the trick involves presenting as *found* an orangutan which is *lost* ("at large"). This un-equality conceals another: for, given the essentially deductive logic that has brought Dupin to this point, his wager here is in presenting as *real* an orangutan that is as yet only a shadowy entity, a "side-long," "*outré*" solution to a problem which, otherwise, would be intractable ("hermetically sealed"). Success in duping the sailor is therefore crucial to the enterprise, and the unsettlingly Derridean overtones to Dupin's certainty as he awaits "the man"—"It is true that he may not arrive; but the probability is that he will" (255)—confirm that the success of the call is premised necessarily on the possibility, inscribed within it, as its forked condition, that it will fail, that the orangutan will remain *un*found, *un*real, its flame-colored body so perfectly concealed "among recesses of thought"—and of diegetic reality—and so "altogether inaccessible" (239) as to be their vanishing point. That is to say: it cannot be found because it was never lost, there was never anything in the place from which something is now lost, nothing *in the first place*,[22] it is, then, something like an *orang-*

utan of undecidability, and in never completely arriving in/to the text, it must ruin the text's "count" of its bodies (*que le pasteur ne puisse plus compter ses moutons*). This orangutan, with no "prior reality" (to use Blanchot's term, see further) can return to representation only as "struck-through," under erasure, "undying," as what "has faded, without ever having been present," as per a supplemental fate which, as Akira Lippit has lucidly shown, has been shared, in a certain history of Western thought (Heidegger, Breuer, Freud, Bergson, Derrida), by the animal and the unconscious.[23]

But the first of the "puzzling questions"—"What song the Sirens sang . . ."—leads us into waters more muddied yet.[24] Recalling another, all too well-known instance of Odyssean cunning—by which the hero, strapped to the mast of his sail, while his crewmembers rowed with wax in their ears, had succeeded in resisting the Sirens' fatal call—the allusion connects Poe's story to what is a darker place in the Homeric text, if we remember that in the encounter with the Sirens, as with a series of "mythic monsters" through the journey, epic reason had to vie with "figure[s] of repetition" that were remnants of an archaic mythic world, and which presented so many "claims from prehistory."[25] The question (what song the Sirens sang), which Robert Graves had also used in his opening to *White Goddess*, is posed again by Maurice Blanchot in *Le livre à venir*, who writes: "Some have said that it was an *inhuman* song—a natural sound [. . .] but on the borderline of nature, at any rate foreign to man; almost inaudible, it evoked pleasurable dreams of an endless descent which, in normal circumstances, can never be realised. Others suggested that it had a more mysterious charm; that it *simply imitated* the song of a normal human being; but since the Sirens, even if they sang like human beings, *were only beasts* (very beautiful beasts, admittedly, and possessing feminine charm), their song was so unearthly that it forced those who heard it to realise *the inhumanness of all human singing*."[26] Ulysses's perfidious encounter with the Sirens ("He took no risks but admired the Sirens with [. . .] cowardly, unemotional, calculated satisfaction"), exemplifying "the disturbing deafness of he who is deaf because he hears," is no allegory for Blanchot. The encounter inscribes, rather, the "hidden law" of every *récit* (60, 62): "Every narration secretly resists the encounter with the Sirens," and "for such resistance Ulysses' caution [. . .] is always exploited and improved upon" (61). The "hidden law" is summarized as follows:

> Narration is movement towards a point which is not only unknown, ignored and strange but such that it seems to have no prior reality apart from this movement, yet it is so compulsive that the narration's appeal depends on it to the extent that it cannot even "begin" before it has reached it, while it is only the narration and the unpredictable movement of the narration which provide the space where this point becomes real, powerful and appealing [*attirant*]. (62)

The fascination and peril Blanchot describes is one that is perceptible in Poe's story, wherein the detective, to arrive at the truth of the tale, must in effect *repeat* a trajectory (that of the imagined intruder) of which there can be *no representation prior* to this repeating, and must yet make it through to the other side, by turning this repetition, powerful and alluring, into knowledge. If this reiterative structure makes the story a lucid precursor to (and revelator of that of) all detective fiction—where detective and murderer classically mirror each other—the casting in it of *an animal* as the mirrored/mirroring other reveals (and perhaps alone could reveal) the more obscure, or most extreme, stakes of what Dupin's journey—not to say "every narration"—inherits from Ulysses's. For if in both cases the "irresistible pull" of the Sirens' song must be opposed, it is because the self-identity of the human subject *is assured by*, is, indeed, *conditioned upon* that "disturbing deafness" toward what in an inhuman song could imply "the inhumanness of all human singing." The choice that must be made is, in Blanchot's terms, between the respective fates of Ulysses and Ahab in *Moby-Dick*:

> It cannot be denied that Ulysses half-heard that which Ahab saw. But where he was able to resist what he heard Ahab was overcome by his vision. In other words, the first rejected the metamorphosis into which the other vanished. After the test Ulysses is still what he was and the world, if less rich, is firmer and safer than before. But Ahab will never be himself again and, for Melville, the world threatens to collapse into that worldless space which draws him with the lure of a single image. (64)

In forgoing "the lure of a single image," and in offering, in its place, the passage from Cuvier, Poe inverts the Sirens' inhuman song into naturalist knowledge *of* the inhuman, received by the narrator as "sufficiently well known to all." The untranscribed intertext serves in fact to "seal" the story, substituting itself for the animal body at the precise place where, reconstructed from its parts, it was closest to view, and thus closest to being *become*. The danger averted by Ulysses was nothing less than that of "metamorphosis," suggests Blanchot ("the first rejected the metamorphosis into which the other vanished"), therein anticipating the writings of Gilles Deleuze and Félix Guattari, for whom *Moby-Dick* was, undeniably, the story of a becoming-animal.[27]

What song did the Sirens sing? Kafka, writer of animal stories if there was one, had read the Homeric episode differently, assuming that Ulysses too, like his sailors, had stuffed wax in his ears. Of course, he wrote, "it was known to all the world that such things were of no help whatsoever. The song of the Sirens could pierce through everything, and the longing of those they seduced would have broken far stronger bonds than chains and masts."[28] Yet, while Ulysses "trusted absolutely to his handful of wax and his fathom of chain," the Sirens themselves, when he approached, "did not sing, whether they thought that this enemy could be vanquished only by their silence, or because the look of bliss on the face of Ulysses, who was thinking of nothing but his wax and his chains, made them forget their singing" (431). Kafka offered two successive hypotheses. The first: "Ulysses, if one may so express it, did not hear their silence; he thought they were singing and that he alone did not hear them" (431). And the second: "Perhaps he had really noticed, although here the human understanding is beyond its depths, that the Sirens were silent, and held up to them and to the gods the aforementioned pretense merely as a sort of shield" (432). Which hypothesis are we to believe? Was Ulysses's "disturbing deafness" more disturbing for hearing the song while refusing its risks (Blanchot), in thinking that he alone didn't hear the song when in fact in his forced deafness he heard its true silence (Kafka's first hypothesis), or in pretending he had silenced it when in fact it was truly silent (Kafka's second hypothesis)? "Now the Sirens have a still more fatal weapon then their song," wrote Kafka, "namely their silence. And though admittedly such a thing has never happened, still it is conceivable that someone might possibly have escaped from their singing; but from their silence certainly never. Against the feeling of having triumphed over them by one's own strength, and the consequent exaltation that bears down everything before it, no earthly powers can resist" (431). Pitting the "fatal weapon" of the Sirens' silence against the equally irresistible human "feeling of having triumphed over them" forces Kafka into a further folding of the fold (not hearing their singing > not hearing their silence > pretending the silence heard was the singing *not* heard), and into devising an escape clause whereby Ulysses, hearing the Sirens' silence, *only pretends to believe* they are singing. Can there be a more devastating commentary on the relationship between *logos* and the inhuman other than this erasure of silence? And then there is the troubling question of the address of the pretense: for in holding up the shield of his pretense to the Sirens and to the gods, Ulysses successfully held it up to Homer too, that is to say, there is no place within the narration (save in the vanishing point of the conscience of the pretender—"here the human understanding is beyond its depths") where such a pretense could be recognized as pretense. And so, though the Sirens were silent, we must remember them forever to have been singing.

WITHOUT THE ANIMAL

Through Kafka the problem is reversed, or becomes reversible: whether we impute silence to the animal or song, whether we represent it as lost or found, the risk is always that of an unequality,[29] that fold, itself so inextricably embedded within representation as to form its imperceptible inner lining. Approaching *Moby-Dick* as but a variation on *The Odyssey*, Blanchot had described in vivid terms a cosmic agon between human protagonist and inhuman other, each vying for the very world. Their impossible coexistence in one space is precisely, writes Blanchot, literature's "secret desire":

> The drama enacted between Ahab and the whale, which might loosely be termed metaphysical, is similar to that between Ulysses and the Sirens. Each protagonist seeks to encompass everything, to be the whole world, so that their coexistence is impossible, while at the same time their one desire is for coexistence and encounter. It is precisely the secret desire to confine into a single space Ahab and the whale, the Sirens and Ulysses that turns Ulysses into Homer and Ahab into Melville and makes the world which results from this juxtaposition the greatest, most terrible and wonderful of worlds—alas a novel, only a novel! (63)

Which should, surely, bring us back to *Sans l'orang-outan*. If La Fontaine's fable had the animal standing outside the door, and then, in its dismemberment, at the gates of the village, if Poe's story had it, by ingress and egress, cross the boundaries of the house, and then the boundary separating forest from market, the particular conceit (or deceit) of Chevillard's novel is in imagining the animal as a body crossing or "passing" an altogether more radical threshold, beyond which it vanishes exhaustibly from the "real." It should perhaps not surprise us to find in such a "fable," like in the other two, an imaginatively recounted update from the historical human/animal "front": just as wolves were real threats to livestock in the seventeenth century, and the orangutan was in Poe's time a plausible example of the sort of exotic animal being increasingly "translated" (as per the French term used for such displacements) from "exotic" habitats in Africa and Asia into zoos and collections in European metropoles, Chevillard's novel indexes a time when, due to deforestation and continued poaching, the Sumatran species of the orangutan is estimated to be critically endangered and the Bornean species endangered, so that, to a purely logical eye, extinction can seem, as Chevillard both irreverentially and fiercely suggests in precipitating it, a mere *matter of time*.[30]

The obsession of *Sans l'orang-outan* is in fact, from the outset, the (fearful) nonsymmetry between presence and absence laid bare by the event of extinction: "There are no more orangutans anywhere [*nulle part*], that is everywhere [*partout*], in every point of space it is no more" (35). To equate here *nulle part* (nowhere) and *partout* (everywhere), exact lexical opposites, is to acknowledge an outer limit where the symbolic must answer for itself (and, in so doing, collapse back on itself). If orangutans certainly did not occupy, while alive, every point in space, at present they *are* absent from every place and at every instant (31). Indeed, in drawing relative presence into absolute absence, the orangutan's vanishing exerts phenomenological pressure on the inverse categories by a "passing" that makes perceptible, *as if retroactively, on the other side*, in its now total negation, corresponding to nothing that could ever have existed, a (struck-through) form of total presence. A kind of reverse-mirror logic inserts the orangutan everywhere that it is not. Reversing the direction of the movement by which fables, in Keenan's thesis, carry nameless bodies toward location and accountability, this fable recounts the production of the perfect bodyless name—that is, the orangutan as *ghost*. Having perfectly crossed over to the other side, the orangutan can now occupy the novel's pages in unfettered unequality. Through a radical unaccountability that is at the same time a dissolving of all bounds to its agency, the orangutan turns out—and in this *turning out* is a *return* as well as a *turning inside out*—to have held the very world together, held the very human together, so that in its disappearance everything slides toward chaos and catastrophe: "Wherever [the orangutan] was, wherever it is no more, vertigo pulls at me, my legs buckle, all my bearing abandons me, I know only to fall [*je ne sais plus que choir*]" (46).[31]

What I have been calling the "reeling" in *Sans l'orang-outan* takes many forms, like so many variations on a theme, so that the detail of it is of less interest than certain structures—as I have suggested, germane to Chevillard's prose—that it makes apparent. One, already noted, is the crisis of measure, or of measurement, and particularly *vertical extent*, which the outstretched body and long forelimbs of the orangutan had long assured:

> Don't we already feel the difference, and that gravity, for instance, no longer weighs down only ripe apples? As if the orangutan—I cry pronouncing his name—held us standing by the hair from his branch. He pulled us upward. He opened the sky for us, made the clouds part, brought the moon closer. The orangutan carved a path for us among the stars. A clear path for our rockets, for our prayers. The trapdoor has closed again. The ceiling is collapsing. (22)

Sealing the pact between earth and sky, the orangutan had also ensured the distance between humans themselves, so that in its absence lands and homes collide, and humans fall together and merge in dangerous resemblance and aberrant intimacy. Its ability to climb and to grasp had served as prosthetic extension of human capacities, so that its abandonment of the world precipitates a collapse of phenomenological and moral meaning, a withering of the distance of prehension and comprehension, a shriveling up of the human reduced to foraging upon a newly hostile, arid earth: "Our arms no longer grasp anything. Our bodies are lost" (11); "we are amputated of several limbs" (16). The principle through all this seems to be, in part, that the *difference* organizing human life had been premised on the *identity* of the orangutan to itself: "Orangutan he was *without measure*, without remainder nor reserve, without shame nor scruple, headily, with provocation, some would say, orangutan without competition, it was useless to line up, defeat was certain, the orangutan prevailed effortlessly over all suitors, in his category, he feared no one" (24, my emphasis). The string of "sans" ("without") declines the in-difference of the orangutan in its unqualified (or un*quantified*) coincidence with itself. This is a portrait of an *equal animal*, then, though the trick is that the price of such equality is its absence. What it had stood as guarantor of, retroactively, was the unequal self-identity of the human: "Without the orangutan, I am but the shadow of myself" (153).

Asked in a 2004 interview what place he gave to the animal, Chevillard replied:

> The animal is for me a reference point, a fixed point in a moving landscape. One can always refer to it to know what life is foremost about, what it is before we build our fabulous career plans. Man adapts infinitely [. . .] while the animal executes the program of the species to which it belongs. That is its force and its limit. Sometimes we find ourselves envying this strength and even this limit of whose debt we are not entirely clear, far from it, of course. The animal reminds us of it. Man's evolution, this perpetual revolution rather, is less frightening and dizzying because he has the faithful and stable animal at his side (sometimes even on his shoulder).[32]

Yet such a view (closing on a likely reference to portraits of the type *writer with cat*—one thinks of Borges and of Perec) is too stable to account for how Chevillard in fact treats his animals—witness the ever-morphing Palafox, the hedgehog of *Du hérisson*,[33] or the orangutan at hand. In this sense, perhaps, he was being asked the wrong question on this occasion (whether he believed more in involution than in evolution, less in the human than in the animal). Earlier in the same interview, reflecting on the proteiform character of Crab in *La Nébuleuse du Crab* (*The Crab Nebula*) and *Un fantôme*, Chevillard advanced notions that might well have more bearing on the orangutan: "Crab was for a long while for me that personal pronoun that the writer is missing, between the 'I' [*le 'je'*] and the 'he.' Michaux says that the *I* [*le* moi] is an equilibrium position [*position d'équilibre*]. Crab embodies all the oscillations and vacillations of this *I* [*moi*] suddenly out of balance. Every whim that passes through him effectively transforms him: he becomes liquid if the slope favors it" (181; my translation). Henri Michaux, whose influence on Chevillard's oeuvre is undeniably profound,[34] had written in his postface to *Plume*: "I [*MOI*] makes do with anything. *A flexion in a sentence*, is that another I (*moi*) attempting to emerge?"[35] In a later interview Chevillard would offer an uncannily similar description of his own creatures: "They are the subjects of my sentences but *the inflection of the sentence modifies their being* and they can no longer resemble themselves at all by the time it ends. A sentence is a whole adventure and because they are its subject, they are inevitably transformed by this adventure that constitutes their only experience in this world. For them there is no outside the book. These characters are phenomena of writing, appearing in language, they live and die according to its laws."[36] Calling them "literary ectoplasma," he goes on to clarify: "They are not persons. They do not exist as neighbors. They are empty, ductile forms, polymorphous figures." He would also return in this interview to the idea of unusual pronouns: "My characters, Crab or Palafox, for instance, are rather incongruous rhetorical figures or new personal pronouns that parasite language and indeed take advantage of its extraordinary resources, of its terrible efficacy, to develop following their own law" (97–98).

I must wonder here whether *Sans l'orang-outan*, which appeared shortly after this interview was published, was not a virtuoso culmination of just these principles. For was a narrative of extinction not *precisely* the means, the necessary *fable*, by which to ensure that "orang-outan" was no longer a location that could be occupied by any real "third person," let alone by a "first person," and to confer upon it, rather, the charge and *impropriety* of one of those "new personal pronouns that parasite language," "between the 'I' and the 'he'"? This indeed would account for the reeling (as language and reference scramble to organize themselves vis-à-vis this incongruous entity), and also for the disquieting effects of the inversion, in Chevillard's prose, by which the animal, far from being pure body or fleshly real, becomes, on the contrary, pure textuality. Which makes for a radical reading indeed of Keenan's thesis regarding fables' way of illustrating the "generation of the pure name," a fate that places the orangutan in the same shadowy realm as the Mauritian dodo, "as forgotten as orang and outan, orang dash outan, also written outang with a g, optionally, whereas one doesn't joke with the g at the end of orang, it's Malay, more or less Malay, literally *man of the forest*, orang-outan or orang-outang" (53–54).

It goes without saying that the fable is not just a fable but an inscription of the ecological costs of a modern history of the human, a stretching of the exactions of a certain "exotic" logic to their furthest brink. In fact the way had been prepared by an earlier novel, *Oreille rouge* (2005; *Red Ears*), whose protagonist, sojourning in Mali, had been disappointed not to ever see any hippopotamuses. Escorted by his guide and self-appointed hippopotamus expert Toka on the animals' trail, he was instead repeatedly treated to expert speculations on why they were no longer there, and on their grazing and reproductive habits.[37] The verbose knowledge he is provided on these occasions reveals itself, toward the end of his stay in Mali, to be information extracted from an encyclopedia. Had Toka himself ever seen a hippopotamus? Had anyone ever seen one? Oreille rouge returns to Paris shrilly and unscrupulously proclaiming he has. Where he does see them, ultimately, is at the local zoo. Therein is exposed the logic of the captive animal, perhaps not so different from that of language. As Walter Putnam puts it in an essay on the long history of displacement of exotic animals to Western metropoles (infelicitously titled "Can the Subaltern Growl?"), "The authenticity of the captured animal is, of course, guaranteed by the idea of other specimens 'born free' and leading wilderness existences that we could actually view given sufficient time and resources."[38] The "return movement" Putnam describes, "a form of inverted colonial penetration" (124–25) by which animals were turned into "mimetic capital" and a "surplus of meaning for the cultures that exhibited and observed them" (140–41), tells the story both of a gaze and of a conversion from wild, unaccountable animal body to *sign*. The provocation of *Sans l'orang-outan* is, in such a perspective, in imagining what would happen if there were no longer any "specimens 'born free' and leading wilderness existences" and if, once the last "captured animal[s]" had perished, the "surplus of meaning" were all that remained. The novel *is* this surplus of meaning. To this extent, its connection with the animal is that of a mischievous (and dangerous) remove, that of a representation which has cleaved itself free of the burden of its referent. No doubt the *sans* of the title *Sans l'orang-outan* should be read in this maximal capacity, and every inscription therein of the word "orang-outan" as a spectral floating of a name without an animal: "For our grandchildren the orangutan will be a specter, born of legend and drivel, yet they too will suffer from this absence but not knowing what to link it to, what its abolished object is, they will experience a permanent dissatisfaction, an inexplicable malaise that nothing deriving from man will appease, they will err without understanding in those zones of turbulence where the orangutan stood erect leaning on its fists, while they themselves lose footing, while their bodies flounder" (38).

We are left, then, with something like *a wolf in orangutan's clothing*, an animal of undecidability which, released from the regulatory constraints of the economy of presence, of the need for a referent, can, as extreme *animot*, occupy every possible place: it is god of all things and source of all misfortune, interstitial pronoun and theme of endless variations, available for exercises of all sorts: from a gymnastics on the level of narrative and sentence to the contortionist exercises in becoming-orangutan to which humans are seen subjecting themselves in the last section of the novel, under the emotional/cynical guidance of the unconsoled narrator. If wild animals "born free" in their faraway native habitats were long the alibi (which derives, we recall, from the locative case of the Latin *alius*, thereby signifying "elsewhere") lending mimetic credentials and referential direction to exotic animals captive and relocated in the metropoles (including through circulating representations thereof—toys, images, stories, words), the extinction of the orangutan, when read through the etymology of its name ("man of the forest") that Chevillard recalls in passing, becomes that of an *über*-alibi. For was this sylvan man not the "born free" specimen which, from the beginning ("depuis le temps"), assured the possibility of (deferred) meaning to the existence of his deforested counterparts? If we follow such a hypothesis, the orangutan emerges as the very embodiment/disembodiment of something like an originary supplementarity, or what David Wills would call an originary "prostheticity,"[39] founding the human. Chevillard will give this the name *prehistory*,[40] and *Sans l'orang-outan* features a number of passages which "remember" human's originary orangutan-ness, a remembering that is turned both toward the past and toward a possible future or a place outside of time itself (as per the supplementarity of the logic of *pre*-history, as insistence that history cannot fully account for itself, that its field cannot be closed): "We have lost all sense of balance today. We teeter dangerously. We no longer adhere. Every surface pushes us away or absorbs us. We used to be flexible, bendy, undulating like our reflections in water. We had pockets full of elastic. We intervened wherever there was a threat of boredom or paralysis, as soon as the wind fell, as soon as narrative stilled itself in its form, as soon as the cadaver went still, we would appear" (154–55). The "we" in these instances is a kind of composite human-as-orangutan *first person*, which attempts to straddle the abyss: "Yes, all that we thought we grasped slips away: it called for the four hands of the orangutan" (60). This location, in the absurd last section of the novel, where humans train to be orangutans, is seen to be a fatal one. Continually failing to live like orangutans, the trainees succeed at most in dying the deaths of orangutans: "Balmer was the first to perish like we will all perish, I hope, as a true orangutan" (169).

In such human deaths works the hoped-for reversal of a *switch*—Wills, commenting on Heidegger's thinking on the human, writes of a "destining switch at the origin, a sending that is a diverting, a natural that as it were precludes the human, or an inventing that as it were precludes the natural" (*Dorsality*, 33)—that the narrator of *Sans l'orang-outan* deems responsible for the death of the last orangutans:

> There was an error. There was a mistake, it is clear. That crater had opened up to swallow *us*, and to rid the world of the threat posed by our death drive. [. . .] But a mistake was made by the universal forces blinded by their wrath and deceived by the resemblance between man and orangutan and which drove the latter into the abyss, the naive and urbane orangutan, that inoffensive sleeping and fruit-eating primate very exceptionally capable of brutality towards the termite. (52)

Orangutans, in this view, died mistaken for and *in the place of* humans. But the first possible misrecognition, preceding and unnoticed under cover of this switch in death, was a switch in life. In its furthest wager, the novel suggests that the forces of natural selection and history, deceived by the human/orangutan resemblance, had privileged humans in an arguable case of *mis-address*: "The orangutan was, much more than we, the man of the situation. [. . .] But the orangutan needed to disappear for our millennial imposture to be exposed, which rested, granted, on a mistake that we did not consciously seek nor want, the great red ape [. . .] consented to our domination even while he could grind our skulls in his fist like a nut, or, more gently but firmly, put us back in our place among the creatures of our order. He withdrew to his forests, vaguely disgusted, far from our agitations" (172–73). Chevillard's orangutan at its fullest subverting force—as animal of undecidability—is best summed up in this torsion, by which the possibility of a mis-taking, a misprision, an originary "diverting," creeps into the human's claim to its own location. The human is human only via this "millennial imposture," having managed to "profit as a parasite from existing structures," to use the phrase with which Chevillard had once described Palafox's occupation of the real, and of narrative itself (*Pala-*

fox, 25). In *Sans l'orang-outan* it is the "existing structures" of nature and history themselves that are suggested to have been available for parasiting—and this, in turn, to be the work of all fiction, starting with history itself *as fiction*.[41] Inextricably exorbitant to itself, the human needed the orangutan in order to better resemble *itself*, to better defend its own place: "Two hands will never be enough to defend a man. With four, we would alas not have a greater chance of survival, as we have seen. I suppose we would need a dozen hands" (87). The orangutan as supplementarity is itself a logic of endless *mise en abyme* and deferral, as if being human depending on being more orangutan than the orangutan. Dis-placed by the human ("He withdrew to his forests, vaguely disgusted"—note that in this reversal that produces "the man of the forest," the forest does not precede the human but is produced by it, as what it invents and exiles), the orangutan inhabits that "perfectly empty" "space of exception" that Agamben describes as "the articulation between human and animal" (38):

> Insofar as the production of man through the opposition man/animal, human/inhuman, is at stake here, the machine necessarily functions by means of an exclusion (which is also always already a capturing) and an inclusion (which is also always already an exclusion). Indeed, precisely because the human is already presupposed every time, the machine actually produces a kind of state of exception, a zone of indeterminacy in which the outside is nothing but the exclusion of an inside and the inside is in turn only the inclusion of an outside. (37)

We recognize in this account the description of the very *fold* that has accompanied this reflection at every turn. The orangutan and the human together form, in Chevillard's novel, a continually reversible chiasmus of inside/outside. If the chiasmus is disturbed by the extinction of one of its terms, its sheer structuring force is dramatized in the solution it as if irrepressibly devises: diegetic and symbolic "reality" accommodates animal vanishing with an "all the better to invent it with" confidence (and here we find in terms quite different from Escola's reading our own trail leading from La Fontaine's tricked wolves to the cunning villain of Perrault's *Le Petit Chaperon Rouge* [*Little Red Riding Hood*])—seizing, in the flight of the animal from its name, the opportunity to lift all principles of realism, fixity, constraint, or accountability on the name now unburdened of its animal. "The orangutan has passed to the other side and no sign from him any longer reaches us. Even the great male, even Bagus, filling with air like a bagpipe his hypertrophied goiter, called a laryngeal pouch, I note the word before we forget it, and cupping his hands around his mouth, his brown hands of smooth palms, of nimble fingers, does not succeed, from where he now is, in extending his cry to us" (31).

To conclude, what of the *unequal* voice that the witnesses, in Poe's story, had heard on the night of the crime? That would have been, as revealed by the Maltese sailor who arrives to tell the tale, "the fiendish jabberings of the brute" as it had left the scene. But can an orangutan fiendishly jabber? Uncannily, a recent documentary film by French director Nicolas Philibert about a forty-year-old (now more than forty-nine-year-old) orangutan at the Jardin des Plantes, seems to pick up exactly where the Poe story ended and provides the most poignant answer to this question. Remember what Berger had remarked about the zoo: "The view is always wrong," "like an image out of focus," because "*you are looking at something that has been rendered absolutely marginal*; and all the concentration you can muster will never be enough to centralise it" (23–24). Overlaying upon long takes of a silent listless caged animal the ceaseless chatter of zoo visitors as they speculate on its thoughts and demeanor, Philibert's *Nénette* (2010) at one point features an offscreen zoo attendant who explains that the bulging throat pouch on the male orangutan (Nénette's son Tübo, who was born at the Jardin des Plantes and has since died) is the appendage enabling it to emit a cry that can travel vast distances in the wild. But, he then clarifies, the animal has no need to do that here. Indeed, for what and with whom and across what surviving distances would Tübo have thus communicated? The "laryngean pouch" ("I note the word before we forget it" [*Sans l'orang-outan*, 31]) is his alibi, by which he is seen to still possess the lost distance he never had to begin with. This discreetly devastating moment of *Nénette* (its *punctum*) leads me to wonder whether the "fiendish jabberings" of Poe's orangutan and the "cry" of Chevillard's Bagus, exiled beyond the reach of sound, are not "unequal," precisely, because they are points where *animal distance* has collapsed *into text*, irrecoverable anteriority captured as catachrestic irony. And whether these are not just other words to describe the "fabulous complication" through which the human story has, "depuis le temps," simultaneously sought the animal and been unable to bear its existence.[42] Man, Protagoras had once dared declare, is the measure of all things; Chevillard's fable, taking fabulist economics to their complicated end, reveals this "measure" to be riddled with supplementarities, unsettled (unequaled) by the continual ghostly "passing" of an orangutan across intimate thresholds of human meaning and being. And so perhaps I can locate here, for now, my answer to my question as to why the question of the animal must imply a slipperiness of the meter. (Perhaps, had the orangutan been able to jabber, it would have said something like La Fontaine's "veteran mutton-eater": *Is this the way they change their metre? / And do they take me for a fool?*)

CHAPTER 3

Vague Dog

Marie NDiaye, with Beckett, Levinas, Deleuze, Leibniz

So as to be here no more at last,
To have never been here, but all this time above,
With a name like a dog to be called up with
And distinctive marks to be had up with . . .
—Samuel Beckett, *Texts for Nothing*

I sing the dog of calamities, whether wandering alone in the circuitous ravines of immense cities, or having declared, batting clever eyes, to some abandoned man, "Take me with you, and perhaps our two miseries will add up to a kind of happiness."
—Charles Baudelaire, *Spleen de Paris*, trans. Keith Waldrop

WHAT CAN YOU EXPLAIN TO DOGS?

What would it mean to say that a story or journey, to arrive at completion (or that I, to enter again my house—the house of the I), may need to get past a (/the) dog? Unthinkable dangers beset homecoming. One may have traveled too far or too long—or not far or long enough—to make the return. In returning, one may be other than the one who left, the ghostly double of another who never left at all—or another who never *existed* at all. One may not look (or smell) the same, and die unrecognized at one's own gates. Thus Ulysses, having reached Ithaca after twenty long years of war and voyage, is almost torn to pieces by the fierce hounds of his loyal servant, the swineherd Eumaeus, who must intervene "by shout[ing] at the dogs and sen[ding] them flying with a shower of stones."[1] Yet the specter of this gruesomely ironic death so narrowly averted ("he would have come to grief then and there, at his own farm, if the swineherd had not intervened") is incompletely exorcised in the averting. The dogs may have been driven off, but something about their fury remains, recalling the Red Queen's riddle in Lewis Carroll's *Through the Looking-Glass*: "'Take a bone from a dog: what remains?'" Answer: "'The dog would lose its temper. [. . .] Then if the dog went away, its temper would remain!'"[2] What can you explain to dogs? Hidden narrative reasons may not be able (or enough) to call them off. Remember how Acteon, cursed by the goddess Artemis to take the form of a stag, is thereupon devoured by his own beloved hunting dogs. *The Iliad* abounds with references to dogs feeding on bodies fallen in battle, preying at that place where the protections of identity are lost. And this can mean simply where recognition has lost confidence.

Yet, by way of canine lessons, we are less likely to remember the unrecognizing hounds of book 14 of *The Odyssey* than the emblematic scene in book 17 where, on entering the premises of what used to be his home, Ulysses, still incognito in beggar's clothes, is feebly greeted from a distance by an old, ailing dog.

> Argus was his name. Odysseus himself had owned and trained him, though he had sailed for holy Ilium before he could reap the reward of his patience. In years gone by the young huntsmen had often taken him out after wild goats, deer, and hares. But now, in his owner's absence, he lay abandoned on the heaps of dung from the mules and cattle which lay in profusion at the gate, awaiting removal by Odysseus' servants as manure for his great estate. There, full of vermin, lay Argus the hound. But directly he became aware of Odysseus' presence, he wagged his tail and dropped his ears, though he lacked the strength now to come any nearer to his master.[3]

So moved is Ulysses by these signs of recognition from his loyal dog, that he sheds a discreet tear—remembered (and multiplied) in the title of Roger Grenier's book on dogs, *Les larmes d'Ulysse* (on which more anon). Inquiring after the handsome hound ("He's a beauty, though one cannot really tell whether his looks were matched by his pace, or whether he was just one of those dogs whom their masters feed at table and keep for show"—what mistrust! What could there remain to test? But after the compromising tear cunning must quickly reestablish its mastery . . .), Ulysses receives confirmation from Eumaeus of what a prodigious hunting dog Argos used to be in times past and how neglected since having lost his master. No matter that there is no trace of Argos in the epic text before this moment. In these memorable few lines of book 17 this feeble, faithful dog lives a whole lifetime, stretching far beyond dog years to reconnect past and present and to seal by his knowing gaze not only his master's identity, but also the integrity of the epic—the assurance of self-sameness against the odds of vast distance and years. This crucial function accomplished, the sickly dog can expire peacefully ("As for Argus, he had no sooner set eyes on Odysseus after those nineteen years than he succumbed to the black hand of Death," 267).

There are reasons to prefer to Grenier's lachrymose title its English translation (by Alice Kaplan)—*The Difficulty of Being a Dog.* Argos was less a dog, arguably, than a principle (loyalty, recognition—*anagnorisis*), and perfectly equal to it. But then were the hounds of Eumaeus dogs any more than Argos? Did they too not stand expressly for certain narrative or thematic principles (*non*recognition, loss of immunity, hideous irony, prehistoric claims)?[4] What does a dog see when it recognizes us? What does it see when it doesn't recognize us? Or is it that for every dog there is another that is equal in strength and opposite in direction? What does this mean for humans? What does it mean for dogs? Is a dog ever "literally" a dog? How many dogs does it take to arrive at an axiomatic or paradigmatic truth about dogs? Can anything be a dog?[5]

Queer speculations, these. But it is into such a region of murky verdicts that the dogs of Marie NDiaye will lead me in these pages. First there were the unambiguously anti-Argos threshold figures that opened *En famille* (1991; *Among Family*), an early novel where the protagonist, having arrived at her grandmother's house, is dismayed to be met with ferocity by creatures that should have known her well:

> When she arrived in front of her grandmother's house at the end of the village, the two dogs she had so often petted in the past, now old and blind, summoned enough strength to throw themselves furiously at the gate. Every time she tried to poke her face between the bars, they barked with a violence she had never known in them before. She called them softly by name. They redoubled their fury. She put down her suitcase, hoisted herself onto a large rock at one end of the gate—out of reach of the dogs—then squeezed her chest be-

> tween two bars and shouted towards the house for someone to open for her. She was upset that the dogs had not recognized her, seeing it as a sign of serious failure on her part. (7/9)[6]

Barring the protagonist's entry to the family home, momentarily blocking her admittance to the space of the story if not of the symbolic itself, the dogs are the first expressors of the central drama of *Among Family*. The "serious failure on *her* part" nods to the logic of the tortuous story that will shortly unfold, wherein Fanny's wretchedness at being ostracized by her family is made more abject (and illegible) still by the speculation that she herself is obscurely responsible for her fate. But then, there will be occasion, through what follows, to think about why, where there is a dog, there is often a disturbance of accountability, of person, an uncertainty of *who/whom*. Alice Kuzniar, in *Melancholia's Dog*, suggests that melancholia may see itself in a dog precisely insofar as it casts as a riddle the question of *whose* melancholia it is.[7] If the aggressive dogs of *Among Family*, here and later in the novel, seem to raise the question of whose house it is and of whose fault it is, a graver prospect, as I follow them beyond this novel, is that dogs' unique capacity, vis-à-vis a weakened protagonist or identity claim, is to unnerve the sense of *whose story* it is.

The grandmother's dogs (at which Fanny "without thinking" throws a stone as she leaves, injuring "the gentler one in the eye" [25/21]) are not seen again, plausibly dying soon thereafter; but their function, in addition to supplying that opening note of ontological anxiety ("hadn't she played with them throughout her childhood?" [10/10]),[8] is to prefigure a subplot of canine discontent that will periodically act up at the protagonist's expense. Oddly, repetition will only increase the uncertainty as to whether the anger being directed at Fanny is that of particular dogs or that of the whole species. Gathering like knots in the novel, they are the places of a blind fury, an allergic objection to her presence (though whether it is to her appearance—which the novel marks as different while suppressing the marks of its difference—or to her *disavowal* of this appearance is importantly indeterminable). The difficulty in locating the hostility (the dogs' or the world's? individuals' or the species'?) is most vividly attested in the case of a "huge, yellow dog" which, taking up its post at the window of a restaurant's sordid basement kitchen the day that Fanny starts to work there, keeps a growling watch on her. Fanny's response to this is narrated in these strange lines, fairly representative of NDiaye's treatment of her main characters: "She trembled to think of the day when he, or another, would finally punish her. 'What can you explain to dogs?' she muttered. 'I played with them, I cleaned their kennel without shame, but as soon as the family turns its back on me, they devour me . . .'" (83/68). Moving from the "he" to "another," then to indeterminate "dogs," to circle finally back to the treacherous dogs of her family home, Fanny's thinking here produces, by the time it reaches the final "they," a monstrous aggregate of known and unknown dogs, joined in a single as if endlessly looped nemesis, communicating, inheriting, *accruing* ingratitude and vengeance. The short-circuiting through these third-person pronouns toward unreason is made barely less strange by the seamless move from narrativized thought to direct speech, in what is a representative sampling of the technically *good* faith of a narrator at every point committed to not overstepping or calling out the character's *bad* faith. Indeed, here as in much of NDiaye's prose, the narrative voice, strained, literalist, eager not to be noticed (and as a consequence excessively noticeable), hugs the character's thoughts so closely as to appear to have access to no other knowledge or reason—so that nothing in the text, in this instance, allows us to discredit, as unsound or merely symbolic, Fanny's apprehension that dogs are occupying *interchangeably* the place from which her retribution will come.

Which certainly makes the bludgeoning to death of this *particular* dog a limited solution:

> She kicked it violently under the muzzle, thinking: another will take its revenge!—then pushed it to the ground, deaf to its yelping. The dog now seemed old and tired-out. Was it really a threat or had she been mistaken? It might have made a more reliable and faithful companion than Eugene, who'd had ulterior motives for going with her. Already tired out from her struggle with the dog, she finished it off with a kick in the stomach, then with the tip of her toes slid the heavy rain-soaked carcass from the sidewalk into the gutter, where the gushing water carried it gently away. She ran away guiltily, but comforted herself with the thought that she would no longer be afraid to look up at the basement window. This ugly beast had made her toil in the kitchen even more difficult! Besides, one summer's day in the yard, hadn't she seen Uncle George coldly shoot his most faithful

> hunting dog then dump its body on a manure pile because it had just devoured three chickens? He had not eaten lunch with any less appetite than usual, and Grandmother's dogs always jumped with joy at the sight of him and greeted him by licking his hands. If her uncle George—who knew how to handle dogs—did not hesitate to punish them with death, neither he nor any other member of the family would blame Fanny for killing this filthy animal. (88–89/72)

Indeed, the feared retribution from dogs is here not so much vanquished as given further grounds ("another will take its revenge!"), and the flurry of mutually negating postulations of self-doubt (was it perhaps a friend?) and desperate self-justification (would my family members, always rightness incarnate, not have done the same?) that follow succeeds in neither locating nor diverting responsibility for the violence of the killing. Rather, it sheds ungainly light on a self dispossessed of sure reference, as much in relation to the dog as in relation to itself. In the irresolution regarding what or who the yellow dog was, as becomes clear in the overwrought analogy with the deed of Uncle George (a particularly dislikeable representative of the family bent on excluding Fanny from its ranks), Fanny risks playing out her own story, except here she positions herself on the other side, and, excluding the dog, seems not to see that she has only given sharp illustration to the logic by which her family can "coldly" "punish [. . .] with death" their own "most faithful" member (155).

In the course of the novel Fanny will go through yet more circles of self-exile—where dogs often seem to wait menacingly on the sidelines.[9] But it is a section titled "The Wedding Preparations and Fanny's First Death" (184/150) that confirms the gravest consequences of the canine subplot as a radical other to plot—that is, as a deplotting of positions, a zone of potentially lethal syntactical indifferentiation. In the "dreadful dog episode," as it is later called (230/186), Fanny, who has been sitting hunched in a nook previously reserved for the family dogs, feeding like a dog on scraps from meals passed secretly to her by her mother (otherwise unmoved by her daughter's predicament), bounds out at the sound of the name "Léda"—which she associates with a missing-fairy-godmother-like aunt whose reappearance, she believes, would put an end to her own stigma—only to find that it is the name her cousin/fiancé has given to his new "big, strong dog." The dog promptly attacks her, tearing off "big hunks of flesh" while Fanny makes "[not] a sound except [for] a slight, very slight squeal!" (186/151). The exclamation mark, while mimicking those that would usually have accompanied utterances in direct or free indirect style (e.g., "She kicked it violently under the muzzle, thinking: another will take its revenge!"), here bespeaks the dreadful rudderlessness of the narrative voice as it loses the body to which it had till then clung so closely and is now exposed in its grotesque nudity. Fanny's Aunt Colette at this point briskly "regained her quick-wittedness, and without distaste—just as she gutted rabbits or cleaned calves' heads—she wrapped what was left of Fanny in an old sheet and went out to throw the whole thing on the manure heap at the bottom of the garden" (186/151).

When finally (for my purposes here), Fanny's fiancé George comes to inquire after her, Aunt Colette tells him where she is ("in the garden," "on the manure heap"), whereupon we read: "But the hens had already gobbled up all that was left of Fanny. Finding nothing but a few scraped bones, a few bloody hairs, George thought Aunt Colette was making fun of him and that he had been mistaken to take her answer literally" (187/152). In assuming a mistake, George conveniently pleads escape from the literality of the novel itself, while the narrative voice for its part assumes unseemly cover in a characteristic slip into free indirect style: "In any case, he had come on impulse; wasn't his love for Fanny passing?" But this non-self-implication, this undecidable allegiance of the narration treats others—in this interlude of Fanny's absence or diminishing—only as it at other times treats Fanny: espousing the turns and boundaries of her own thinking, even as it passes its own turns and boundaries for hers—so that neither is it ever sufficiently disentangled from her thinking to (need to, or seem to) judge it as curious or misguided, nor can *its* thinking ever be confidently judged as curious or misguided by *us* (for perhaps it is only *her* thinking?). The novel is replete with such instances (often in the interrogative). Consider for instance how Fanny represses her hurt when Lucette pockets her only picture of her aunt Léda—"After all, she owed the people here—hadn't they, after the usual precautions, treated her less like a stranger than her own family had on Grandmother's birthday?" (63)—or her hesitant happiness to see her father so delighted at the post-dog transformation of her features (whereby she has presumably lost the difference that was her stigma): "But wasn't she happy, despite her confusion, to be so enthusiastically received by her father . . . ?" (195).

Gérard Genette wrote astutely once of Gustave Flaubert (a writer whose influence over NDiaye is indeed striking) that his mastery of free indirect style allowed him to "make his own language speak this both loathsome [*écœurant*] and fascinating idiom of the 'other' without being wholly compromised or wholly innocent."[10] No words (*écœurant* here equally translates as "sickening" or "nauseating") more fittingly describe NDiaye's prose—and, even beyond particular instances, the general politics, not to say *malady*, of a narration whose defense is in its continual claim to be merely ventriloquizing or speculatively inhabiting a point of view, rather than itself (necessarily) sharing or condoning it. The real drama, one might say, of *Among Family*—and, more disturbingly, of much of NDiaye's prose—is that in the character's desperate desire to belong, to merge her "imperfect flesh" with the family's (wishing in one instance "to become perhaps one of the faithful dogs" [65/52]) is possibly but an elaborate allegory of the condition of the narrative voice: without moral bearings because without a place, without a body or memory of its own. At times when it is not sticking closely to Fanny—because she is indisposed or because while recounting external facts it has seemed to lose access to her thoughts—it flaps about untrustworthily, as if needing to do or say *something* while waiting to merge again, attempting accordingly not to say anything that would overly implicate it (thus often resorting to mere questions or conjectures), yet with every word only revealing how indifferently it might serve friend or foe. Thus, when Fanny is in the doghouse, we read of her mother who repeatedly passes by, stopping sometimes to absently feed her: "Did she even remember what she would have found in the nook if she raised the curtain? Probably not, considering how distracted and distant she was . . ." (182/148), and, further on the same page: "Would she even have wanted to believe that a daughter of hers could be in the nook? She was careful that no one saw when she half-opened the curtain, but it could have been out of a sense of propriety" (182/149). The French text here reads "par pudeur," which if anything describes the narrative voice that a kind of *pudeur* (or self-consciousness, reserve) keeps from probing any further. That "nook" behind the curtain is in fact a nook—a limit-point—in narrative consciousness itself, which it (conveniently) disguises as an unreachable point in the mother's mind.

But then if the whole trick is to present words or thoughts or events as if they were being simply relayed, without narrative reservation or dismay, what immunity can a story claim at all from violation or violence? It seems not impossible that the dog that devours Fanny is a body arisen directly from this promiscuity of the narrative voice, from its compulsive urge to literalize its own nonidentity (and thus play at disappearing). For several sorts of circles are seen to tighten around Fanny in that episode, all overdetermined by the dogness of the dog: reduced to the fate of a dog, she is torn to pieces by a dog; her memory, earlier, of Uncle George killing his dog and "dump[ing] its body on a manure pile" here turns prophesy, with the twist that in this scenario *she* is the dog; "Léda," whose name she had so desperately invoked and even wished at one point might at least name a dog ("'You've never even met anyone by that name? Not even an animal?' Fanny would insist, discouraged. 'Not even a dog?'" [143/116]), turns out homonymically to name a dog (so that it is a speech act that provokes what follows: "Someone, perhaps the fiancée, cried out: 'There's Léda and Eugene!' and they saw Fanny jump out" (151), an "Argos moment" gone terribly wrong); Fanny, who had so ardently sought assimilation ("to *become* perhaps one of the faithful dogs" [65/52]), is indeed, most intimately assimilated by a dog ("as if it wanted to taste all of her before deciding to swallow" [186/151]). Lured by a mirage of identity between long-lost aunt and new pet, literal meaning and figurative, dog as other and self as dog, it is as if the narration of *En famille* itself lost in that moment—or *pretended to lose*—the capacity to protect one from the other, or to tell the difference.

A KIND OF GRIMACE

Bad dogs, bad faith, blind spots, and barred entryways riddle NDiaye's novels. *My Heart Hemmed In* (2007; *Mon coeur à l'étroit*) shares with *Among Family* a protagonist (Nadia) whose consciousness—governing the narrative—is arranged around a cryptonomic suppression of the truth regarding her class origins and ancestry. The novel anthologically repeats and anticipates others: like in *Among Family* the negated truth generates an anathemic logic making it difficult to know what has been suppressed;[11] as with Clarisse in the later *Ladivine* (2013), the invention of a new life for Nadia will entail the false premise that her parents are dead; obstructed through every available symbolic channel, the repressed returns to haunt Nadia through a series of disconcerting, senseless degradations that are so many cracks in the edifice: an open wound in her husband's side, the souring of her relationships, enigmatic or accusatory responses from her environment, an unexplained and possibly monstrous pregnancy, itself prefigured by *Rosie Carpe* (2001). In the midst of this generalized unraveling of Nadia's carefully disposed world, enter her son's dog Arno, whose vicious anger toward her forms a salient point of hostility—not to say a vague counterknowledge seeming to challenge what she (thinks she) knows.[12] Vague because like in *Among Family*, it is impossible to name or limit whatever knowledge the dog might possess. The son, perplexed, wonders whether Arno is picking up on Nadia the scent of another male dog, whereupon she retorts that the dog probably senses the less-than-wholehearted welcome her son and his wife are extending her, a point he appears to concede (239–41).

Arno's small role in *My Heart Hemmed In* is ultimately inconsequential, more noteworthy is Nadia's inordinately articulate aversion for him, and for her son's keenness to talk about him: "Doesn't he know I don't care about dogs? That for me dogs don't exist? That any word spoken about a dog bores me to tears [*m'ennuie intolérablement*—equally "*bothers* me intolerably"]" (239/222). In this statement of aversion both categorical and undecided as to its own vehemence (disinterest? boredom? or unbearable distress? but with dogs per se—or all talk of them?), the most puzzling phrase is surely "for me dogs don't exist." Is that to say that dogs too have been buried alive (along with her parents, her first husband, her true origins) in the "ugly depths [*vilain repli*]" of Nadia's heart (273/252)? If one really wanted to give this dog its meaningful place in the novel (or in the universe), one might surmise that Arno (who happens also to be from Bordeaux, like herself) senses in Nadia (like the dogs of the earlier novel had in Fanny) the dishonest concealing of a secret. For do dogs not instinctively abhor lies? Indeed, an insistently ethical reading would make cynics of NDiaye's dogs (and in so doing restore cynicism to its etymological truth). Diogenes was known to say that while other dogs bit their enemies, *he* bit his *friends*, in order to save them. "This paradoxical pedagogy," writes Michèle Clément, "illustrated by the inversion of the use of the dog, which no longer protects from the outside but from the inside, is the foundation of cynicism."[13] Peter Sloterdijk has commented on the critical pertinence of the dog figure to the cynic, serving as "the biting conscience of every dominating self-satisfaction," ever ready to denounce those "ashamed for the wrong reasons, for their *physis*, their animal sides (which, in fact, are innocent), while they remain unmoved by their irrational and ugly practices, their greed, their unfairness, cruelty, vanity, prejudice and blindness."[14] Michel Foucault in turn, in his *Courage of Truth* lectures, would reflect on the Cynics' reappropriation of that "life which does in public, in front of everyone, what only dogs and animals dare to do, and which men usually hide."[15] Cynics took "to the point of its extreme consequence and reversal" the philosophical ideal of the true—unconcealed—life, theirs was the shameless, scandalous embodiment of a "diacritical, barking life," one able to tell apart truth and falsity, master and enemy (243–44). But Foucault noted here "a very strange paradox," a "double attitude," whereby philosophy, even while readily reclaiming cynical thought as its "universal core," tended to reject the Cynic, as embodying truth too radically, vulgarly. Thus cynicism forms the heart of philosophy, while "the Cynic is driven out; he wanders [*le cynique est chassé, le cynique est errant*]," inadmissible, unbearable, on the margins of society.[16] "Cynicism is thus this kind of grimace that philosophy makes to itself, this broken mirror in which philosophy [*le philosophe*] is at once called upon to see itself and fails to recognize itself" (248/270).

Might this forceful insight extend to NDiaye's world, so darkly moral? Should we imagine that the dogs are the grimace these novels make to themselves, a cracked mirror held up to their heroines? Between *Among Family* and *My Heart Hemmed In*, a 2004 story titled "Brulard's Day" presents in support of such a hypothesis a remarkable scene where a dirty, pitiful, nauseating, improbable crossbreed, the ugliest dog Brulard had ever seen, which her husband acquired soon after she suddenly left him (because he considered seriously that the dog might be *her*), assumes the character of an unsettling mirror:[17]

> Pendant les quelques secondes où les yeux du chien furent à hauteur des yeux de Brulard, celle-ci eut l'impression brutale de voir s'y refléter ou s'y noyer sa propre âme anxieuse. Il lui sembla que le miroir sombre des pupilles du chien ne lui renvoyait pas l'image de sa propre figure réduite mais autre chose, d'inattendu, d'inexplicable—comme si, se dit Brulard déroutée, elle avait soudain changé d'aspect au point de ne plus se reconnaître, ou encore comme si l'oeil noir incompréhensible du chien réfléchissait l'être véritable et secret de Brulard, dont elle-même n'avait pas la moindre idée, qu'elle ne pouvait décrire même en le découvrant ainsi révélé dans le regard de cette bête pitoyable. (131–32)
>
> For the few seconds that the dog's eyes were level with Brulard's, she had the brutal feeling that she could see her own anxious soul reflected or submerged deep inside them. The

> dark mirror of the dog's pupils seemed to be showing her not her own miniaturized face but something else, unexpected, inexplicable—as if, Brulard told herself at a loss, her appearance had suddenly changed beyond all recognition, or as if the dog's incomprehensible black eye were reflecting Brulard's true, secret being, of which she herself had no notion, which she couldn't describe, even on finding it thus revealed in the gaze of that pitiful creature. (104)

Certainly, this little dog, "good-hearted and peaceable" (127/101), is a more touching canine presence than any other in NDiaye's oeuvre, bearing out Michael Sheringham's hypothesis that it might be a transitional object enabling Brulard's cognitive evolution (if destroyed soon thereafter by a Great Dane in a horrid manner).[18] Even so, looking more closely at the mirror scene, one is struck by the string of terms signaling indetermination ("something else," "unexpected," "inexplicable," "incomprehensible") which, while they make as if to describe Brulard's face in the "mirror," more accurately index it as *in*describable. As if mimicking her own inability to conceive, let alone analyze, her "true, secret being" ("of which she herself had no notion, which she couldn't describe"), the long sentence (beginning "The dark mirror . . .") confounds itself in subordinate clauses ("as if," "or as if," "of which," "which") and spirals back upon itself as if to further shut out its object ("beyond all recognition"). This piece of unwieldy, baroque, "bad" prose is characteristic of what happens to NDiaye's language when it approaches something suggested (or suspected) to be a truth. Bad prose also because Brulard's governing point of view through the scene seems not to supply coordinates strong enough to dispense with the repeated reiteration of her name—witness in the French the unnecessary (almost jarring) "celle-ci" where an "elle" (as it becomes in the English "she") should have been enough, but also the "se dit Brulard" ("Brulard told herself") where a "se dit-elle" ("she told herself") would have been just fine, and, again, the "être véritable et secret *de Brulard*" ("*Brulard's* true, secret being") where, likewise, given the perspectival regime, a possessive (*son*/her) should have amply sufficed. It is almost as if the passage were staging a subtle separation between theme and syntax, between, on the one hand, the dog that draws Brulard toward a defaced, unnamed outside of the text and, on the other hand, a narration that pretends not to be implicated, indeed, plays at defamiliarizing itself *from* Brulard, peeling itself away minutely from the sinking soul ("s'y noyer sa propre âme anxieuse" / "her own anxious soul [. . .] submerged"). Might it be that, as with the "dreadful dog episode" of *Among Family*, the *face-à-face* with the dog is a function (and dramatization) primarily of the narration's own unhomeliness, its unhom*ing* powers, that is, its power, in detaching itself ever so slightly from its protagonist, to sustain a gap between her and herself, even as the story's central, unending effort is that of behaving as if there weren't one? And that *this*, somehow, is what the dog is—a sort of figure for this irreducible, unspeakable gap—*before* it is given a "fleshed-out" place, as it were, as a dog? So that when Nadia muses desperately, in *My Heart Hemmed In*, that "for me dogs don't exist," there is reason to suspect that the statement expresses not merely a character's incidental disinterest or distaste, but a more fundamental, transdiegetic, atavistic dread of what force dogs may incarnate, of the untamable narrative drift by which the name or idea of a dog *produces* a dog—*narration's dog*, which, even as it stands close and fleshly, odorous, breathing warm, thick breath, baring the dark black of its eyes or the moist inside of its gums, is at the same time perhaps no more than the dogly form given to the story's own autoimmunity, an indifference at the story's heart that unhinges the terms on which identity and recognition would depend. An inhospitability, if you like, that works unaccountably against what might be deemed the traditional symbolic interests of the novel: essentially, protagonism, separation of voices/perspectives, immunity of the human (premised notably, one could say, on the distinction between person and prey/flesh). While "Brulard's Day" and *My Heart Hemmed In* both attempt to close on a redemptive note, the pessimistic end of *Trois femmes puissantes* (2009), published eighteen years after *En famille*, suggests that the dog, wittingly or not, thematized or not, itself fierce or not, continues to be positioned as the breathing, living, recognizing/nonrecognizing, grimacing totem (or alibi . . .) of narrative adversity, and even auto-*av*ersity, that is, narrative's capacity to turn *on* itself. In the third of the powerful women (yet what form of power is this?),[19] Khady Demba, we find at long last a NDiaye protagonist no longer alienated from or disavowing her name and her story. Yet even she will be fatally denounced—along with other clandestine immigrants attempting to escape a detention camp, and before they are caught by guards—by dogs that materialize in the last sentence unnecessarily: "As they moved forward dogs began barking and shots rang out" (292).

NOWHERE IN ITSELF

The problem with dogs' special gift for recognition is that it may aggravate the burden of human self-identity. This is at least as much a historical entanglement as a conceptual (or empirical) one. Inasmuch as the presence of domesticated dogs is attested as far back as 12,000 or 18,000 (not to say, as some would, 100,000) years before the Christian era,[20] certainly the histories of domiciles and dogs cannot easily be untwined. "Man took the (free) wolf and made the (servant) dog and so made civilization possible," Donna Haraway writes pithily, even as she points to the murky distribution of agencies in this "cross-species socialization"—for was it man who domesticated the free wolf or was it some "wolf wannabe dogs" who, seeking profit from "the calorie bonanzas provided by humans' waste dumps," adapted accordingly?[21] Jean Rolin notes that canine evolution is "a painful question" and the subject of "violent polemics" among specialists; many of them fiercely disagree with Raymond and Lorna Coppinger, who believe that wolves genetically predisposed to show a lesser *flight distance*—those who, when approached, were less prone to run away—were naturally selected to survive on the waste of early human villages and thus domesticated themselves (101, 245/247). A recent study goes so far as to impute the friendliness of dogs (and their divergence from wolves) to variations in two specific behavioral genes, in turn found to be linked, in humans, with Williams-Beuren syndrome, a congenital disorder of which one core symptom is hypersociality.[22] For me it is a fable of Jean de La Fontaine's titled "Le loup et le chien" ("The Wolf and the Dog") that most poignantly memorializes this hotly contested event of the mesolithic or superior paleolithic age. In this fable a hungry, skinny wolf is almost persuaded by an enviably plump dog to return with it to the homestead, where he will enjoy access to plentiful food and comfort in exchange for some "light work" (a spot of barking, chasing, fawning . . .). But on the way there, he notices with great foreboding the discolored patch left on the dog's neck by its collar. Understanding its implications ("[. . .] What! Run you not, then, / Just where you please, and when?"), the wolf parts ways with his "fat relation," the fable's last lines sealing his declaration of freedom and his flight—in Elizur Wright's translation: "['. . .] It ought to be a precious price / Which could to servile chains entice; / For me I'll shun them while I've wit.' / So ran Sir Wolf, and runneth yet." There runs a wolf committed to flight distance—a distance that stretches out poetically at the fable's close (can the wolf ever run far or fast enough?).

As against the wild "wit" of those wolves resolved to remain wolves and free (and we may consider at what cost, the French wolf being today, technically speaking, an extinct subspecies),[23] the dog's consent or aptitude for domestication and its provisions—"[. . .] 'you only need / To bark a little now and then, / To chase off duns and beggar men, / To fawn on friends that come or go forth, / Your master please, and so forth' . . ."—has been arguably limitless, its suitability as man's best friend having everything to do with an asymptotically *compressed flight distance*—the dog, in a sense, cannot get close enough. Whence, too, the slippery, compromised coordinates of the history of human-canine coevolution. Whose story even is it? And who disappears, the longer one probes into it? Even dogs may love us less for our presence than for the traces, waste, and warm gaps we leave. So suggests Allan Stoekl, in a beautiful reflection on ecology as "a movement of ghosts, speculative and specular entities":

> We don't even know whether we (humans) domesticated dogs, or whether they domesticated us. Perhaps there's no coincidence that human agriculture and social hierarchy—and the appearance of the first towns—developed around the time dogs were "domesticated." Did "we" somehow make the dog (formerly the wolf) particularly responsive to human intentions and desires? Or did the dog transform and essentially create humans, making possible the domestication (and herding) of other animals, and the protection of private property? The "human" may simply be an after-effect of canine self-preservation.[24]

Why do we insist on seeing the dog as a creature of home and familiarity? Following it seriously may lead rather to startlingly unfamiliar tellings that would exile us altogether from home. Indeed, the sovereignty of the human vis-à-vis its own story—not to speak of stories at large—starts to seem a feebler claim once one starts to consider that dogs might be the cosponsors of things as distinctly "human" as agriculture, social hierarchy, or private property.[25] Oh, but surely the capacity to *tell* stories is properly human, you despair—so that at least in the "author function," in assumed enunciatory positions, in our literature and in our conversations, we stand alone and whole? Not *quite*, if we are to consider the remarkable hypothesis, cited by Haraway (albeit with skepticism), that human language itself, to develop, had awaited the dog: "Some commentators think that even something as fundamental as the hypertrophied human biological capacity for speech emerged in consequence of associated dogs' taking on scent and sound alert jobs and so freeing the human face, throat and brain for chat" (31). Michel Serres in turn, musing on the beginnings of human language, imagines as the first voices those of women, mothers, as "they command the dogs to turn their defensive barking in the direction of the jackals and invasive wolves" and thus "protect the fruit of their wombs and the meat and milk that feeds their children." Thus, language, even as it "is born to protect births," as humans' claim to immunity from the wilderness, is inseparable in its beginnings from a turning of dogs away from, or on, wolves.[26]

Credible or incredible, such conjecturings certainly make of the dog "a painful question," gnawing away at even those analyses that would take it on. Humanists and deep ecologists, as Haraway notes, have equal and opposing stakes in the location of that wolf/dog boundary, in pulling it this way or that (28, 30). In her privileging of anecdotes of "metaplasmic," "naturalculturural," "becomings-with," "sym-bio-genesis," "worldings," "species coshapings," and global, reciprocal, entangled "ethics of flourishing,"[27] Haraway herself is wont to absorb (rather than to "problematize") the difficulty dogs may pose to our concepts. This she foregrounds as her ethics and her method, which require that "there be no deviation from the animal stories themselves. Lessons have to be inextricably part of the story." For Haraway dog writing is a serious strand of feminist writing, and its rule, derived from lapsed Catholicism, is premised on the belief "that the sign and flesh are one" (*Companion Species*, 17). Thus she writes *with* the dog, which, if it is "material-semiotic" and even a "figure," is no "alibi for other themes" nor a "surrogate[. . .] for theory": "They are not here just to think with," she writes, "they are here to live with" (5). Dog writing is then unavoidably autobiographical, at least in the broadest (or the most fundamental) sense—to write about dogs is to narrate one's own entangled fleshly-symbolic situatedness. If such webbed, hyphenated, neologistic, technoscientific-cultural, cross-species interfacial writing risks its own brand of utopianism, it responds to something real and continually confounding: the fact that the distinction between figure and ground—not to say representational language itself—tends to go slippery around dogs. This emerges clearly in a meditation by Carla Freccero (whose thinking here closely follows Haraway's and serves as a methodological lesson in it) on the mauling to death of a woman in a San Francisco apartment building in 2001 by two Presa Canario dogs owned by proxy by a prison inmate. The gruesome incident, immediately framed in terms of gender, sexuality, race, and class (the victim was lesbian; the dog's fury or motivation in certain discourses was represented as masculine; the case was filed by the victim's lesbian partner, raising the issue of the rights of partners in same-sex unions; Pelican Bay prison's treatment of its prisoners placed it on par with detention spaces in Iraq, etc.), turned into a legal and epistemological flash point, raising abyssal questions regarding responsibility, human-animal relations, and intersections of gender difference and racial difference with species difference. Distentangling the multiple "becomings" the case involved and which humanism—or for that matter any *one* interpretive frame—is "unable to contain," Freccero's essay "Carnivorous Virility; or, Becoming-Dog" offers a case study, by the by, of how, the harder one tries to read such an incident, the more in fact *the dog vanishes.*[28] Besides, was it ever *literally* a dog? (Is a dog ever literally a dog?) Here humiliation at being treated *like* dogs in prison led to a warrior subculture reclaiming the dog as a symbol of raw male counterpower. But in this identification and the discourses it engenders, the dog can only be pure essence (essentially innocent or genetically ferocious) or pure instrument, that is, it either subsumes human selfhood altogether or is swallowed up in its mediation of it (186).[29] The sexuality/race lens yields similar anamorphoses: metonymies of fetishistic investment (locating in the dog a compensatory, racialized, narcissistic masculinity) get to express themselves within metaphors safely heteronormative (which reinstate themes of protection, guardianship, family). Thus on the one hand implications of homosexuality and bestiality haunting the man-dog relationship are evaded, while on the other a complicated American history of racialized power is also disavowed. Considering the two "haunted ontologies" (191), Freccero concludes that "both transform the human-dog encounter into a potent and condensed figure of (human) sexual/sexuality and racial conflict distributed across multiple cultural institutions or 'state apparatuses,' from the legal system to the prison system to the populist imagination represented by the media" (190). Haraway too speaks of companion species as *figures*: "As ordinary knotted beings," she writes, "they are also always meaning-making figures that gather up those who respond to them into unpredictable kinds of 'we'" (*When Species Meet*, 5). But it is interesting to see, with Freccero, that in a crisis, the dog's becoming-real, becoming-excessive, becoming-monster (what she calls, after Derrida, "carnivorous virility") works hand-in-hand with its becoming-figure, a becoming-blurred, not to say a becoming-ghost (counterpart to "the ghost in the machine of transnational capital and the prison industrial complex" [183]?). Even as the dog mauls a person to a ghastly death, it would seem to disappear in and to the event. Either the event is about the dog, and the dog exhausts it (for *what can you explain to dogs?*); or, more likely, it never really was about the dog, and an inexhaustible picture of the world is revealed, but the dog curiously falls out of it.

I take this to be one of the kinds of vanishing that Colin Dayan is describing when she writes, in *The Law Is a White Dog*, that "the dog exists nowhere in itself."[30] In this strange and moving book, Dayan retraces and connects the various fictional, analogical, phantasmatic, compensatory ways in which the dog, and particularly the stray, has through European and American legal history prefigured, accompanied, belied, and survived (as its ineradicable residue) the arrival of the human at personhood. Through the evolution of the law, she shows dogs to have had the status of inconvenient, *imperfect* property—that is, hovering complicatedly between animals over which the property right was complete (economically useful farm animals, principally) and wild animals for which there could be no claim to property (and therefore to liability) at all. Naturally it was when a dog stepped out of line (by straying or biting) that it confounded laws pertaining to property—while at the same time spectrally rehearsing predicaments increasingly meted out to humans considered vagrant or deviant. Imperfect property: that is, more person-like than property, yet less than person (240–42, 248). But less than person in a way that specifically demonstrated how a person too could be turned into something less than person, dog-like (241). "Only with dogs before us and beside us can we understand the making and unmaking of persons," writes Dayan (209), pointing to the various ways in which slavery, capital punishment, and torture have logically depended on the animal analogy even while disavowing it. Banishment, expulsion, and radical depersonalizing, in modern history, are in fact never exceptional instances where the law is suspended, forgotten, or weak, but rather where it reveals its never-renounced archaic, ritual, magical side, its power to make unreal the claims of personhood. An overdetermined figure in Dayan's analysis, a paradox, "so empty of substance that it can accrue to itself all kinds of projections," the dog is a fleshly, unhomely reminder of a kind of originary figural trickery, involving continual migrations, morphings, mirrorings, dematerializings—there is nothing simple to what "dog" (and by extension "person") might mean. Even as dogs allegorize dispossession and abjection—in popular imaginaries (such as that of Haiti) they may be seen as the ghosts of people divested of natural rights or personal properties—they are equally the vessels of a twisted vengeance, identified just as naturally with brutal state authority and sometimes wanton persecution—as in the case of slavery, racialized policing (hence *white dog*), concentration camps, and high-security prisons. No wonder the dog is ambivalent. It would have to be, to follow Dayan here, at least as ambivalent as is the legal, social, material history of modernity that has produced personhood and made it possible to bear rights even while simultaneously inventing forms of disfigured personhood, stigmatized bodies, stripped of the right to have rights, specters banished from the city or the very world.

PLACEBO (LEVINAS'S DOG)

Can dogs bear the figural excess gnawing at them, commandeering their properties to contradictory ends, invoking their name even as it drives them out of their bodies? In a sense this was the problem faced by Emmanuel Levinas in the much-commented short essay "The Name of a Dog, or Natural Rights," the first third of which the philosopher had to devote to getting past considerable parabolical and allegorical drag before suggesting that the dog of Exodus 22:31 ("*You shall not eat any flesh that is torn by beasts in the field; you shall cast it to the dogs*"—"So who is this dog at the end of the verse?") is in fact, simply, "a dog. Literally a dog!"[31] First a catalog of dog proverbs and locutions must be rolled out, most of them specific to the French idiom: *un chien dans un jeu de quilles* (a dog in a bowling alley, or bull in a china shop), *qui veut noyer son chien l'accuse de rage* (he who wishes to drown his dog charges it with rabies, i.e., justifies the action after the fact), *métier de chien* (a dog's work), *temps de chien* (dog weather, i.e., horrid weather), *temps à ne pas laisser un chien dehors* (weather in which one wouldn't leave a dog out, i.e., horrid weather), *faire le chien couchant* (to act like a lying dog, i.e., in a servile, obsequious way), *entre chien et loup* (between dog and wolf, describing twilight, where the difference is not clear).[32] "But enough of allegories!" writes Levinas at this point. "We have read too many fables and we are still taking the name of a dog in a figurative sense" (152). To identify the dog at the end of the Exodus verse, a dog to which men may be somehow *indebted*, he would proceed to work his way, through the dogs of Egypt in Exodus 11:7—who, on the night of the "death of the first-born," "will not growl!" allowing the Israelites to flee their bondage—to Bobby, a "wandering dog [*chien errant*]" who, while Levinas and others were being held in a Jewish prisoner-of-war camp in Nazi Germany, would await the prisoners as they returned from forced labor each day, "jumping and barking in delight." "For him, there was no doubt that we were men," writes Levinas (153), to then conclude:

> Perhaps the dog that recognized Ulysses beneath his disguise on his return from the Odyssey was a forebear of our own. But no, no! There, they were in Ithaca and the Fatherland. Here, we were nowhere. This dog was the last Kantian in Nazi Germany, without the brain needed to universalize maxims and drives. He was a descendant of the dogs of Egypt. And his friendly growling, his animal faith, was born from the silence of his forefathers on the banks of the Nile. (153)

"The Name of a Dog" struggles with the enigma of what a dog is. The essay, and, within it, this passage in particular, the only place where Levinas would grant the possibility of ethical recognition—or for that matter give any serious ethical thought—to an animal, has drawn a great deal of commentary,[33] none more thoughtful than that of David Clark, who has reflected both on the pressures by which the strongly humanist claims underpinning Levinasian thought neutralize (and even derealize) Bobby and the sense in which they stand nevertheless to be unsettled by him. No doubt because so much lay at stake there, this dog cuts a necessarily paradoxical, self-limiting figure, Clark suggests in a first essay on the subject, a "depthless surface," a "cyborg," both "lifeless and alive," having and not having a face.[34] While for Levinas, importantly, it is with the face (itself paradigmatically human) that ethics starts,[35] Bobby, because he is an animal, necessarily "enjoy[s] an excess of life over face" (57). Ultimately, Clark decides, Levinas's Bobby is too poor of face to carry anything more than a provisional and "limited testimonial function," "in earnest of the true human witness whose account—in the form of Levinas' essay—has always already usurped Bobby's place in our reading of it" (70). The dog's impact, he ventures in another striking formulation, "is finally only a placebo effect, or perhaps a form of animal triage in a time of terrible need."

With the words "placebo" and "triage" something of the puzzle of Levinas's essay seems to carry over into that of Clark. Why these words, and what do they have to do with dogs? As broadly medical terms they expand an initial metaphor by which Bobby serves temporarily as "the good medicine" that does "a certain purifying work," "restores a minimal health to the camp" (even while he must be excluded after his work is done). But they seem to spill just as easily over this metaphoric field, both because of the etymology of "placebo"—from the Latin for "I shall please" (first-person future of the verb *placere*, used to name first a kind of vesper, then a flatterer, then a drug that heals less than it consoles)—and because of the implications of "triage" (usually used where lives are threatened, resources are scarce, and what is still curable must be attended to by level of priority), by which it is the ethical capacity of witnessing (and by extension humanity itself, and by restriction the philosopher's own testimonial-narrative agency) that here plays the part of threatened life that must place its bets with care. In this instance, finding itself without human agents or the habitual parameters able to sustain it (the prisoners having been "stripped [. . .] of [their] human skin" [153]), witnessing projects itself in extremis onto a stray dog. "Pour lui—c'était incontestable—nous fûmes des hommes" (234; literally, "For him—there could be no doubt—we were men"): inserted in a forceful way within the statement, the claim of certainty here ("c'était incontestable") expresses starkly how humanity, placed under severe threat, reroutes itself through the dog's eyes—in a last effort to save itself. To be clear, the text does not strictly say that for Bobby the prisoners are undeniably humans (this who could say?) but rather that Bobby *undeniably behaves as if* they were (a distinction lost in Sean Hand's fine translation: "For him there was no doubt that we were men"). Surrendering themselves to Bobby's eyes, the prisoners must assume at all costs that he sees men and that the joy he demonstrates is joy at precisely that; without the power to suppress doubt in the dog's mind, they suppress it (as if one could stand for the other) in their own ("c'était incontestable"). The essay's argument—of a piece with the men's very survival—requires so critically that Bobby bear humanity across to the future that it must rely on a presumed and unequivocal one-to-one correspondence between truth (who/what the men are) and affect (Bobby's manifest joy), a last-ditch behaviorist wager, as it were, secure in the fact that *there is no telling apart* the dog's behavior from what would have been shown to (them had they been) men—any difference or "doubt" simply has no place or status in world or thought, is *nowhere* to be found (sealed away in the dog; the dog itself may not know it). It is in this grave and singular sense that the dog shall please: following that curious form of agency by which a medicine or treatment is "*believed by* the patient to be therapeutic (and *[is] sometimes therefore* effective)" ("Placebo," *OED*; my emphasis). The chief characteristic of the "placebo effect" (a beneficial effect after taking a placebo) is not that it is somehow false but rather, more interestingly, that it cannot be attributed to the placebo's properties. Thus, the placebo effect is where the placebo itself vanishes. The placebo is that to which nothing of its therapeutic effect can be strictly *traced back* (even while such a link cannot be positively *dis*proved). Bobby's witnessing, likewise (at any rate, this is how I read Clark reading Levinas) turns on the condition that it not look back at itself—lest it discover it is missing (within the given script, i.e., Levinasian humanism, or Western philosophical thought as a whole) *the ability to* witness ("with neither ethics nor logos" [233/152]). This is, one could say, a witnessing that is "nowhere in itself"—Bobby witnesses, but somehow, when called out, "is" himself not.

In his second take on the Bobby essay, Clark would unfold some of these radical potentialities traced in the first, recalling that for Derrida "something withdraws from sight—or is out of earshot—a secret, as it were, at the heart of testimony, namely the trace of a singularity and non-substitutability of the work of the witness—and that is not witnessed, not as such. To witness without witnessing—is this not Bobby's in-human or other-than-human role in Levinas's testimonial essay? Perhaps Bobby offers Levinas an immemorial trace of that trace, without which witnessing would not be possible; he recalls the languageless spur to language and thus, for Levinas, to responsibility."[36] Earlier in the essay, disagreeing with readings of the Bobby essay that too hastily assume a Kantian humanism to be precluding the possibility of an ethical opening to the dog, Clark had pointed out that *even* for Kant, the ethical obligation is in fact "in-human," "'something other (than man as such),'" so that Levinas's references to Kant through his essay are in fact "his way of exposing his text to the alterities that disturb Kant, and indeed make him *other* to himself" (26). Inspiredly, Clark recalls the emergence in Levinas's writings, around the time of the Bobby essay, of the important, ambiguous, unsettling figure of *le tiers* (the third), "a kind of witness to witnessing," a necessary, irreducible figure of *thirdness* by which the dyadic field of ethical obligation is always opened out to absent, faceless others, "compelling us to ask," writes Clark, "whether there is not always an other other" (33–34). He wonders at this point, paronomastically, across languages: "And when *le tiers* was on Levinas's lips, did he ever hear or think another word encrypted here, namely *das Tier* [German for "the animal"]? Did he ever say the one word and, without meaning to, hear the other? For example, when as a French speaking prisoner in a German labour camp, his gaze met that of a dog who acted as witness to his humanity . . . and something more or other than his humanity?" (34). Even if this message (which makes of Bobby "a strange kind of avatar" [33] for *le tiers*) was "almost inaudible" to Levinas himself, Clark's reading makes sense of why and how Bobby might have haunted and even possessed the philosopher, whose disavowal of him could symptomatically never be complete (31).[37]

VAGUE DOG

"The Name of a Dog," as has been amply noted, marks several exceptions within Levinas's oeuvre: the only place where he so directly broaches the possible relation between ethics and the animal, it is also the most personal and testimonial of his essays. But then it is also arguably the most literary of his writings, in its sifting through of allegorical and rhetorical overdeterminations of dogs, in the way it positions Bobby on its edge and allows his presence to multiply precede him, in its clinging close to language, its self-conscious shifts of angle and register as it advances toward the pithy core of its tale, its exclamation marks,[38] its Baudelarian provocation and wavering of tone. (Interestingly, the last prose poem Baudelaire would ever write, "Les bons chiens" [The Good Dogs], closing *Le Spleen de Paris*, was an ode to street dogs . . .). The transcendence "with neither ethics nor *logos*," the barking born of silence, the emphatic distance taken from the Homeric precedent, effect so many decouplings and redistributions by which Bobby's presence is given as defamiliarized and, consequently, somehow *flickering*. Eluding a conceptualizing narrative, and thereby eluding philosophical recuperation, Bobby is placed rather under the sign of paradox—to read his act demands a different sort of reading of texts and concepts, one that would suspend their provisions and combine the parts differently. No doubt this is why Levinas's essay has elicited commentary that is itself far-fetched, risky (witness here Llewelyn, Clark, Hantel, Katalyn, or my own "wandering" prose). To read "The Name of a Dog" is to be in turn haunted by that scene and that dog and the grave part it is entrusted with.

For my part I am troubled by an enigmatic question Dayan raises with stray dogs in mind: "If the natural creature possessed of personal status [and renounced upon entering social-legal personhood] dies not to be reborn in the spirit but in the body of civil society, what kind of body is this?" (42). Indeed, behind the apparent (cover) question of what kind of mind Bobby's is (how can there be a Kantian without ethics nor logos, etc.?) is possibly a more fundamentally troubling question: what kind of body his is. As Karalyn Kendall has noted, "Bobby, for all his jumping and barking, cannot seem to show his face in 'The Name of a Dog.' He appears quite literally in name only, for Levinas's account of Bobby's behavior offers no sense of a specific canine body of a given size, shape or color" (192). So much so that Max Hantel (even as he proposes to read Bobby as the "Anomalous" described by Deleuze and Guattari, "radically open to transversal relationships," with "only affects" [117]) detects a "wagging tail" at no point mentioned in the text, reading it (quite wonderfully) as an index of tension, of oscillation, by which Bobby himself, as he beholds the prisoners, "runs to unknown becomings": "The tail wags in this moment, suspended between, on the one hand, the possibility of a comforting reterritorialization and, on the other, the risk of tracing new paths with no guarantees" (121). A tail with two hands perhaps, but a tail for all that.

Which, were one to wonder idly (given the hands) whose tail it is, and/or (given the tail) whose hands it is, may be the point. Namely, the question "What kind of body is this?" may yet be awaiting a properly literary answer—that is, an *im*proper literary answer, if one considers that the literary may be precisely what ceaselessly undoes the law of the proper. Levinas may insist that Bobby is "literally a dog!," but the difficulty with the literal is precisely that it may be simply indifferent to realism, allowing a dog to appear "in name only" (Kendall, "The Face of a Dog," 192), which is to say, equally (indistinguishably), something quite *other* to appear in the name of a dog. The proverbial locutions and figurative usages (dog in a bowling alley, etc.) that Levinas had attempted to clear out of the way had at least each offered some sense of what a dog is, of what *they* meant by "dog." Whereas, *literally* speaking, as it were, there is no such thing as a dog—*or there are no bounds to it*. It must coalesce somehow as an effect of its parts, must start and end unaccountably, however weakly or improbably assembled. Bobby hangs together as a dog around his jumping and barking, the rest of his body is supplied by an unheaved corpus, where concepts and predicates (the constituent parts of an entire Western tradition of humanism and ethics) slide into new places and reassemble, forming new seams, leaving new gaps. Not just a prosthetic dog, but, in "the name of a dog," a sort of *joint* where the corpus, or the world, comes together in the last instance and something in it does not quite add up, must be repaired by paradox (so that meaning, so that the world, may survive). In that place, a dog without ethics can act ethically. There a dog without reason can attest to the dignity of the human person. There can be thought where there can be no thought. There can be humanity where humans are "stripped [. . .] of [their] human skin." And perhaps in a way not entirely unrelated (this being as I proceed the weird heart of the matter) to the way in which there can appear a dog where there could just as well have been no dog: "And then, about halfway through our long captivity, for a few short weeks, before the sentinals chased him away, a wandering dog entered our lives" (153).

Wandering dog: so very evocative a term! More commonly, one might say "stray dog." The strayness of Bobby is important to Levinas (who notes that the dog "survived in some wild patch in the region of the camp" and makes a point of marking the difference between this dog encountered "nowhere" and Argos, that dog with master and home in "the Fatherland"). A stray dog is by definition a dog with-

Figure 3.1. *Street dog I*, Bangalore, photograph by the author.

out a proper place. Wandering—*chien errant*—in French (and thus in the many West African and Francophone Caribbean cities where dogs wander), the stray dog goes *vague—perro vago* in Spanish, *cão vadio* in Portuguese—in the many Latin and Central American cities where stray dogs abound. Vague dog. *And then, about halfway through our long captivity, for a few short weeks, before the sentinals chased him away, a vague dog entered our lives* . . . The detour through the Spanish and Portuguese presents the interest of recalling a meaning "vague" once carried in English and French, and first had in Latin, the very one implied by Kant in the Third Moment of the "Analytic of the Beautiful" when he wrote of two forms of beauty: *pulchritudo adhaerens*, "dependent beauty," beauty that is premised on a concept, and *pulchritudo vaga*, "free (or *vague*) beauty," whose examples (e.g., beautiful creatures of the skies or the seas) "signify nothing by themselves," "are not attached to a determinate object in accordance with concepts regarding its end, but are free and please for themselves."[39] *Vaga* comes from *vagus*, signifying in Latin "wandering, inconstant, uncertain, etc.," of which the most "literal" remnant in English is the now-obsolete use of "vague" to mean "vagrant" or "vagabond" (*OED*). *Pulchritudo vaga*, for Kant, "presupposes no concept of what the object should be" and is subject to an aesthetic judgment therefore purer than that elicited by an object appreciated *as* that particular object.[40] Interestingly for me, Alain David, in an essay on Levinas titled "Cynesthèse: Autoportrait au chien," even without noting the specific relevance of the term "vague" to stray dogs (indeed, in a moment where the Bobby essay seems to have been forgotten), deems Kant, in his forging of the notion of *pulchritudo vaga*—"this beauty of erratic forms, whose smiling calm proceeds from the sense in which these forms concern no anguish nor attachment to a ground"—to be invoking in his way the rhetorical figure of hypallage (and so we encounter the dear figure again), as "free expression, liberated from the veneer [*gangue*] of forms, a displacement of qualities that no longer refer back to nouns, unsuitable [*disconvenant*] to all."[41] The figure of hypallage—as in the example he offers of "the yellow sweetness of tea, instead of the sweetness of yellow tea," a wandering, a vagueness, of the attribute—in David's terms "describes perhaps that interruption that has become pure adjectivity (indifferent to substantives [i.e., nouns] which are still beings, subject to being and to death) and meaning [*signifiance*]." *Ibant obscuri sola sub nocte*, or "They went darkly beneath the solitary night," goes the famous Virgilian example of a hypallage, where Aeneas and the Sybil borrowed their darkness from the night and in return gave it their solitude. (But the other term, the second half of the chiasmus, is often absent in the hypallage, whence such phrases as "restless night.")

Is it not such a vagrancy of properties, precisely, that allows Bobby to become an outpost for what meanings are condemned and suppressed in the human? In jumping and barking, the dog all but speaks. If he knows, is himself this *knowing*, he must do so, given (and in order to "pass") the constraints of Levinas's ontological grammar, in the errant (not to say aberrant) mode of a night that is solitary or restless. Hypallage as a figure wields rare poetic and political force, evincing eloquent, obstinate indifference to the proper. Moreover, and importantly, it is not an affair of anthropomorphism or even prosopopaeia (even if it can produce these as two of its possible surface effects), because it concerns that literality of language at which, before (or beneath or despite) "proper" attributions, that is, before (and even so that) they can be "correctly" attributed or *mis*attributed, qualities know no place, so that they are indeterminate or *vague*. It is against such a suggested literality of language (a *poiêtic* dreamtime of roaming forms, colors, properties) that the assignment of a quality, its attachment to a ground, its affecting of a body, when it happens, carries the power of what Paul Ricoeur would call a "métaphore vive" (language's "live" power, with every metaphor, to *create* the real), and what Deleuze and Guattari would call *becomings*: blocks of events, affects, knowings, livings, crossing porous thresholds, sweeping through what our distributions and representations persist in demarcating as discrete, unitary subjects.[42] To be clear: it is biopolitical violence that overturns the "proper" in the camp, turning the Jewish prisoners into something "subhuman, a gang of apes," capable only of "monkey talk." But this overturning remains a wielding (in the negative) of the force of the proper. If hypallage is a meaningful response to the unmaking of persons that is concentrationary violence, this is not due to its vested interest in the proper (quite on the contrary, as I have said) but inasmuch as it offers a poetic correlate, as it were, to *nonviolence*: its work never to deprive or remove nor to impose or disfigure but, quietly, to divert, to miscegenate, to cross, to crisscross, to smuggle across, to express in one entity the untethered, stray, and perhaps unavoidably testimonial traits of another. Seen this way, it is the figure of contraband, also of contagion and affect, making readable the sense in which one body cannot *not* be "bodily" affected by another in its proximity and in relation with it. It is in this rigorous sense a (and arguably *the*) figure of deconstruction, in that it reveals the extent to which every subject is expropriated by its "own" qualities, inhabited by traces of that from which it may claim or strive to distinguish itself. Perhaps, to overstate the point only slightly, it is this sort of nonviolence of the hypallage, as the work of what in the distribution of properties remains undifferentiated, vague, homeless, essentially unhomely, that "The Name of a Dog" dreams of opposing to the Nazi ideology of identity and difference; at any rate this would be one way to understand how—and how tensely, how improbably—humanity here, stripped of its skin, can be saved in the name of (i.e., in what goes by the name of) a dog.

Not that animality in Levinas's essay can be anything other than an idea irreconcilably divided-from-within. Transcending itself in the "literal" animal (Bobby), animality nonetheless metaphorically ensures "subhuman[ity]" in humans ("gang of apes"), as per a chiasmatic deadlock that rightly frustrates contemporary readers. Yet the difficulty is real—material-historical, philosophical, political, ongoing—and hypallage resolves it less than it attests (by the tautness of its threads) to it. The work of determining how Levinas's essay may despite its irreducible contradictions be nonetheless advancing thinking on the animal is being painstakingly done by Clark and others; I have at length come to realize that my own haunting is by something else. "There is something far worse than being turned into an animal," as Dayan writes, and "naming that thing requires a great deal of thought" (71). While "that thing" is, for Dayan, dehumanization, or depersonalization, itself "not easy to accomplish" (95), I have come to read her proposition in relation to that of a rather different thinker, Clément Rosset, when he writes that "the fear of dying is only a secondary consequence of the fear of not living."[43] Rosset is, at this point of a book titled *The Real and Its Double*, correcting what he perceives to be Otto Rank's haste in equating the fear of the double with an ancestral fear of death: "Much rather than his imminent death," he writes, "the source of the subject's anxiety is his non-reality, his non-existence. It would not be so bad to die if one could at least be certain one had lived" (56). Human reality, claims Rosset, may repeatedly and mistakenly be searching for its other in various ghostly others when it is rather *itself* its own other, indistinguishably, *or*—what amounts to the same—*the other of nothing*. The argument, initially one about pervasive structures of avoidance and illusion (duplication and secondariness) in humans' relation to reality, turns ultimately on the "disastrous ontological quality" of existence: as first formulated in Plato's *Cratylus*, a being derives infinite value from being unique, just as, by virtue of that very uniqueness that makes it irreplaceable, it is devalued infinitely (51). That is to say that, once a unique thing or being or reality is gone, *nothing* replaces them. What sort of space was that, then, that now reverts to nothing? What kind of body was that, which need not have been in the first place? The "disastrous ontological quality" of being, then, is that of never having been "more than a very weak, very ephemeral participation in being" (52). The problem, in a sense, is that we stop at the dog because we think we know what a dog is (whose other it is, what sort of other). And that we think we know what the dog is because we think we know what the human is. But, Rosset reminds us, our anxiety when faced with doubles, others, reflections, images, traces, is precisely in knowing that the *proof by the thing itself* (the proof of self by self) has never been effective (79). (This was also Derrida's untiring lesson regarding the signature, and regarding [self-]presence.) In fact, one is never sufficiently visible or plausible as a unique being; in the final analysis one cannot establish one's body and existence by oneself, except on paper (through institutions, legal rights, documentation, acts of witnessing, writing) (75–77). How immeasurable a burden of proof this is is made clear in times of crisis—when there are no papers, or when papers mean nothing. Then—and this is precisely that point of unmaking that so preoccupies Dayan—the human person turns implausible, returned to the ghostliness of being the other to nothing. To my mind the drama of Bobby's presence is most soberly registered at that place where he is not even just a wandering dog, or a vague dog, but standing at (and for) that place where human properties and meanings must survive their own being-vague.

PETITES PERCEPTIONS (THE LEIBNIZ-BAYLE-DELEUZE DOG)

Vagueness happens to be an important notion in analytic philosophy and linguistics, where it describes those predicates whose boundaries are inherently unclear: it is hard to say where precisely they begin or end, which objects belong to them and which do not, without coming up against the riddle of borderline cases.[44] Hence the vagueness of a proposition such as "the person was tall"—How tall? Taller than what others? Where is the threshold where tallness begins? (And what would that place—that *first place* of tallness—even look like? Is it not an irrational, slippery threshold, for the fact that the taller one is, as with Alice when she grows, the shorter one *was*, and therefore the shorter "tall" is?)[45] Vague in this sense too, then, seems to describe the weird predicament of a quality's or a concept's being the other of nothing, its way of flickering, of fluttering, of seeming ghostly, as its proof, or center, stands *outside* it. Discussions of vagueness often refer back to a paradox formulated by the fourth-century B.C.E. Greek philosopher Eubulides of Miletus (most famous for his paradox of the liar: "What I am saying now is a lie") known as the paradox of the heap or the sorites paradox (from the Ancient Greek word for "heap"). A certain number of grains of sand (say one million) makes a heap. A heap minus one grain of sand is still a heap. Proceeding according to the two premises, grain by grain, down from one million to one, one arrives at a single grain of sand that is, absurdly, still a heap. Conversely: one grain of sand + 1 does not make a heap; keep adding according to this logic, and we get to one million grains of sand that are still not a heap. The sorites paradox has elicited a "desperately wide range" of theoretical solutions.[46] Establishing a fixed threshold or boundary between heap and pile (or tall and not tall) is unsatisfactory because it would be arbitrary and would illuminate nothing about the truth of how terms such as "heap" or "tall" function meaningfully in natural language despite their vagueness. In the extreme one can decide simply (this would be the skepticist's answer) that there are no such things as heaps. An epistemicist's answer is that there is a boundary separating heapness from itself but that it cannot be known. A more pragmatic or political approach (for instance, when addressing the vagueness of legal terms) would be to seek a group's consensus on what constitutes heapness or tallness. For some philosophers vagueness is a property of language, rather than of truth.[47] Starting in the 1960s others argued in favor of "fuzzy hedges," "quasitransitive relations," and other descriptions of transitional zones of partial, weakened, or indecisive difference/identity ("truth gaps" and "truth gluts") between heap and nonheap where something may be neither wholly heap nor wholly nonheap, or both heap and nonheap, or where the difference, at any rate, may not yet be distinguishable.

Samuel Beckett had mulled in several places over the sorites paradox and other paradoxes resulting from nonfiniteness or vagueness. In extensive notes taken in the 1930s on early Greek philosophy, he likened them to Zeno's paradox—also concerning thresholds only asymptotically (i.e., never quite yet) arrived at—and sometimes misattributed the sorites paradox to Zeno.[48] "Finished, it's finished, nearly finished, it must be nearly finished. [*Pause*] Grain upon grain, one by one, and one day, suddenly, there's a heap, a little heap, the impossible heap," goes the much-quoted opening line (Clov's) of *Endgame* (1957). A more diffuse treatment of Eubulides's riddle in the wartime novel *Watt* (published in 1953) makes of the imperceptible slipping of sand grains nothing less than a theory of the (slightest) event.[49] Things here are slippery in more than one way. Chris Ackerley, who has written substantially on *Watt* and who points to Beckett's exposure to Gottfried Wilhelm Leibniz's *Monadology* in the very years—and initially through the same source, Wilhelm Windelband's *A History of Philosophy* (1901)—in which he encountered the Pre-Socratics, suggests that in Beckett's thinking the sorites paradox came to be quasi identified with Leibniz's *petites perceptions*.[50] Following Leibniz's doctrine of preestablished harmony, the soul (or soul-like substance, which he would come to name the monad) was a "perpetual living mirror of the universe"[51]—in Windelband's words, "The monad knows the world because it is the world."[52] This relation was worked out in detail through the theory of *petites perceptions*, by which the monad "has very many more representations than it is conscious of."[53] A crucial point, for in Leibniz's view "herein l[ay] the great mistake of the Cartesians, that they took no account of perceptions which are not apperceived," that is, perceived consciously.[54] He would offer up, as against the Cartesian *res cogitans*—which had in turn led both to a denial of souls to animals and to an insistence on the separation of soul and body, both of which Leibniz would dispute—a newly dramatized understanding of "the life of the soul [as what] transcends all that is clear and distinctly conscious, and is rooted in obscurely presaged depths" (*A History of Philosophy*, 2:464). Now, a dog enters the scene precisely here, what is more, owing to a French connection. For it was the French philosopher Pierre Bayle, exiled in Holland, author of the *Dictionnaire historique et critique* (the first edition of which [1697] featured his first comments on Leibniz), who had challenged Leibniz to explain how his theory might account for the sudden transition in a famished dog from pleasure to pain when it is unexpectedly, while eating some bread, struck by a stick. Wherefrom would the pain issue forth, Bayle asked Leibniz, if monads, "windowless,"[55] cannot be influenced from without? Are we to believe that this passive state spontaneously arises from the dog itself, in other words, independently and (thereby) even potentially in the absence of the stick?[56] The engagement between the two philosophers over several years of published writings and correspondence (1687–1706) is now understood, despite disagreements never quite overcome, to have been determining in prompting Leibniz to take his thinking to its furthest and sharpest scope.[57] In the *Histoire des usages des savants* as well as in notes following the 1702 edition of the *Dictionnaire* he would take pains to respond to Bayle in some detail, resulting in this explanation:

> The causes that make the stick act (that is to say the man positioned behind the dog, who is getting ready while it eats, and everything in the course of bodies that contributes to dispose the man to this) are also represented from the first in the soul of the dog exactly in accordance with the truth, but weakly, by little, confused perceptions, without apperception, that is to say without the dog noticing it, because the dog's body also is only imperceptibly affected by it. And as in the course of bodies these dispositions finally produce the blow pressed hard on the dog's body, in the same way the representations of these dispositions in the dog's soul finally produce the representation of the blow of the stick. Since that representation is distinguished and strong, . . . the dog apperceives it very distinctly, and that is what makes its pain.[58]

Leibniz would clarify the need to "distinguish between the spontaneous and the voluntary"—the dog does not will the change, yet it supports it through its own spontaneously evolving and productive representations: "The principle of change is in the dog. The disposition of its soul moves imperceptibly towards giving it pain; but this is without its knowing, and without its wanting it. The representation of the present state of the universe in the dog's soul produces in it the representation of the subsequent state of the same universe, just as in the things represented the preceding state actually produces the subsequent state of its world."[59] The point is that what happens on the level of inner representations mirrors and actualizes what happens on the level of represented (events of the world), so that the passage from pleasure to pain is made possible precisely by the fact that, somehow, even before the blow falls, "both the stick and its wielder are expressed in the mind of the dog."[60] Thus the event itself, when it occurs, has the character of an accumulation, where enough *petites perceptions*—like grains of sand—have added up for the threshold of consciousness to be crossed, and virtual and actual, inner and outward reality to correspond: in the words of Gilles Deleuze, who would return repeatedly, in his book on Leibniz, to the dog, "pain has not abruptly followed pleasure, but has been prepared by a thousand minute perceptions."[61]

In Deleuze's hands the Bayle-Leibniz dog would become a figure for the ceaseless disquiet of animate life, continually alert to those minute slippings—"When no one is looking, no one listening, in tiny packets of two or three millions the grains slip, all together, a little slip of one or two lines maybe, and then stop" (*Watt*, 43)—that may in a situation or event already be carrying it toward its disfigurement: "If Leibniz attaches so much importance to the question of the souls of animals, it is because he knows how to diagnose the universal anxiety of the animal watching out for danger [*de l'animal aux aguets*], that seeks to grasp the imperceptible signs of what can turn its pleasure into pain, its hunt into flight, or its repose into movement" (*The Fold*, 56; translation modified). Deleuze would write some pages later of the *petites perceptions* that they "constitute the animal or animated state par excellence: disquiet [*l'inquiétude*]. These are 'pricklings' [*aiguillons*], or little foldings that are no less present in pleasure than in pain. The pricklings are the representative of the world in the closed monad. The animal that anxiously looks about [*l'animal aux aguets*], or the soul that watches out [*l'âme aux aguets*], signifies that there exist minute perceptions that are not integrated into present perception, but also minute perceptions that are not integrated into the preceding one and that nourish the one that comes along ('so it was that!')" (86–87). If we remember that in Leibniz's monadology soul and world mirror each other, what starts to appear is that the *âme aux aguets* (the soul "on the lookout" or "on guard"), as Deleuze so vividly calls it, is the rigorous correlate to the Baroque conception of world. The dog looks out (*is* this looking out without seeing, as it were) at a world that is essentially one, but differing infinitely in degree and direction.[62] The world that provides sustenance at one moment may in the next moment injure or menace with death; a soul such as the dog's must, in reflecting the world, carry within itself at the same time a multiplicity of perceptions and possible perceptions.[63] Yet, because the *petites perceptions* are largely unconscious, the dog's knowledge is a peculiar one, unrepresented to itself, a wary dwelling and watching through the expressive work of which the world—*as* endless change, constant foldings and unfoldings, events continually in production—repairs its own apparent differences and ceaselessly actualizes itself as (infinitely) one.[64] Indeed, the dog exemplifies (it is an example but also a fable) the soul that for Leibniz is the place of a "concentration of the universe" (*GP* 4:53), with "the means sufficient to unfold the history of that universe through its perceptual states."[65] It is in this fairly radical sense, then, that the (Baroque conception of) world needs the (Baroque conception of) dog. And perhaps the dog more vividly, more intuitively, than any other animal precisely (this being the unsaid in Bayle and Leibniz and of particular interest to me) because, positioned as it is vis-à-vis the human world in a way that is uniquely experimental, hopeful, vulnerable, *entre chien et loup* (drawing from that same world alternately its assurances and its abjection), a dog finds its life nervously indexed exactly on that threshold (that vague boundary) where food is always on the verge of turning into stick (and/or vice versa), and pleasure into pain (and/or vice versa), and thus, in the *petites perceptions*, its very survival continually at stake.

"If someone asked me 'What is an animal for you?,' I would answer, 'It's to be on guard [*aux aguets*].' It's a being that is fundamentally on guard [*c'est un être fondamentalement aux aguets*]," Deleuze said famously in *L'abécédaire*, those eight hours of interview recorded in the very year he published his book on Leibniz.[66] He would concede (when pressed) that this may serve as an analogy for the state of the writer, of the philosopher, only to then return explicitly to the predicament of animals: "[The animal] doesn't do anything without being on guard. It's never at peace [*on laisse jamais tranquille un animal*]. . . . When it eats, it has to notice [*surveiller*] what's happening behind its back, if something is happening to the side, et cetera. It's terrible, this existence of being on guard [*c'est terrible, cette existence aux aguets*]." To me it is clear,[67] even while Deleuze may throw us off the scent by commencing the "A for animal" entry with a general condemnation of familiar/familial animals and with a statement of strong distaste for dogs in particular (their bark the "stupidest noise," "the embarrassment of the animal kingdom," etc. [24]), that it is not the wild or unfamiliar animal that he is thinking of here when he defines the animal, and associates with it foremost the character of "être aux aguets," but rather that very wretched dog that eats while a man approaches stealthily from behind with a stick. In its transmission from Bayle to Leibniz to Deleuze, that unseemly scene will have gathered dramatic allegorical force, emblazoning in its details the experience of embodied, temporal, injurable life, and registering the exact sense in which that experience can be—in the word's original sense, derived from terror—"terrible."

Terror is arguably the price to pay for the (i.e., Leibniz's original) refusal of the abstract, discrete concepts of classicism. "Instead of sticking to abstractions, we have to restore the series," Deleuze writes in *The Fold*, then goes on to describe the man approaching the eating dog, "tiptoe[ing] up from behind," "rais[ing] the instrument," and correspondingly, in the soul of the dog, the "thousand minute perceptions—the pitter-patter of feet, the hostile man's odor, the impression of the stick being raised up" (56). The terror is in realizing that opposites are not opposed, but in a continuum, differing only in degree. The same world can by turn be hospitable or hostile, the change creeping in imperceptibly till it is (as if) suddenly effective. There, then, lies the secret lesson of the *petites perceptions*, a secret that Leibnizian philosophy, in its response to Bayle, would come to locate, for didactic purposes, in the dog. The infinite unity of the world becomes the dog's to bear. What would not have escaped Beckett as he connected the sorites paradox and the *petites perceptions*—particularly in his early novel *Watt*, which, as Germaine Brée was the first to suggest in 1963, "appears as an intentional parody and refutation of Leibniz's 'best possible of worlds'"—is that what is located in the dog describes, equally, *our own dog life* to live, without ground, without home.[68] "To think, when one is no longer young, when one is not yet old, that one is no longer young, that one is not yet old, that is perhaps something. To pause, [. . .] and consider: the darkening ease, the brightening trouble; the pleasure pleasure because it was, the pain pain because it shall be; the glad acts grown proud, the proud acts growing stubborn; the panting, the trembling towards a being gone, a being to come; and the true true no longer, and the false true not yet" (*Watt*, 201). If there is a lesson of the dog, it has to do obscurely with this vagueness, which in the extreme instance, in substituting creeping, unstoppable continuities for oppositions, is what secretly connects (this is why we dread it) what a thing or being is to what it is no longer, or not yet.

THE RELATION WOVEN NIGHTLY (BECKETT'S DOG)

When Watt wonders, thereby weirdly anticipating Levinas's question ("So who is this dog at the end of the verse?"), "But was a dog the same thing as the dog?," and, a little further, "a fortiori were several dogs the same thing as the dog?" (96), I find a clue to why dogs keep appearing at those places where concepts and humans go vague. Beckett's protagonist, while in the service of the most enigmatic Mr. Knott, is here mulling at length over the riddle of a certain instruction pertaining to his employer's daily one-dish meals, namely "to give what Mr. Knott left of this dish, on the days that he did not eat it all, to the dog" (91). There is no dog in the house, "so that it was necessary that a dog from outside should call at the house at least once every day, on the off chance of its being given part, or all, of Mr. Knott's lunch, or dinner, or both, to eat." The matter, like all matters in this novel of series and permutations, presents "great difficulties" (91): some days Mr. Knott would eat everything he was served, on others he would leave some unforseeable part of his lunch or dinner or both, on others yet (rare) he would eat nothing at all (which would be "of course wonderful days, for the dog"). The problem is that "the average hungry or starving dog, if left to its own devices," would not willingly depend for its daily survival on a food source so erratic (92). Twenty-five pages of elucubrations follow, in the course of which, piece by piece, is assembled the arrangement, and indeed the world system, that must logically be implied by the mysterious injunction: A dog (kept) continually hungry must present itself every day at an appointed hour (after Knott's second meal) to eat however much food there remains to eat, there must be a keeper for this dog, there must be a second hungry dog on reserve in case the first dog dies (a fair probability since on some days there will be nothing for it to eat, and on others the food would be "a little on the rich and heating side, for a dog," and since in any case the dog is kept on a chain with no exercise [112]), and eventually a third in case the second dies, "and so on indefinitely"; there must also be a backup for the keeper in case the keeper dies, and a third in case the second dies, "and so on indefinitely"; there must be monetary incentive to ensure the daily service and no departure from it, therefore the keepers must be (kept) poor; and so on. Watt's ratiocinations lead ineluctably to "the solution that seemed to have prevailed": on the one hand, "a kennel or colony of famished dogs"; on the other, "a suitable large needy local family of say the two parents and from ten to fifteen children and grandchildren passionately attached to their birthplace" (98–99). There are few more chilling examples in modern literature of what can happen when logic takes the place of narrative or world. One thinks, for example, of the way competitive games order life on the dystopian island of Georges Perec's *W or The Memory of Childhood*. Beckett, "an engaged and traumatized witness" to the "genocidal disasters brought about by twentieth-century thinking," wrote *Watt* during the period from February 1941 to February 1945, the first part of which he spent working for a resistance network in Paris and the rest in flight from the Gestapo and hiding in the Vaucluse.[69] That the shadow of a concentrationary world should fall so darkly on the novel is then hardly surprising; for Ackerley, *Watt* "testifies eloquently to a world in ruins."[70] More remarkable is the fact that the pages given laboriously over to "this matter of the dog required to eat the food that Mr. Knott left" (99) should be the principal place where this shadow falls.[71]

Writing on Beckettian exhaustion, Deleuze himself would cite this "great serial novel, in which Mr. Knott['s] only need is to be without need," where the exhaustive is the field of a subjecthood itself exhaust*ed*, that has "renounce[d] any order of preference, any organization in relation to a goal, any signification."[72] The distinction between terms, at this exhaustive/exhausting point of language, writes Deleuze, serves no end "except to create further permutations. It is enough to say about an event that it is possible, since it does not occur without merging with nothing, and abolishing the real to which it lays claim" (153). Admittedly, the dog is not the most exemplary instance of an exhaustive series in *Watt*.[73] It offers, nonetheless, emblematic grounds for showing that Beckettian exhaustion is not, as Deleuze would have it, strictly or necessarily without value or investment, but on the contrary can be the radical means by which to delimit the properly *unbearable*.

To begin with (by way of secondary evidence), there are places in *Watt* where, within a series, a particular permutative outcome is suggested to be unhappy. There is the fact that when Watt thinks, through a series of possible configurations, of what Knott's relationship to his daily food arrangement might be (varying around the axes: Is he responsible for it? Does he know he is? Does he know the arrangement exists? Is he content with it?), he expressly leaves out all those configurations wherein Knott might not be content, as François Martel has noted without venturing any particular reading of it.[74] That the possibility of Knott's unhappiness—vis-à-vis an arrangement that has "never varied, since its establishment, long long before" (88), a harmony *preestablished*, shall we say, to follow Ackerley's reading of *Watt* as a rehearsal or parody of Leibnizian thinking—does not bear thinking finds within the novel a likely (if nonexplicit) explanation. For it is Watt himself who, while in Knott's service, shedding "tears of mental fatigue," is responsible for the daily brewing of his preestablished stew, whose ingredients and dosages had been "calculated, with the most minute exactness, to afford Mr. Knott [. . .], the maximum pleasure compatible with the protraction of his health" (88). Here, then, is why *Watt* is a novel about "the tragedy of the monad that tries to accommodate itself to the 'establishment'":[75] to be a servant of the preestablished order is to find certain kinds of relations to it, and thereby certain regions of world and self (those not in harmony with it), silenced as unthinkable, or rather, too painful to think, for they would instantly put in question the harmony of the whole; worse still, they might show universal harmony to be premised on a making-unreal of singular predicaments. It is in these terms that I would understand, likewise, the extraordinary passage (again read for its logic but not for any "meaning" by Martel—oh the happy age of formalism!) where, before a picture in Erskine's room featuring a circle and a center, Watt runs through all the possibilities of what it might be a picture of, to find himself inconsolable at the last:

> And he wondered what the artist had intended to represent (Watt knew nothing about painting), a circle and its centre in search of each other, or a circle and its centre in search of a centre and a circle respectively, or a circle and its centre in search of its centre and a circle respectively, or a circle and its centre in search of a centre and its circle respectively, or a circle and a centre not its centre in search of its centre and its circle respectively, or a circle and a centre not its centre in search of a centre and a circle respectively, or a circle and a centre not its centre in search of its centre and a circle respectively, or a circle and a centre not its centre in search of a centre and its circle respectively, in boundless space, in endless time (Watt knew nothing about physics), and at the thought that it was perhaps this, a circle and a centre not its centre in search of a centre and its circle respectively, in boundless space, in endless time, then Watt's eyes filled with tears that he could not stem, and they flowed down his fluted cheeks unchecked, in a steady flow, refreshing him greatly. (129)

The last configuration easily, pithily formulates the missed relation between, on the one hand, a preestablished world order that indifferently seeks *any* body or self to stand at its center and assure in turn its harmonious functioning, and, on the other, that body or self that looks for a world that might be *its* world and home. That "it was perhaps this," that *this* should have been the outcome arrived at as the best of all possible worlds, has Watt crying tears that the world cannot in fact receive nor contain, since the world seeks and knows not him but "a" body whatsoever in his place. Thus his tears flow "[un]stem[med]," "unchecked," unworldly.

Under cover of the "outrageous parody of scholasticism" of *Watt*,[76] it seems to me that Beckett would prize open small windows (in a supposedly windowless world) in precisely this way, that is, as bits of meaning and feeling that the world and its telling have no place for. So with the business of the dog by which "Watt was, for a time, greatly interested, and even fascinated," "attach[ing] to this matter an importance, and even a significance, that seem hardly warranted" (116). As the arrangement works out its perfected form, tiny excesses accrue here and there: the man sent from the house to seek out a/the dog cuts "a wretched and ridiculous figure" (94); the dog, once it is established to be the same from day to day, becomes "the same poor old dog" (96) and then the "faithful emaciated dog" (97);[77] in one flawed scenario, "the man and dog come *running* to the door, when there was nothing [to eat for the dog], or onward *plod*, when there was something" (97; my emphasis). In other words, as the scene gains consistency, small semantic elements appear that seem to indecently exceed the strictly logical necessity at work. But then again, are these elements really excessive or erratic? When one pays closer attention to them, they gather rather as points where the imagination (Watt's or *Watt*'s) most clinically registers what is necessarily implied, indeed *required* by the system—places where *suffering* forms in truth the system's central animating principle. For, at the center of the system that ensures that Knott's "remains," as they are called (115), go to the dog, is a dog kept famished, prevented from seeking its nourishment through any other means, and forced to eat no more and no less than what Knott leaves. So that we should perhaps not be surprised to see materialize, around the "real live famished dog as large as life" (100), also a stick and a disciplining scene:

> Passing on then to the solution that seemed to have prevailed, Watt found it to be roughly this, that a suitable local dogowner, that is to say a needy man with a famished dog, should be sought out, and on him settled a handsome annuity of fifty pounds payable monthly, in consideration of his calling at Mr. Knott's house every evening between eight and ten, accompanied by his dog in a famished condition, and on those days on which there was food for his dog of his standing over his dog, with a stick, before witnesses, until the dog had eaten all the food until not an atom remained, and of his then taking himself and his dog off the premises without delay. (98)

Here the scene is reconstituted at its most elaborate, featuring all its necessary components. Earlier and later, the stick and witnesses are omitted, or only tacitly implied in a "standing over" (95, 96, 113). Ackerley has connected a reference to a stick elsewhere in *Watt* with a Schopenhauerian thematic of self-extension of the body in relationship to itself and its environment.[78] The stick for Schopenhauer (and for Stephen Dedalus) serves to verify the existence of a thing. But the stick of the "standing over" is no Schopenhauerian stick, it would seem to be rather, alas, a stick of the Bayle-Leibniz sort, held aloft while a dog eats. With a twist, if one considers that the power of the stick here is not to interrupt the dog's eating but quite on the contrary to ensure that it "eat[s] all the food until not an atom remain[s]." It is worth remembering here that for Leibniz, hunger/satiation, like pain/pleasure (and even appearing to provide the model thereof), were not simply linked through reversal or separated by a frank caesura, but spilled forth into each other like paradoxical communicating vessels: "How could a feeling of hunger follow one of satiation if a thousand tiny, elementary forms of hunger (for salts, for sugar, butter, etc.) were not released at diverse and indiscernible rhythms? And inversely, if satisfaction follows hunger, it is through the sating of all these particular and imperceptible hungers."[79] Leibnizian thinking stands not to survive *Watt*'s "concrete and burlesque" twist,[80] whereby what determines the end of the dog's meal is no longer an inner threshold of satiation, where a thousand *petites perceptions* culminate, but rather an outer injunction and limit (the stick, enforcing subservience to the dish, that must be emptied), by virtue of which the faithfulness of "the faithful emaciated dog" names its forced consent to being hollowed out of itself as it were—made all appetite and no perception/affection. Thus preestablished harmony gives way to what Beckett would call some pages later a "preestablished arbitrary" (134). Is it that monadological thinking cannot account for biopolitical violence, or that it had in fact allowed for it from the beginning?

Perhaps the key to Beckett's provocation to Leibniz (appearing as he does here almost as a second Bayle) is in the insistence that "not an atom remained." Atomist or protoatomist though Leibniz was, he had no place for emptiness or nothing, suggesting rather folds or what later materialists would call fractals, waves, quanta.[81] This is fundamentally, one could say, what made him "a philosopher of habitat and ecology."[82] To this Beckett opposes the zero-sum economy of the pot that must at all costs be completely emptied. An imagined scenario (not efficient enough to prevail) where a person might be employed every night to take "the pot full" to dog after dog "until all the food was eaten, and not an atom remained, and then to bring back the pot empty" is followed by this rare parenthetical meditation on the nonsymmetry of fullness and emptiness: "(And is it not strange most strange that one says of a thing that it is full, when it is not full at all, but not of a thing that it is empty, if it is not empty? And perhaps the reason for that is this, that when one fills, one seldom fills quite full, for that would not be convenient, whereas when one empties one empties completely, holding the vessel upside down, and rinsing it out with boiling water if necessary, with a kind of fury)" (95). It is this seemingly excessive but in fact strictly economic (econom*istic*) "fury" that will find concrete expression in the stick, whose work is to ensure that the pot is emptied every night, as it were, *into* the dog, "until not an atom remained." The perfect economy of Knott's establishment is thus ensured by this dog, alternately starved and forced to eat, not so much a monad within the world, as the dark hole where what does not quite "add up" in the world can be evacuated. Such evacuation—the rounding off of "remains" to zero, the production of clean borders and emptiness—is not achieved without fury.

That the nightly scene of the dog's feeding is one that affects Watt—the dog's plight emerging then as perhaps even what is *most* unbearable, more so even than Knott's possible discontent (its symmetrical double,[83] but whose main effect is to exile the dog further from thought)—is evidenced in the fact that though "it was part of Watt's duties [. . .] to witness the dog's eating the food, until not an atom remained," actually "after the first few weeks Watt abruptly ceased, on his own responsibility, to discharge this office" (113). The refusal entails certain intricate measures (a code involving a light lighting the doorstep where the food is kept, when there is food, etc.) and possibly "the gravest consequences, both for Watt and for Mr Knott's establishment," we learn, yet "he could not have done otherwise, believe it or not, than he did" (114–15). No reason will be provided for Watt's declining of his witnessing/disciplining role, though it is made clear that it is certainly not because he loves dogs ("greatly preferring rats"), nor any one dog in particular (Kate, in service when he joins Knott's estate, he finds "of repulsive aspect" [111–12]). But it can be guessed that Watt's refusal, despite his fear of being punished for it and/or that it will bring about great harm to the establishment, is of an obscurely similar order to his great sorrow at the last of the circle/center hypotheses. The "relation that the dog wove nightly" (116)—and by extension the establishment or the preestablished/arbitrary world system—enlists Kate as it would any other body in her place, it runs, as per the original injunction/riddle governing Knott's food arrangements, on a notion (and a keeping-in-optimal-operation) of "the dog," with no relation whatsoever to any questions concerning who or what "the dog" might be—"But was a dog the same thing as the dog? [. . .] a fortiori were several dogs the same thing as the dog?" (96). What stands at the place of "the dog" is a bleak and godforsaken life. Released from sight, unmoored eventually from words and thought, Kate will flicker between existence and nonexistence, unthinkable center of the world, appearing nightly in a pool of light, to then return again to darkness: "He had turned, little by little, a disturbance into words, he had made a pillow of old words, for a head. Little by little, and not without labour. Kate eating from her dish, for example, with the dwarves standing by, how he had laboured to know what that was, to know which the doer, and what the doer, and what the doing, and which the sufferer, and what the sufferer, and what the suffering, and what those shapes, that were not rooted to the ground, like the veronica, but melted away, into the dark, after a while" (117).

Dog sustenance would again turn (endlessly, abyssally) into suffering in the doggerel opening act 2 of *Waiting for Godot*, where a dog steals a crust of bread (it is a sausage in the original French text) from a kitchen only to be beaten to death for it (with a ladle), whereupon the other dogs bury it and inscribe on the tomb the tale of the dog that steals a crust of bread from a kitchen only to be beaten to death for it, and so on, a recursive loop of a song that, if not for the return of Estragon (who himself was beaten during the night that he spent in a ditch), would continue endlessly.[84] Beckett's dogs are curious creatures, as if underdeveloped and excessive at the same time. If they are "despised for their obviousness"[85]—and we might remember here that "obvious" comes from *ob viam*, "in the way"—it may well be because they express too obviously a tetheredness to that threshold where doing can turn into suffering, eating into aching—not to say the extent to which something like subjecthood (as initially subject*ion*—remember Bentham/Derrida's "Can they suffer?") starts precisely at that threshold—that the self would rather "despise and refuse" in itself. Which might account for the moving moment in *Krapp's Last Tape*, where Krapp (there too in a *mise en abyme*, since it is Krapp listening to his past self on a tape) can no longer separate his own (refused) sadness at his mother's death from the (too obvious) disappointment of a little dog:[86] "There I sat, in the biting wind, wishing she were gone. (Pause.) . . . I was there when (. . .) the blind went down, one of those dirty brown roller affairs, throwing a ball for a little white dog as chance would have it. I happened to look up and there it was. All over and done with, at least. I sat on for a few moments with the ball in my hand and the dog yelping and pawing at me. (Pause.) Moments. Her moments, my moments. (Pause.) The dog's moments."[87]

NOT I

Deleuze would not enact the same "refusal to be present when the dog ate the food" (*Watt*, 115) as Watt. This extraordinary thinker of becoming-animal, when revisiting a second time in *The Fold* the Leibnizian scene of the dog always-on-the-verge-of-being-flogged, slips curiously into the first person: "However abruptly *I* may flog *my* dog who eats his meal, the animal will have experienced the minute perceptions of *my* stealthy arrival on tiptoes, *my* hostile odor, and *my* lifting of the rod that subtend the conversion of pleasure into pain" (86–87; my emphasis). A disconcerting point of view to say the least, until one considers that such a distribution of positions was perhaps already foretold in Bayle-Leibniz. For to insistently locate the drama of the *petites perceptions* in a dog was to not sufficiently guard against the fantasy of an essential difference between humans and animals. A difference if not in terms of capacity (for in this respect the dog is meant to stand for the soul in general, including the human soul), at least in terms of predicament and narrative position—for as soon as a stick appears, a man appears to wield it, and this man is presumed to be self-identical, that is, assured of the consciousness of his intention and thus of inhabiting for all intents and purposes the realm of reason and apperception. Of course one could maintain that the "I," in its exaggerated exteriority ("my stealthy arrival on tiptoes, my hostile odor"), forms here at most a sort of prop, a weak defense and foil, and that the perceptual-affective energy, the sensory intensity of embodied life is, in the scene, entirely that of the dog. But the point is that Deleuze, even as he holds up Leibniz's dog as a figure for the universal anxiety of the soul, in assuming in this lapse the position of man with stick, at the same time symptomatically illustrates the force—narrative, representational, gravitational, biopolitical, but also/even pedagogical—that will always attempt or appear to preserve, or to prefer, subjecthood at a distance from the "être aux aguets"—even if this means a subjecthood rather impoverished or ungainly (sad stick man, "stealthy" and "hostile").

True, even while the deepest thrust of Leibniz's thinking (and that of Bayle) was anti-Cartesian and even while by "animals" he meant "all living creatures up to and including man,"[88] he did locate in humans alone (or at least in "the wisest people") the ability to reflect on the reasons for why what happens happens—while "brutes" (that is, animals), like pure empiricists, base their knowledge entirely on what has already been known to happen and thus could happen again, "without being capable of determining whether the same reasons hold good": "It is because of this that it is so easy for men to catch animals," Leibniz would write, pointing out that "men become more skillful by discovering countless new contrivances, whereas the stags and hares of today are no more cunning than those of yesterday. The sequences of brutes are but a shadow of reasoning, that is to say, they are but connexions of imagination, transitions from one image to another" (*Philosophical Writings*, 152). Granted, as Garin Dowd notes in a lucid essay on Beckett and Leibniz, "the dog [. . .] has an archival capacity" (Dowd quotes Leibniz: "When dogs are shown a stick, they remember the pain which it has caused them in the past, and they run away").[89] Still, in the hierarchy of monads it is a properly reflexive capacity that is needed for a soul to become a rational self: "It is by knowledge of necessary truths and by their abstractions that we are raised to acts of reflection, which make us think of what is called the self, and consider that this or that is within us."[90] Thus, if for Leibniz the dog can remember and even learn to avoid, to become a rational self is to go further still, it is to transcend one's dog life as it were, those mere appetites and aversions, pleasures and pains, it is ultimately to turn the stick into a heuristic device—as, say, Beckett's Malone would do awhile, using it to reach out and enumerate his possessions and thus to verify the extent of the self—not to say a concept: "How great is my debt to sticks! So great that I almost forget the blows they have transferred to me."[91]

Yet has one ever completely arrived at such a transcending? What if the drama of the "être aux aguets" simply got transposed onto another level? For is the self not a function of the continual (attempted) dividing off of the "I" from the "animal that therefore I am," the dog condemned to live in fear of the stick, at its mercy? And is a life—or a story—not the space of a continual striving (or dreading) to know "which [is] the doer, and what the doer, and what the doing, and which the sufferer, and what the sufferer, and what the suffering" (*Watt*, 117)? To be *aux aguets* is to lie in wait (*guetter* shares its root with "wait"), so as to surprise *or* to avoid being surprised (*Littré*). Within this waiting that describes wakeful, watchful life, the ambusher strives, through strength or cunning, to distinguish itself from the ambushed, the human from the animal, the narrator from the narrated. The "être aux aguets" describes an intense, anxious vigilance as possibility unfolds and divides. To understand it as a state of destinal suspense, a tense place where living beings stand waiting and wary, is to feel an unease at the thought of which of us—or which part of us—might not or does not survive the unfolding.

And what of NDiaye's dogs that led me down this winding, riddled, eccentric path, through Levinas, vagueness, Beckett, Leibniz, Deleuze, and the "être aux aguets"? They pose an enigma that I slowly gather the means to interpret: the presence of a dog in a story may point foremost toward the drama of what struggles—what has historically struggled—to be apart from it, to *not* identify with it. *Not I*: so one might formulate this drama, remembering one of Beckett's most troubling monologues (1972; *Not I*) but also so many limit-like points in his writing, where a speaking voice recognized both that it could not stop speaking (and thus continually producing inescapable images of itself, yet which were not sufficiently itself for it to stand there once and for all for itself: "For why [. . .]? And whose voice asking this? Who asks, Whose voice asking this?"),[92] *and* that it could never be sure that it was itself really speaking: "I never spoke, I seem to speak, that's because he says I as if he were I, I nearly believed him, do you hear him, as if he were I, I who am far, who can't move, can't be found, but neither can he, he can only talk, if that much, perhaps it's not he, perhaps it's a multitude, one after another, what confusion"[93] This *not I* is not exactly short for the *I am what I am not and I am not what I am* that for Sartre described the structure of bad faith, that irresistible human flight from the knowledge of (and responsibility for) who/what one is.[94] In Beckett it describes a more unearthly paradox, by which, through the "I," we enter both language—as speaking subjects—and the indifference of language to who is saying I and to what it means to be mute or to die: "Unless another still. Nowhere to be found. Nowhere to be sought. The unthinkable last of all. Unnamable. Last person. I. Quick leave him."[95] Still, ultimately both have to do with the fact that with the possibility of thinking/saying "I" comes also the possibility of feigning, evading, hiding, dividing, surviving (as) the I. It is what Derrida, discussing autobiography, would seem to gesture to as the I's *unfalsifiability* (my term), which is precisely its ability to be used (potentially endlessly) falsely yet to never be called out, nor called on to bear the burden of its own proof.[96] With the power to think/say I (a power essentially founded, as Derrida would recall, on a domination over animals)[97] comes also the paradoxical possibility of claiming "(I am) not I"—an extreme measure taken when the self cannot bear its place or charge (and flees it, in a sort of irreducible *flight distance*), or, experienced or conceived in a more ordinary or originary sense, a deep truth about the I (playful or grave, alienating or dialectical, making life livable or unlivable), which is that it can never wholly and only and definitively speak for itself: "He has me say things saying it's not me, there's profundity for you . . ."[98] What if, taking literally Derrida's claim (as he reviews Western thinking on the animal, from the book of Genesis to Kant to Lacan) that "power over the animal is the essence of the 'I' or the 'person,' the essence of the human" (130/93), one were to consider the "not I"—which, in Beckett, as Rolf Breuer notes, works as a grammatical/logical "trick" where the point is actually to *not think or say I*—as that paradoxical place where language *might think the animal* (i.e., that to which it has denied speech and thus the possibility of "I"),[99] as if turning itself inside out, reaching for its furthermost, unbearable outpost (that place where language virtually annuls itself) in order to name (even while seeming to negate) my (the I's) secretly shared passivity and finitude (and even muteness) with animals, my ability to suffer and to die.[100] Here we encounter an abyssality that Derrida would comment on everywhere, and which in his hands never failed to leave defeated all arguments for what is "proper" to the human: if it is possible to pretend, it is not possible to limit the object and level of pretense: thus one can pretend to pretend, and this possibility is no less available to animals (*pace* Lacan) than it is to humans.[101] Similarly, from the moment that it becomes possible to say "not I," it becomes equally possible to say "not not I" and so on, so that—and all the more since the only witness and arbiter for such identifications and disidentifications is the I itself—it may no longer be possible to arrive at an I free from all that is "not I," nor, even more importantly, a "not I" sufficiently cleaved away from the I not to still be it. I may always simply be pretending that something/someone is not I, or pretending *not to be* I (or, in Beckett's language, pretending to be *not I*),—or, indeed, pretending *to be* I (and therefore in truth *not I*)—who is to say? (And whose voice saying "Who is to say?")

These riddles may seem a far cry from NDiaye's work but in fact such abyssality covertly animates many of her stories: in characters who insist on proceeding as if they were "not I" (because the "I" is marked with the shame of [bodily or historical] difference) but around whom language starts to work as the repressive (and French Republican) law itself works,[102] that is, in making the repressed difference itself invisible, unutterable, and thus permitting exclusion or violence on its basis to equally function outside all symbolizable frames. Thus, in *My Heart Hemmed In*, when Nadia says, "We're exactly like you," the pharmacist replies: "So you think, [. . .] the disgust and hostility you inspire in some people, not me, oh not me [. . .] Forgive me, this is so hard . . . You have something in your face that people can't stand to see . . . not on any face . . . and it's something truly repugnant, not for me, no, not yet" (28/21). In a sense, the difficulty of these narratives is that in them a "not I" has effectively substituted itself for an "I" (or one could say the reverse, depending on whether one is concerned with the level of speaking or being), but subsequently these two (the "I" and the "not I") have effectively swapped names. The trick is so perfect (this is the unfalsifiability of the I) as to not be unmaskable through language or representation; indeed, it actually grounds all representations.

To say, then, that it takes a dog to see through it, to call out the phantasmatic (and also perfectly conventional, socially stipulated, normative) separation between I and not I—that first speech act and immunological act on which identity and narrative are assumed to be premised—is to lend the name or shape of "dog" to that which within a story cannot be represented through the story's own distributions (subject/object, known/unknown, I/not I)—because these distributions are founded precisely on a fierce *un*thinking or *un*knowing of it ("for me dogs don't exist"). Thus, in César Aira's short story "The Dog," as a man on a moving bus starts to realize that the dog following relentlessly and barking fiercely is in fact coming *for him* because it has not forgotten his cruelty to it many years before ("what I'd done to him was truly, unspeakably disgraceful"), he admits: "I realized that I had been counting on a certain impunity. I had assumed, as anyone in my place might have done, that a dog being first and foremost a dog, its individuality would be reabsorbed by the species and finally disappear. And with that disappearance my guilt would vanish too."[103] Further, he grasps at other possible arguments against this being the same dog: "Dogs don't live that long" (47). But it is clear that, more deeply still, he wishes to argue (to the other bus passengers, to the symbolic order, to himself) that it is *not him* that the dog recognizes and is coming for: "All I had to do was deny my knowledge of the animal, and no one would contradict me. I gave thanks for words and their superiority over barks" (52). The dog in this story (as in certain others that have preoccupied me here) is a thing as if hewn from a substance other than that of the story, the story's buried and unspeakable heart: "What I saw in his eyes was not the fury I'd been expecting but a limitless anguish, a pain that wasn't human because it was more than a human could bear" (48). If dogs did not exist would we have invented them, perhaps, to carry what exceeds what we can bear?[104] (Who says we have not?) Is this why we "are—sometimes only momentarily—incapable of beholding a dog"?[105]

Is it that the expressivity of dogs is underwritten always by the brevity of their lives? In a passage of *Un chien mort après lui* that has haunted me for years, Jean Rolin notes his hyperalertness to stray dogs in cities and texts. The dogs turn here both utterly prosaic (they are the emblems of the unfinishedness of the work of the political/municipal, often signaling poverty, failed urban management, conflict, or a period of social transition) and quasi mythical, things always about to disappear, merging with their own disappearance:

> By dint of [*À force de*] searching texts for occurrences of stray dogs, one ends up developing, or fancying that one is developing, a sort of instinct, or experience, that makes one sense several lines ahead their imminent appearance. But it can so happen that the early signs are misleading and that this expectation [*attente*] is disappointed, the scene or pas-

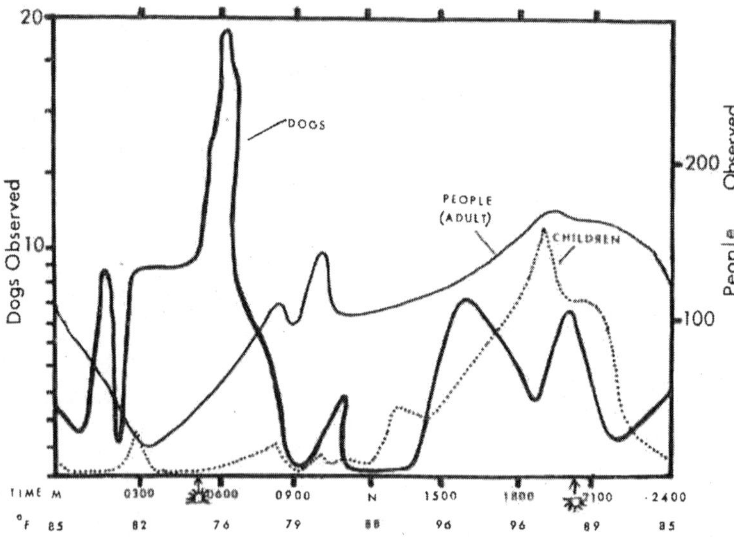

Figure 3.2. From Alan Beck, *The Ecology of Stray Dogs*.

> sage in question giving you then the impression that there are dogs missing [*il y manque des chiens*]. (94)[106]

Stray dogs have vanished from many cities today. In others, dogs' brief, chary lives, their vivid circadian rhythms, continue to form a parallel, ancient, shadow ecology to those of people. (So attests this chart so oddly moving in Alan Beck's *The Ecology of Stray Dogs*, a study of Baltimore carried out in 1970 and cited by Rolin.)[107] In a more recent book, *With Dogs at the Edge of Life*, Dayan continues as if haunted to write about dogs. The book's last section, "Pariah Dogs," turns to populations of strays (in Turkey, Mongolia, etc.) increasingly subject to control and extermination. Do we know what is missing when dogs are missing? These are "creatures that can still feel, hear, touch and remember all that has been and will be destroyed," writes Dayan.[108] Alerted to what dogs could do and be in NDiaye's world, I too, like Rolin, came to feel I could sense where dogs could (or even should) have been but were missing (*Il y manque des chiens*). Sometimes, thinking too literally, madly, like a NDiaye character sensing a truth obscurely, I wondered whether there are not two kinds of stories in the world as there are two kinds of cities, one that at its very start eliminates dogs, to better clear space for a self-assured, self-possessing, masterful I, and another that (like NDiaye's) does not make dogs impossible entirely, one where the self dwells more tensely, provisionally, in the spaces they concede.

Now, obviously, a dog in a story need not stand always or simply in a reliable relationship with some inconvenient truth the subject or narrative regime has suppressed. When Hearne wrote of people "incapable of beholding a dog," she was in fact referring to what she called "natural bitees," "people whose approaches to dogs (and perhaps to people as well) are contaminated by epistemology. They attempt to *infer* whether or not the dog will bite, jump up on them or whatever. Instead of 'reading' the dog, as handlers say (the German philosopher Martin Heidegger might call this listening to the dog's being), they cast about for some premise from which they can draw an inference that will give them certainty about the dog's behavior."[109] Assuming conceptual, even ethical, consistency from NDiaye's dogs, for a long time "cast[ing] about for some premise" where they could all find their common cause, I too, I now see, made a natural bitee. But then a dog may make it difficult to think certain things apart from it, it comes in the way, borrows the forms of other things—or lends them its own qualities. At long last I started to see that it was less dogs per se than this difficulty (sometimes) of beholding the dog that had been egging me on. "Egging," an old word, having everything to do with a nearing to the edge,[110] as in Dayan's dark title (*With Dogs at the Edge of Life*). The dog most difficult to behold may not be the most fierce or frightful dog, the cleverest Cynic or Nietzschean nor the most ethical dog. It is more likely to be a radically ambiguous, unwhole, even pitiful thing ("surviv[ing] in some wild patch," like Bobby, of a story or a life). In its presence the I feels its field (its I vs. not-I allotments, its self-persuasions regarding what it is and what it is not) unnerved, as if faced with its own "outside," as if unsure about the direction of the banishment. Do I face here what I have abandoned or what has abandoned me?

DOG OF THE OUTSIDE

Take the "yellow dog" of NDiaye's *Rosie Carpe* (2001). As Lagrand ponders over why he is so accepting of the filthy, parasitical brother of Rosie, it occurs to him that Lazare "might be the yellow dog in human shape, the lonely, sullen stray, which his mother had taken in in the past, washing and feeding it without ever beating or cursing it."[111] In his shame and disgust vis-à-vis Lazare it is likely "his dog he was ashamed of, his own dog he was disgusted with," for when his mother had abandoned him, the dog too had plausibly disappeared with her: "He was taken in by his grandparents and had then lived with them, but without the dog, and there had never been any question of a dog after that, neither the one that had disappeared as suddenly from Lagrand's existence as his own mother, nor of any other, for the couple were both suspicious of dogs—the old couple, whose life consisted of tiny, daily defense strategies against the evils of the unknown, judiciously condemned all dogs as detestable" (232–33/206–7). Here too, then, we find a dog serving as potential transitional object, a catalyst for insight into past or self, an entity part unloving part unloved, part abandoning part abandoned, seeming to carry over something of the ruptured or disfigured maternal relationship (if not, further back, of a lost father).[112] NDiaye is by her own admission fascinated by mothers abandoning their children, a pattern in turn linked through her oeuvre, as Andrew Asibong has compellingly shown, with that of female protagonists' recurring affective deficiency or "deadness."[113] But given the dogs adding up in

NDiaye's world, how tautologically they seem to appear (a dog is a dog is a . . .) and how totally they can be refused (Lagrand's grandparents' blanket condemnation of dogs recalling Nadia's in *My Heart Hemmed In*), given also what tense and shadowy things dogs turn out to be the closer one gets—there is a case for wondering whether the NDiaye dog is not always more generally and fuzzily—totemically?—connected with unhappy personhood (a dimension common to all novels). Certainly *Rosie Carpe* goes furthest in suggesting that animals may stand at precisely those points where the self is least certain of its properties and identifications—and perhaps in just the way that Deleuze suggested when, commenting on Leibniz's "animal monadology" ("an infinity of creatures" within me, of which "the animals that I meet outdoors are nothing but an enlargement"), and shortly before referring to Beckett (this time to Malone, as "consummate proof" of Leibniz's system), he wrote: "In fact, it is very difficult for every one of us to make a list of our own belongings. It is not easy to know what we own, and for what length of time" (*The Fold*, 109). Lagrand will slide into a fearful torpor after driving past a fly-infested cow carcass on the road, and seeing one of the flies attempt to sit on his own hand: "But I'm not that dead cow, he told himself, thinking slowly and with difficulty" (203/179). There are other comparable moments: Rosie, hearing the hungry oxen bellow in the ravine as they do throughout the novel, finds herself "no longer knowing if she were there, seated in front of the house, or farther down in the ravine beside the bulls and moaning with them" (160/140); in the mirror, she will later see an alarmed sheep where her own face should have been (301/272); at the hospital Lagrand fears that the nurse is about to "split his head open" so that he will see "his own blood spurt onto the tiles" ("And yet no knife struck . . .") (270–71/243). In *My Heart Hemmed In* a few years later a scattered trail of italicized thoughts would attest to similar fears, identified distinctly, in some places, with those of an animal in the throes of death or anticipating its own slaughter. Dominique Rabaté has commented on these bits of uncontrolled inner speech or "parasitic thought" scattered through *My Heart Hemmed In* and in the second story of *Trois femmes puissantes*, a technique of a piece with NDiaye's "second manner" (characterized by strict focalization and the use of the first person) and whose first use he dates to the bleak play *Rien d'humain* (2004). For Rabaté these are bits of erratic content that manage to slip past the strict surveillance by which characters tend to police their thoughts and speech. "Something insists on being uttered, despite the codes of exaggerated politeness, or in their folds."[114] If these are rare "moments of liberation," they are especially instances, writes Rabaté insightfully, of a character's surrender to the forceful irruption of something too long repressed.

But then hadn't bits of unmoored, stupefied thought infiltrated NDiaye's prose quite early on, hadn't the "fascinating and sickening" use of free indirect speech[115]—but also of exclamation marks and question marks—in *En famille* already presaged it? I wrote earlier of "narration's dog" and places of strangeness where narration could turn on itself or away from itself, but it is time to draw closer to the edge, and to the question of how or why in the vicinity of a dog there so often occurs, in NDiaye, a disturbed arithmetic—we could call it an *unwholeing*—of perspective not to say person. *Rosie Carpe* offers an extreme illustration of this, soon after the analogy is drawn between Lazare and the yellow dog: Lagrand, having received Lazare's murder confession and absorbed his guilt of the random killing of an old man, becomes so confused as to ask himself, even while thinking, *who* is doing the thinking: "He felt full of Lazare; he seemed to be Lazare himself coming home and finding death brought into this house by Lagrand's hand. This is just horrendous, he thought—but who, he carried on to himself, was thinking this? Was it Lagrand or Lazare? [. . .] Nothing about his body could belong to Lazare, who looked like a dog deprived of rations [*chien sans pitance*], with a figure at once thin and limp, long and ill-defined, whereas Lagrand, he knew, was a superb horse, dusky and shining, taut and muscular" (238/212). The (self-)consciousnesses of two characters appear to cross here, and, more subtly, in several other passages in free indirect style that unduly repeat Lagrand's name ("lui, Lagrand"—remember this very tic in the Brulard story), as if indexical uncertainty (him or another?) were imperiling thought's very adherence to thinker. But the name (repeated like a talisman) cannot, any more than the shining horse, constitute decisive enough resistance (not I, not I . . .) to the sordid pull of the "chien sans pitance," literally a dog left or kept hungry. NDiaye has said herself that Lagrand is a character "endowed with the ability to literally put himself in the other's place, to suffer for him,"[116] and the word "literally" used by a writer so careful with her words should surely not be taken metaphorically. Lagrand—significantly, NDiaye's first identified Black character, created fifteen years into her writing career—will struggle with an "unbearable compassion" (266/238) as he identifies successively in the pages that follow with the old man killed by Lazare and his friend Abel, with Lazare and with Abel, so that he must "literally"—that is, through explicit, inescapable, narrative veerings—reinhabit thinkingly the scene of the murder which Lazare and Abel had committed without thinking.

But Lagrand's function as all-gathering narrative consciousness (and moral conscience) in the novel, and the suggestion that he must think not merely for himself but also for others still do not fully account for the strangeness of the "who [. . .] was thinking this?" Recalling Beckett's "And whose voice asking this? Who asks, Whose voice asking this?," such a question seems to breach a limit and to betray more fundamentally the presence—supernumerary yet impregnable—of something like *narration* itself, known more often and less disquietingly as *the narrator*. Through the capacity always latent in internal monologue or free indirect discourse to fold back on itself, to disown its own illusion, Lagrand interrupts his own supposedly internal thought process to wonder whether thoughts are not being imputed to him, or implanted in him, which more logically belong to Lazare. But this being a novel (an unrigorous, self-comforting way to start this sentence, for would this not be even more terrifying in life? This being here the veritable point), what means of appeal, verification, or resistance might a character have left when seized with the suspicion that their thoughts are not their own, that there is another behind them—or, perhaps worse, no one at all?

Writing on *Rosie Carpe*, Elisabeth Arnould-Bloomfield has convincingly shown that while the novel through its enunciatory framework amplifies Rosie's trauma and passivity (her life seeming to be told from her point of view but in fact under the strict—and too eloquent, to the point of uncaring—mastery of a narrator), Lagrand's consciousness is able to substitute orphically (or psychoanalytically) for hers precisely through what the novel suggests is an "identical figural unconscious."[117] Noting the remarkable nonrealism of this traumatic substrate shared between the two characters (where motifs are repeated across points of view, word for word and noticeably), Arnould-Bloomfield argues that here the narrative meets its own radical exteriority—gesturing toward the forms of traumatic reality, but equally, in keeping with Blanchot's notion of disaster, to the trauma at the origin of the novel itself as expressive form (26–28). The question of "who is thinking" indeed connects poignantly to that of trauma—whether understood as "an event that has happened to me but to which I can never be present"[118] and which therefore I might not be able to think, or in the thinking of which I might not be me, or, more generally, as the exteriority with which speaking affects being, and which Foucault had once called, writing on Blanchot (and modern fiction more generally), *la pensée du dehors*.

"Literature," he wrote, is "language getting as far away from itself as possible," that "returns thought to the outside" and itself stands outside what it says, "for it undoes every figure of interiority."[119] Of or from the outside, literature thus understood presents a thinking on life that is not formed in our image, that "makes to draw one toward it," in Foucault's words, with an "indifference that greets [the person it attracts] as if he were not there" (28). We recognize here the terms in which Foucault had invoked Beckett's *The Unnamable*, which made a long-lasting impact both on his thinking and on Blanchot's: "'What does it matter who is speaking,' someone said, 'what does it matter who is speaking.'"[120] Speech of or from the outside takes the form of a "continuous streaming of language. A language spoken by no one: any subject it may have had is no more than a grammatical fold" (*The Thought from Outside*, 53–54).

There is a connection here between *the outside* and dogs so literal that it embarrasses. But then what if NDiaye's (much-speculated-upon) reluctance to write explicitly about race correlated directly with a long reticence to write about the right sort of dog?[121] For it seems that after the disagreeable encounter with the ugly, filthy, "yellow dog" outside the kitchen basement window in *Among Family* (which Fanny, remember, pounds to death, to then wonder: "Was it really a threat or had she been mistaken?") there are, by way of *homeless, unowned* dogs in NDiaye's writing, only the childhood "yellow dog" vaguely remembered by Lagrand in *Rosie Carpe* (significantly the softening of the treatment of the ugly yellow stray comes in the same text that carries the first reference to Blackness) and, most explicitly, the dog of the second half of *Ladivine* more than twenty years later. Most of the dogs of *Among Family*, the dog of *My Heart Hemmed In* and that of *La femme changée en bûche* (1989; *The Women Turned into a Log*), those of "Une journée de Brulard" (and even the first half of the dogs of *Ladivine*) are dogs attached to houses and/or masters. I like to imagine that it was only when NDiaye visited Ghana for a ten-day reconnaissance with filmmaker Claire Denis that she had occasion to "discover" stray dogs, to be affected by those singular, unaccountable forms of presence and watchfulness.[122] The stray dog is "very provoking" (as Humpty Dumpty would say) not just because it answers to no one but because one might imagine its very allegiance to the world of persons (ownership, authority, property, propriety) to be weak. In the stray it is as if the drama of what a dog is were kept vividly alive: diverging continually (because too hungry, or too friendly) from the wolf; living in continual hopes of food and fear of pain (and fear of fear); the "être aux aguets" par excellence, warily observing its host world at every moment for the first sign of betrayal or ambush. Stray dogs provoke also another kind of unease that is at the same time a relief—at the thought that, like stories or utterances, dogs are never rounded up or rounded off once and for all, there are always traces, shadows, specters, unassimilated "bits," fleshly remainders of a making of the world that is ongoing, unfinished. To watch a dog in the street, curled up in a fitful sleep, barking with *mythical* anger at a passing car, trotting and stopping nervously, attempting in its own interest mildness and fierceness alternately, is to realize obscurely that something about our reality is being continually negotiated *at* this place, that the dog is the nervous border of our world, itself its live and raw skin. Vis-à-vis the human, the street dog (the Third World dog) is both absolutely other and absolutely implicated. So much so that it seems to confound these two directions (which the fold and which the un-fold?) and expose our very intimacy to the outside. It is in this sense that it may emerge as too plain a figure to see for something as vague and vast as thought itself (*la pensée du dehors*), a reminder that meaning (as what makes world), before its *domestication*, before it is consigned to particular places (who thinks what, when, where, why), is unhoused, unowned, wandering, ghostly, not in our image; and that even after (or despite) its many spoken-for assignments, perhaps a part of it remains thus unapportioned, vague—there is at every moment more potential for thought than world.[123] Or to put it differently: the (humanly significant) world has never been sufficiently wrested away from the outside, and dogs haunt us as determined, distorted survivors (prisoners of war?) of the receding forest.[124]

FIND IT (THE LAST DOG)

It is high time (unless it is too late) to consider the last of NDiaye's dogs—last at the last count, and which initially so disturbed the count that I was faced with a crisis. Either "the dog" really was thoroughly unaccountable, and could mean anything from one iteration to the next (but there was something jarring in such a conjecture, for surely a writer so serious and careful could not treat a thing so flippantly), or there was much more work to be done, a longer journey to be undertaken—at the cost of questioning everything I thought I knew—in order to make sense of it. Whence this (dog-damned) chapter.

Ladivine (2013) is centered on yet another paradigmatic female protagonist—Malinka/Clarisse, daughter of Ladivine Sylla—in elaborate denial of her name and origins. In the first section of the novel, told from her tense point of view, Malinka renames herself Clarisse, marries Richard Rivière and moves to Langon, has a daughter whom she names Ladivine, and lives for many years a carefully constructed and depthless life *en famille*, as if frozen by her own lie: for she started while young to claim that her mother was dead—instead she secretly meets "the servant" (as if for form's sake, with restricted exchange and affect) in Bordeaux once a month. After her daughter Ladivine has grown up and left home, Clarisse is suddenly left by her husband (who has ultimately realized he never knew her) and her world falls apart. She takes up with a younger, unseemly man by whom she does not feel judged, whom she introduces to her mother and who one day brutally murders her.

There is a significant "dog" (which may be two dogs) in this first half of the novel. When the couple is still newly married, a mighty wolfhound belonging to Malinka/Clarisse's father-in-law saves her baby daughter Ladivine's life, and Clarisse, feeling a "strong sense of a bond not to be rashly broken, a secret union,"[125] notices that the dog has "the same eyes as Malinka's mother's"—that is, *her own mother's*, but here and in other places the narration is at its most contorted, bending backward, permitting Clarisse to continue to not coincide with her own body and history.[126] Are such primary distortions not in the end the reason why "the dog" (as identity-vane [as in a weather vane], indicator of degree zero identity-stability?) cannot ever in NDiaye's world be entirely identical to itself?[127] Years later, Richard's father is found dead in his shop, his face half devoured by the dog—whether killed by it or not is unclear. *Wait, the same dog?* No, the mother replies ("'the first one died ten years ago at least'"), "'but it was the same breed, and they looked so much alike you forgot it wasn't that other one. Not to mention that your father gave it the same name'" (102/67–68). The mother's words on the subject are ominous: "'Do you have nothing to feel guilty about? Are you absolutely certain your life is in order? [. . .] because your father ended up paying for something or someone, and he was the most virtuous man there ever was. So, yes, I dearly hope you'll take care to live a life no one will ever curse you for.'" The dog is put down, but the mother warns that it will return, "'that one or another, exactly the same, with the same name, and it will attack anyone who deserves it'" (103–5/68–69). While a strong homology connects this episode with the undifferentiated, overdetermined canine nebula/antiplot of *Among Family*, it appears that, twenty-two years later, this overdetermined "nemetic" function of dog is being revisited either parodically or in dead seriousness (this will forever remain for me an undecidable) in order to be called out as (always having been?) equivocal. "Dogs don't 'turn on their masters,'" Vicki Hearne—who knew dogs like no other—once wrote, "but the *light turns on itself* if you aren't respectful."[128] For Hearne a dog bite was always the site of a failure of language, not to say *the failing of* language, that is, when humans wield language or meanings carelessly or in ways they do not "mean."

The second section of the narrative is recounted from the point of view of Clarisse's daughter Ladivine, three years after her mother's death, on a family vacation–turned-nightmare in an unnamed city of the Global South, where, as NDiaye concedes in an interview, "people are dark and where it is very hot."[129] As events turn from uncanny and unnerving to hostile Ladivine feels more and more alienated from her family and more and more in dark affinity with the place—and with a big brown dog seeming to keep watch over her. She wonders, even while never feeling "the slightest fear or unease," whether it is "spying on her or protecting her," a "guardian" or a "calamity" (154, 158, 206/103–4, 136, 139). Could someone, in order to protect her or someone in her family, have taken to "temporarily inhabiting the flesh and the skin of a huge scrawny dog" (142/95)? The prospect is initially disagreeable. But as Ladivine II's innermost thoughts begin to accommodate the dog, it assumes an "all-knowing [*omniscient*]" gaze (238/162), seeming to be the harbinger or agent of something imminent, "perhaps waiting for some sign from her, no, not even that, a breath, a thought, and with that it would come take her away to some mysterious place with no name" (241/164). Followed by it, Ladivine would sometimes slow down, "because the anxiety she imagined invading its canine heart [were the dog to lose sight of her] saddened her own" (143/96). Later, when she is desperately wanting to leave the hotel as everything becomes gnarled and inhospitable, she is convinced that the dog knows it ever better than she: "Wouldn't it know, couldn't it decipher her sentiments better than she herself, and didn't it inhabit Ladivine Rivière's skin more intimately than she herself, who sometimes felt she'd become nothing more than Clarisse Rivière's bereaved daughter?" (273/186). We note again, like in so many passages in free indirect mode through NDiaye's novels, the way the most intimate names (here her own, her mother's) have of becoming tokens of their distance, thought thus expressing its emergence from a place *outside* the intimacy of self-identity, or already hurtling away from it. Indeed, here it seems that a leaving of her world is well under way, Ladivine's self is already migrating toward the dog. Looking into its eyes, she is convinced "she ha[s] the eyes and the gaze of that dog," is "tempted to let them swallow her up," indeed, she "yearn[s] to be it" (221, 224/149–50, 152). Fifty pages before the end of the novel, she responds to an irresistible call (which she takes to be her mother's) and enters the deep forest. At this point the word "dog" itself disappears altogether, as the self merges with it and "trots" out of the forest on "her long, slender paws [*pattes*]" (328/224; translation modified). Before narrative perspective leaves her, "Ladivine" (the novel's title, and also the name that Ladivine II unknowingly inherits from her grandmother) names fleetingly the dog as governing point of view: "Once the SUV had started up and gone on its way through the clearing, Ladivine set off running again. / Joyful and proud that she'd found them and could thus place them under her care, she let out little cries she alone could hear, immediately swept off by the rushing wind" (328/224). A passage infinitely beautiful and infinitely hideous. In it is for me both the obscene insolvency of NDiaye's novelistic world and the point of its deepest truth.[130] NDiaye would be pressed in the Devarrieux interview on the notion of dog avatars ("Where does the dog reincarnation idea come from? Did you invent it or is it a belief?"), to which she would reply immaculately: "It is no doubt a belief in the sense that I imagine that it might exist in certain parts of the world, but I do not know this."[131]

Back in Germany, where the dog has somehow followed the family back, Ladivine's daughter Annika is infuriated by its presence and convinced that her mother had "willingly chosen to shelter herself in the skin of a dog, which, though it did little to protect her from the cold, suited her [*lui convenait*] better than the skin of a woman. [. . .] She saw no sorrow in the dog's eyes, only a serene, stern resolve" (330/226). Ladivine Sylla, the grandmother, will in turn welcome "a big brown dog [with . . .] thin, trembling legs" into her home, convinced, as the last sentence of the novel reads, that it is "bringing Malinka's throbbing heart to them" (403/276). Before anyone had died or disappeared, Malinka/Clarisse too had seemed to *recognize* (on the day her husband had left her) "a big red-brown dog, emaciated and ungainly, in the sunlight's almost unbearable blaze[, . . .] sidling toward her, watching her with one eye, its ugly head half turned away." Shouting "'No, absolutely not, not yet!'" she had locked herself in her house, only to then change her mind and exit again (but the dog is gone), for "what did she care now, what could she care about anything now? What could possibly deserve her fear now?" and, a few lines later, as if making the connection with the mother in law's warning about dogs, "Had she not made of the servant's life a bitter bread?" (98/64).

The possibility that it is the same dog that is seen (and/or *been?*) at various moments by Ladivine I, Clarisse, Ladivine II, and Annika—however fantastically and/or even if only in name and kind ("dog")—makes it the only element connecting the (multiply alienated) women of the four generations, and *Ladivine* decidedly NDiaye's dog novel that does less to resolve than to turn into an ever-more-maddening enigma the question of the dog. Secretly and magically empowering matrilineal totem or ultimate flight from/defeat by the world and deathly loss of power and place? In the final analysis is the dog *a friend or an enemy* to NDiaye's women, to her novels, to *the* novel? To offer interpretations of NDiaye's oeuvre, as Asibong's brave book makes clear, is to stake one's own self, for it is to make repeated decisions regarding the pessimal conditions under which a human life is still a meaningful life. Or should I have taken things less "seriously" myself and observed rather the imperturbable wisdom of Jacques Rancière for whom "new fiction [. . .] must have an ending, but it is perhaps doomed to never be the right ending"?[132]

Returning time and time again, gathering in unexpected places, the dog—"But was a dog the same thing as the dog?" / "a fortiori were several dogs the same thing as the dog?"—seems to have waited, repeatedly, in NDiaye's novels, for a decision to be made about who or what it is. What will the ratiocinating protagonist make of it, what sense or latitude will the narrative decide to assign it? The decision must be made each time (in each story) anew, as if "the dog" were something each novel was assigned (like a coordinate, or a quantity) equally, but whose reality or extent of knowing or being each novel had to speculate on anew, almost as a matter of risk. In this regard the dog is arguably like anything and everything (dog, human, tall, heap, love, life, all vague entities unless invested from the inside and bound from the outside). Besides, what is a dog so abstract and intent that it displays no "need to eat or drink, urinate or defecate" (136)? This is the case with the dog—so Bobby-like—who follows Ladivine and ultimately subsumes her—a vanishing dog indeed, if we remember that the dog exists historically and on an everyday basis by virtue of its drawing of sustenance

Figure 3.3. *Street dog II*, Bangalore, photograph by the author.

from our (the human) world (and its excreting into it, if it must be said). What unearthly dog is this?

If we work our way further back still, *Ladivine*'s first mention of dogs had occurred immediately after Malinka/Clarisse (on meeting her future husband) had renamed herself and claimed her parents dead, the first flight from self—though, it should be asked whether there was ever really in this novel, whether there is ever really in NDiaye's world, a *first* flight, a first untruth or concealment. Have these not been tales, rather, about an "originary" *seriousness*, in the Sartrean sense, that leads the self to impute inflexible, essentialized, transcendent truth to what it believes things "are" and therefore to what it believes *it* "is"?[133] Cats dozing in the shadows near Richard's house remind Malinka/Clarisse of a childhood courtyard and "her mother's inexplicable fear of them [cats], almost as deep as her fear of dogs, on the subject of which she'd one day let slip that beneath their skin they contained human beings stricken with a terrible curse. How could anyone believe such a thing?" (43). Note how the dogs, who strictly had no business here, slip into the picture through weak, borrowed, feebly opportunistic means, presaging indeed how all dogs in this story and in this oeuvre will seem to appear—unaccountably, as if, like thought prey to unrigorous associations, the world could not supply enough of a reason for dogs.[134]

But there is another way to see this, which would be to say that this aspect of NDiaye's dogs—this calling for a decision, a wager almost philosophical—*does* have something to do with real dogs, which Hearne describes inimitably when she suggests that to work (as a trainer or handler) with the rationality of a dog is "to be willing, in Stanley Cavell's words, to let [one's] knowledge come to an end."[135] In a search for a missing person, for clues on a crime scene, or a way out of a dangerous situation, the dog's extraordinary sense of scent takes over where human capacities end. Yelling out "Find it!," the human in such situations must somehow be able "to mean what she says without knowing what she reaches toward with her words" (81). We do not know in such situations what we are asking the dog to find, while wanting very badly for the dog to find it. "It is possible to feel quite foolish and uncertain indeed, *pointing at nothing as though you knew it were something*" (81; my emphasis), the human impulse being to avoid such a sensation. "More often than not," Hearne writes, quoting dog trainer and author L. Wilson Davis, "it is the handler [by needing to signify his intellectual superiority over the dog] who defeats the dog, rather than the difficulty of the trail" (81). *Find it:* For as long as the tracking dog believes that you believe in the "it," even as "the 'it' has nothing that the logician in us would recognize as a referent" (81), the dog will try to find it, and will thereby expand what language does, not to say expand the conditions under which language can be effective and truthful: here, in designating with decisive consequence something that does not yet exist for language, for reference, but only (in belief, eventually in scent) for the dog. In these places "pointing" and "retrieving" concern the quasi-mystical, inhuman, outermost boundary of our world, where what is unnameable and unknowable may perhaps still be "pointed at," "retrieved," and may thus enter the world of the named and the known, through uncanny extensions (reference-scent; I-not I), even if this event, till it occurs, is logically impossible. Hearne writes powerfully of her "questions about language" as being "questions that located the boundaries of language in regions often understood to be remote from language" (16). A dog, because it believes intently, can take language—which in Hearne's hands means the world as structured by language, the world as meaningful, the world of meanings—more seriously than we ourselves do. "Our words carry further than we can see," says Hearne, so that we often ourselves fail to obey (to honor, to mean, to know what we mean). At such times it is only other creatures (whether human or nonhuman, but often with humans, she suggests, this is more difficult to achieve) "who can take us back to the origin of our own words so that we can find out what has happened. In tracking, it is only in the dog's answering illuminations that you know whether you have said anything at all, or what you have said, and if the dog doesn't answer, then that is that, for the moment at least, for language" (106).

Do we know what we say when we say "dog"? But the other side of his question is unquestionably, to my mind, this: do we know what we mean when we say "I"? Perhaps it is a question of *pointing at nothing as though you knew it were something*. If that is so one could say that the dog in NDiaye, which from most points of view *does not quite add up* (no, it doesn't, so there), from another point of view is the too-literalized figure for the wager we make when we say I, for the wager of what that word carries and implies without/before our knowing it, or what we pretend we still do not (or do not yet) know it means or does. So as "Ladivine set[s] off running again," it is as if, in the face of the compromised space of the narrative and the besieged and gnarled state of its language, the novel has—giddily or shamefully, desperately or extravagantly (all-powerfully)—played its final card and moved the seat of its consciousness to its furthest and riskiest, most beloved and most equivocal (*entre chien et loup*) outpost. It is an emergency measure (narrative government in exile) or a *hack*. Or it doesn't really matter which (*placebo?*), the point is to get the meaning across, somehow. ("On the internet, nobody knows you're a dog,"[136] but what about in a novel?)

CHAPTER 4

Barely a Hedgehog, Strictly Speaking

Marie Darrieussecq, with Ponge, Kafka, Carroll, Deleuze, Derrida

The mower stalled, twice; kneeling, I found
A hedgehog jammed up against the blades,
Killed. It had been in the long grass.
I had seen it before, and even fed it, once.
Now I had mauled its unobtrusive world
Unmendably.
—Philip Larkin

Of the Cheshire Cat there remains only the Smile.
Of the dream there remains only a memory trace.
Of the molecule there remains only the electromagnetic trace.
Of the real there remains only virtual reality.
Of the other there remains only a spectral form.
—Jean Baudrillard

It all started with a remarkable passage in Marie Darrieussecq's *Le mal de mer*, a short, abstract novel, only her third, published in 1999, about a runaway mother and daughter, vanishing, migraines, and the sea:

> Le sable s'est tassé au bout de ses baskets, des boules dures entre les orteils, râpeuses, qui travaillent à décoller l'ongle, patiemment, minutieusement. De petites griffes poilues se sont accrochées aux lacets, des graines, des débuts d'insectes, des bouts de hérissons.[1]

One day in class I attempted a spontaneous translation:

> The sand has collected at the ends of her sneakers, hard balls between the toes, rough, working to separate the nail, patiently, precisely. Small hairy claws have clutched on to the laces, seedlings, beginnings of insects, bits of hedgehogs.

Do you see? I asked. The strangeness. The beauty. My students were laughing. I reconsidered the passage. "On second thoughts I think it should be *bits of hedgehog* . . . in the singular. English counts differently. Takes the plural more seriously. For some reason with hedgehogs particularly . . ." I was struggling, at pains to understand what it was exactly here that was both absurd and unnerving. "C'est mieux en français? [*It works better in French?*]," one of them ventured helpfully. I thought back to this episode later, when I read Linda Coverdale's translation of the novel, titled *Undercurrents*. I definitely preferred her treatment of the passage to my own, in view of meaning but also idiom, syntactic consistency, and rhythm:

> Sand has clumped in the tips of her sneakers: hard, gritty balls between her toes, that work patiently, meticulously, to pry off the nails. Hairy little tendrils have latched on to the laces, along with seeds, insect parts, burrs.[2]

Incidentally, the British edition, published by Faber and Faber in the same year (less than three months later), also based on Coverdale's translation, presents minute differences, themselves fascinating, for revealing that this very brief account of a body losing its contours may itself have labile edges:

> Sand has impacted in the toes of her trainers: hard, gritty balls between her toes, that work patiently, meticulously, prising off the nails. Hairy little tendrils have latched on the laces, along with seeds, bits of insects, burs.[3]

Yet beyond this play of differences, the passage is in both its versions the unassuming scene of a disappearance. For where was the hedgehog? Hairy claws had given way to "tendrils," bits of hedgehog had been spirited away, leaving only "burrs" (or "burs," but this did not resolve matters now, did it?). A slippage had turned the animal into the vegetal, and the hedgehog, like a figure for the untranslatable itself, had apparently crawled away through the cracks. As a mere metaphor, evoked itself only in part, it was easily replaced by a plantly correlate, those seeds bearing hooks or teeth with which they can cling fast onto passing creatures. But was the "bouts de hérissons" a metaphor to begin with—whose work could just as well be done by burrs? Did "bouts" mean *ends* in the sense of *extremities* such as spines which, as the hedgehog rolled itself up, stood up on end, fuzzily, looking a lot like burrs? Or did the "bouts" convey, rather, *ends* in the sense of *odds and ends*, or *bits* as in *bits and pieces*? Why not even end*ings* of hedgehog(s), stray temporal or narrative extensions, in homology with the beginnings of insects that immediately precede (*des débuts d'insectes, des bouts de hérissons*)? But how should we understand the beginning of an insect, and what on earth is an ending or end or bit of a hedgehog? Are bits of hedgehog too tenuous, too tender to survive translation? These ones had last been seen dangerously close to the sea. Was it that the English text of *Le mal de mer* was indelibly marked by its first instantiation on American soil, where there are no hedgehogs in the wild? Or are bits of hedgehog, on the contrary, so resistant as to survive under any other form or name (burrs, say)? And if it turned out that this were not their original form or name at all, that they had no original form or name, what is the limit to the forms and names under which they may survive? Where are they, and where are they not? Would we recognize them? And what are we to make of them?

The truth is I was not particularly interested in hedgehogs, and would have wished for this last chapter to have an object less elusive. Yet as I followed certain threads through the work of Marie Darrieussecq, as they led in and out of Lewis Carroll, Chevillard, Deleuze, Kafka, Ponge, and others, bits of hedgehog clung to me.[4]

WORLD WITHOUT RUPTURE

Animals have long teemed in the oeuvre of Darrieussecq; with my bits of hedgehog I shall merely hug the edges. There was the sow-woman of *Truismes* (1996; *Pig Tales*), a seamy allegory of female objectification. If animal metamorphosis in that first novel signified abjection, it more interestingly invited, as Anat Pick has perceptively noted, a rethinking of "the trembling space between the human and the animal—*as* the space of the human."[5] The next novel, *Naissance des fantômes* (1998; *My Phantom Husband*), a sort of female *Nausea*, centers on the experience of a woman as her undistinguished, bourgeois, "normal" world comes apart at the seams. "My husband has disappeared": prose and flesh slowly rearrange themselves around the vexing leitmotif and gaping void. Animal motifs, including circling swifts, overfed and ankylosed sea lions, a beached shark, repulsive sea creatures, and zoo monkeys mad with fury proliferate as so many figures of entrapment, conditionedness, and/or distress, seeming to mirror the narrator's sense of her own fate. But more deeply, this book so aptly titled (literally, *Birth of Ghosts*) marks the birth of a singular logic of volatilization in Darrieussecq's writing, a move to a subtler phenomenology, wherein living entities start to appear as bits and parts and potentialities rather than as wholes. This lessening is borne emblematically by the circling swifts, noted precisely in the hours following the husband's vanishing: their "signature" turns quickly, as night begins to fall, into "two hollow wings around a cry."[6] A few pages later, wings alone, sloughing off the birds, become the eerie appendage of a dissolving self: "I said *bonsoir* into the silence and the word folded into itself like two black wings, I heard the echo of my footsteps" (21/12; trans. modified). A wing reappears shortly thereafter to mark the fluttering difference separating the unspeakable words ("my husband has disappeared") from the impossibility of their silencing: "In their place I heard, responding to the uncertain silence on the line, something like the beating of a faltering wing, something that was fleeing and clumsily found a way to take flight" (28/18–19). It transpires later that it was the mother-in-law's dawning suspicion (of the ghastly truth) as she heard the narrator's silence on the phone that had produced the sound of wings: "She had an intuition of his disappearance, that gasping intuition whose wings I had heard flapping like a feeble partridge [*une perdrix abattue*]" (51/41–42). Evidently, this is no longer a situation of stable—Deleuze and Guattari would have called it *molar*—metaphoricity; as in *Truismes*, where a woman's transformation into a sow was ("truistically") motivated by the fact that in her treatment at the hands of male clients and consumer society she was somehow *like* a sow. It is smaller, less interpretable, more incorporeal units here—words, sounds, intuitions—that are found slipping along fleshly inclines. A wing again flaps toward the end of the novel as evidence of a molecular visitation from the husband: "A rustling [*chuintement*] reached me, the flutter of a wing already scattered" (149/141). *Chuintement* is literally "hoot" or "hooting" (from *chuinter*), by analogy a whistling or whooshing (or hissing) as of a liquid or gas through a narrow passage, so that the logic is complete: the dissolving tenor (the husband) not so much carried by as dragging after it (toward the same vanishing) an equally tenuous vehicle, an unrealized owl, just about inferred from its cry and its dispersed wing. Something about the evanescence of these moments (rarely exceeding the sentence) allows such figures not to develop further (the wing stopping short, somehow, of implying a bird), raising the question—as would soon thereafter for me the "bouts de hérissons"—as to whether these are still figures at all.

Indeed, *Naissance des fantômes* could be said to formalize several sorts of decisions by Darrieussecq that would be determining for her oeuvre as a whole. One could say that it is not simply anecdotally that male characters—and in fact all characters—are more likeable in the works that follow. As Darrieussecq's narrators develop a greater familiarity with ghosts, a confidence that disarms the paternalistic rationality her early fiction associates with males and adults ("My husband chased the shadows away simply by his conviction that he was an adult" [44/34]), animal motifs come to be enlisted no longer as allegorical fallout of an order imposed from the outside but rather in an increasingly reliteralized capacity, as possibilities and presences filling the cracks of the real. By the same logic of molting (like the wings that discard the bird, the ghost too leaves the vanished husband as if he were no longer needed, too figurative or realist an alibi), ghostliness becomes a more generalized character of beings and things, their way of being both more and less than themselves. And most significantly—this is where the animal and the ghost are no doubt most intimately intertwined—wholes increasingly give way to parts, beings to potentials of being, so that the space between presence and absence is revealed to be alive with brimmings and burgeonings. Certainly, this particular phenomenology starts to find its coordinates in *Naissance des fantômes*, and perhaps nowhere more compellingly than in the sea—that backdrop that would become so remarkably recurrent through Darrieussecq's oeuvre (as if every story were being drawn from churning watery depths).[7] After the unseemly sight of the obese sea lions and a brief vision of her husband's corpse in the gurgling viscera of a shark amid water filled with hideous creatures, the narrator seems to break through to a different plane of marino-ontological consistency: "Every arching wave, as it broke, expelled as if between plates of whale baleen a breath of mingled spray and mist. Bit by bit the sea lions disappeared. I glimpsed a back swallowed up by the waves, half a chest that twisted away before plunging beneath the rest of the body into the black furnace of the surf. The criss-crossing of moving sea foam that clung to the shoulders of the swell was further undone at every new cycle, each intersection of the network growing finer and more diffuse amid other little pulverized points" (68/59). In this inextricable indeterminacy of parts—as the waves roll through an unseen whale's baleen and on shoulders carried over from sea lions—are momentarily indistinguishable the no longer and the not yet, forms extinguished from forms yet unfinished. The foaming sea, a veritable *chora*, reveals "the bodies of nothing at all struggling to be born into our three dimensions, trying to escape from the pulverization of space but succeeding only in burning out in intuitive glimmers, rolled and crushed beneath the disaster of the waves" (71/62).

Initially dismayed by the lack of solidity of a world from which something as reliable (or so she had thought) as a husband could simply vanish, the narrator of *Naissance des fantômes* is gradually initiated to a realm in which, between interludes of apparent identity, forms swirl indecisively, continually coalescing and coming apart. Beneath the identities fixed by gaze, name, or concept, the world pulsates with gestating energies: "The table is transformed into a haze of table, only to rematerialize immediately as soon as you bring your gaze to bear on it, as soon as you touch it with a finger. [. . .] Even when named, touched, or crossed through [*traversés*], ghosts lose none of their power or indulgence" (95–96/87). Unsurprisingly, the most striking description of this realm of potentialities returns us to the sea, where a roving "you [*vous*]" travels the slippery threads of a web of being: "The universe, without you, is acquainted with certain embryonic states, mists of nonexistent things to which your gaze would give form; you are the fisherman beside the sea, or maybe the sea is you, or maybe you are the potentiality of fish in the sea, but until the fisherman has snagged it the fish does not exist" (95/86). Darrieussecq's imagery evinces here an uncanny affinity with that of Henri Michaux, whose prose poem "Encore des changements" had featured this dizzying sequence:

> It's a lot of trouble to pass from a truncated pyramid to a whale; you must know immediately how to dive, to breathe, and then the water is cold, and then you find yourself face to face with the harpooners, but I, as soon as I saw men, fled. But it so happened that I was suddenly changed into a harpooner, then I had just as long a distance to go over again. At last I succeeded in overtaking the whale, I quickly launched

> a well-sharpened and solid harpoon (after having first made fast and checked the rope); the harpoon darted, penetrated far into the flesh, making an enormous wound. I realized then that I was the whale, I had changed into it again, there was a new opportunity to suffer, and I am not one to get used to suffering.[8]

Darrieussecq's subsequent writings would consistently confirm her intuitive affiliation with a poetics of ontological continuity and becoming that one associates precisely with Michaux and Deleuze. *Bref séjour chez les vivants* (2001; *A Brief Stay with the Living*) imagines a microscopically enhanced "constant seamless view of the world [*monde sans rupture*]," where one might behold uninterruptedly the minute components of organic life—"all the drops of water the particles the troughs in your skin and all the creepy-crawlies, germs, flies, spiders, their honeycombed eyes"—and where it might be possible to "see the world as flies, spiders, cows and platypuses do."[9] *Rapport de police* (2010; *Police Report*), an impressive meditation on the power and the vulnerability—and the very particular sort of truth—of fictional imagination, makes of this *world without rupture* a veritable theory of writing. In this lucid work, Darrieussecq describes "a becoming-writer, which has as much to do with water, the curves of the earth, cries, murder, the multitude of languages and books, the way that flies or whales see, and the knowledge that forests have of us—as with family or grammar trees."[10] To write, she ventures, is nothing less than a metamorphosis, an "alchemy of transformation" (247), an "unhitching [*décrochement*] from oneself" (376), "protean and using all persons" (381; i.e., first, second, third, singular, plural), an inhabitation, both desirous and anxiogenic, of an open, rippling field traversed by a multiplicity of modes of being and seeing. By this time she has read Woolf and Deleuze, or as she puts it more interestingly in a passage that evokes the deep affinities and unknown ancestries that can connect similar writerly imaginations across time and space:

> How many times have people cited Virginia Woolf re: *Le Mal de Mer,* when I had not yet read her? And when I discovered Deleuze (every new reader is a discoverer)—becoming-animal, deterritorialization, the body without organs, folds and rhizomes—I realized not so much that I was a Deleuzian writer, but that Deleuze had read me before I even knew how

> to write, that Deleuze had written me before my birth, for neither Derrida nor Foucault nor Barthes had theorized so well and so early what my imaginary would be! (Spinoza, says my father-in-law. Spinoza was the first to understand your work.) (*Rapport de police*, 180–81)

Stéphanie Posthumus is perhaps even closer to understanding Darrieussecq's work when she suggests, in *French 'Écocritique'*, that these novels be read alongside the "ecosophy" of Félix Guattari, exploring as they do new kinds of subjectivity—ecological, relational, (new) materialist—that the philosopher's later texts such as *Trois Écologies* (1989) and *Chaosmos* (1992) had precisely called for.[11] Certainly, Darrieussecq's characters, of "leaky, porous boundaries" (50), wonder repeatedly what it is like "to breathe with other lungs. To find paths under the bark, through the grass, through other becomings."[12] To hear the rustlings of space, muses the writer of *Le pays* (2005), "she would have needed ears formed differently from her own, the ears of cats, bears or aliens to experience them fully. Her own world had only three dimensions, and she knew only fragments of them" (37). *A Brief Stay with the Living*, Darrieussecq's fifth book, with its sci-fi conceit of narrator as telepathic agent trained to inhabit others' thoughts, attempts in this sense a thematizing of a certain conception of narrative consciousness, as something that would reel shuttle-like between different locations, following unseen slippery bridges and tunnels (Darrieussecq likes to say "passerelles") of being. In a striking instance, the prose, turning frenetic and discontinuous, in brief spurts of interest and distraction, espouses the fitful point of view of a dog. There is a gravity in such switches (where it is impossible to forget Michaux's harpooner and whale, linked by the fateful cable as by an umbilical cord), in the limitlessness of identifications, as if eyes and pores, once opened, could no longer be shut, nor any fate assumed to be beyond the realm of the knowable. In a particularly awful passage at the end of the novel, narrative consciousness has to follow the narrator's sister Jeanne into the depths of the sea where she slowly drowns in her locked car, her thoughts scattering, knowing that she will be last seen (and eaten) by fish. My favorite is a passage near the end of *Le mal de mer* recording the last moments of a hungry basking shark as its directional systems fail and it veers off course. It is the only passage in the novel to focus on this creature, and on a consciousness not human. Because as a species the basking shark (the second-largest living fish) is "almost blind, like most sharks, and endowed with sensory equipment that is in fact quite sophisticated" (128/105), the passage written from its point of view is itself a veering of narration, toward an estranging of habitual coordinates of perception. I wish I could cite the entirety of it here:

> L'océan est devenu la mer, avec des remous, un courant qui se précise en houle vers la côte. Les signaux d'alerte se font de plus en plus violents, la chair bat sous l'alarme, l'eau gicle plus vite sous les larges ouïes. Le corps monte et descend, la terre fait son bruit, casse l'eau, gronde, ronfle, énorme et arrêtée comme un prédateur. Maintenant, sa caudale s'arquerait-elle au maximum, le large est devenu inaccessible. L'alarme se tait, tout est silencieux dans le grand mouvement des vagues. La fatigue a remplacé la faim. Le vide ouvert sous ses fanons usés semble s'être clos peu à peu, la mer ne le traverse plus, elle rencontre un obstacle au fond du ventre, un calme. [. . .] Sa ligne de contact frémit légèrement, perçoit, du côté d'une dépression de sable, la présence ténue des humains, la chaleur de ces phoques nus. [. . .] Ses latérales prennent un dernier appui, la plage est évitée. La falaise est très proche maintenant, elle renvoie de front les émissions radars: une masse argileuse, émergée, travaillée d'eau, de grottes, d'écroulements, de failles, de masses magnétiques et de métal tombé du ciel. [. . .] Les sonars échouent désormais à reconnaître le haut du bas, le Nord du Sud. Un rocher lui incise profondément le cuir. Ses flancs heurtent le sable, les vagues se retirent; le poids des muscles, lentement, l'étouffe, les ouïes s'affaissent sous leur propre ampleur. La terre est rude, impérieuse, enfoncée sous le ventre; le sol vire, sous un soleil fixe. (114–16)

> The ocean has become the sea, with eddies, a current that forms a swell near the coast. Warning signs become more and more violent, flesh thrashes in alarm, water spurts more quickly beneath the broad gills. The body rises and falls, the land makes its noise, breaks the water, growls, roars, lying in wait like a huge predator. Now, even if its caudal fin were curved as much as possible, open water has become inaccessible. The alarm falls silent, all is quiet in the massive movement of the waves. Fatigue has replaced hunger.

> The hollow beneath its worn baleen seems gradually to have closed; the sea no longer flows through it, meeting an obstacle now, a stillness, deep in the belly. [. . .] The lateral lines quiver slightly, sensing, off toward a sandy depression, the faint presence of humans, the heat of those naked seals. [. . .] Taking one last reading with its laterals, the beach is avoided. The cliff is quite close now, reflecting its sound waves straight back: a clayey mass, primordial, weathered by water, scarred by grottoes, runoff, faults, magnetic conglomerations, and metal fallen from the sky. [. . .] From now on its sonar can no longer distinguish between up and down, north and south. A boulder slices deeply into its skin. Its flanks strike the sand amid retreating waves; it suffocates slowly beneath the weight of its muscles while its gills collapse from their own volume. The land is harsh, imperious, sunken beneath its belly; the ground slues about under a motionless sun. (102–4; translation slightly modified)

Certainly it is an unusual passage, where a shark's fatal disorientation is rendered on the level of the narration through a straining of referential bearings. The effects are more radical in French, as the body flailing in the water seems initially to borrow its life (its very means of appearing here awhile as a living sensing body) from an overall homology (verging on a verbal camouflage) with the (equally dense) accounts of the little girl's swimming lesson and the mother's surfing lesson that immediately precede (where, as is the case throughout the novel, neither is named but goes simply, indistinguishably, by "elle"). Here too there are swirling waves, tense flesh, and water and body parts carried by secretive definite articles and equivocal possessives (*sa*, *ses*—agreeing in French with the object, and therefore betraying nothing of the subject—is it still an "elle"?). The "ouïes"—gills, but also, when in the singular, "hearing"—may pass in a distracted reading as somehow metaphorical; "sa caudale" (its/her caudal or tail fin) suggests a fish more unambiguously, but there too, since the word is not common, might simultaneously conceal it—same with "ligne de contact" and "latérales" (lateral lines) designating a sense organ unique to sharks. Eventually "ses fanons usés" (its/her worn baleen) and the cumulative effect of the string of terms bring the marine body into greater focus, and the intriguing "signaux d'alerte" (warning signs), "alarme" (alarm), and "émissions radar" (sound waves) cohere, with some delay, as aspects of the great fish's dysfunctioning navigational systems. In this lapse narration has effectively loosened itself from human perspective to accompany the large, enfeebled creature on its last (and otherwise unwitnessed) journey. It is as if language were momentarily occupied, word by word, by that heaving body, as if narrative consciousness (narrative *life*) had taken up abode for those two pages in a deep-sea body and could not help but undergo and express its loss of bearings. Narration in Darrieussecq is always gravitating toward such otherings, such breaches and holes (rabbit holes, one might say) where it may slough off its human skin and register the vividness of living and dying through other kinds of seeing and sensing. But such becomings seem to suggest equally in her hands that stories have never been only human, that narration is rather a sweeping (as of a powerful all-seeing beam, or a forceful current) that has always picked up other bodies and predicaments along the way—like unsought sharks caught in fishing nets, or bits of hedgehog latched onto shoelaces.

SOMETHING RATHER THAN NOTHING

Naissance des fantômes carries as epigraph a short passage from *Alice's Adventures in Wonderland:*

> She was looking about for some way of escape, and wondering whether she could get away without being seen, when she noticed a curious appearance in the air: it puzzled her very much at first, but after watching it a minute or two she made it out to be a grin, and she said to herself, "It's the Cheshire-Cat: now I shall have somebody to talk to."

This moment in Lewis Carroll's story—when the appearance of the Cheshire Cat rescues Alice from the boredom of the Queen's game of croquet (featuring as it does live flamingoes and . . . hedgehogs!)—is explicitly referenced halfway through Darrieussecq's novel to describe the narrator herself as, from the depths of anguish, she musters a wan, derealized smile: "I forced myself to give a smile that I hoped was loving, attentive, and as convincing as possible, but that must (against my will) have seemed a physical manifestation as strange as the coquetries of the Cheshire cat when Alice sees in the branches only his teeth and the beginnings of whiskers, with nothing else around them" (78–79/69).

A few pages later, it appears that one of the effects of her husband's disappearance is that the narrator's own presence in the world is increasingly insubstantial: "A solid atmosphere lay heavy on my cheeks, arms, legs; a slowly petrifying layer of ash, growing thicker all the time, made a cast around me, enclosed me, stole my fingerprints in order—once I, in turn, had been dissolved by gastric juices—to preserve me in a museum of absences like the hollow bodies of Pompeii" (87/78). The House of the Dead of *Le pays*, where the Yuoangui may visit (and with their memories further fill out) hollow, hologrammatic simulacra of deceased family members takes this becoming-fossil even further. Bodily evaporation likewise characterizes the mother character in *Le mal de mer*, whose vanishing vies with her body as if sharing the straps of its dress.

But such becomings-ghost do not quite account for the reassuring reference to Carroll's Cheshire Cat. The latter's grin offers in fact a more precise, somehow more technical key to what becomes possible in *Naissance des fantômes*, and continues thereafter to animate Darrieussecq's fiction. Indeed, the "beginnings of whiskers [*début de moustache*]" of the Cheshire cat is of a piece with several other burgeonings in *Naissance des fantômes*, from the "tiny incipience of my husband [*un tout petit début de mon mari*]" (27/17) that the narrator hopes to find by answering the phone, to the "possibility [. . .] of my disconcerting husband" (78/69) she anticipates in the silences of a conversation with a friend, to a hallucinatory vision of "an incipient skin [*un début de peau*]" (107/99) and the imagined discovery inside a teddy bear of "little budding teeth and a tongue ready to speak" (97/89). At its most literal such a logic of incipience—or, seen in the other direction, of *lessening* (or lessness, as Beckett might have said)[13]—the very one that would lead (the following year) to the "bouts de hérisson" of *Le mal de mer*, invites us to imagine behind or beside every body that the text carries whole, other bodies that are incomplete, unfinished—unviable "bits" of life, by which, precisely, life is suggested not to be in a relationship of complete unfoldedness and efficient coextensiveness to itself. It is as if a first vanishing in *Naissance des fantômes* had rendered henceforth perceptible, scattering the conventional divide between manifest presence and manifest absence, a continuum of bodily appearance/disappearance, a sliding, fluctuating metrics of creaturely being. Persons (the husband of *Naissance des fantômes*, the brother Paul in *Le pays*, and the son in *Tom est mort* [*Tom Is Dead*]) disappear along the same slippery conduit along which others are born (the babies of *Le pays* and *Le bébé*), and in both directions, provisional, inchoate states of being find their emblems in distilled forms and embryonic animals. The newborn at the end of *Le pays* would develop not unlike the way the Cheshire Cat rematerializes around its toothy grin: "Each [baby] has a face, that is what's so extraordinary; a face clenched like a fist and ready to open, to smile, if given time. / Wet the origami in water and the paper unfolds, insect, animal, or flower" (181; my translation).[14] The baby of *Le bébé* (*The Baby*) is a continuous unfolding, as is even more intensely the disquieting animal of a short story titled "Zoo," initially found "clasped to the curtain, folded [*replié*] beneath its wings," "hanging head down in a fold of the fabric [*dans un pli du tissu*], paws gathered together, eyes closed, still," its face "folded [*plissé*] like that of a newborn" (149). The creature eventually pulls itself away from the curtain (as if from the inner lining of the text itself), gains enough shape and consistency to move around the apartment, to eat at the kitchen sink, and eventually, to earn its own litter box and food.[15] Its sudden appearance had interrupted the completion of a major writing project—so that it is the space of the story (and the notion of what constitutes a story) that is also led to "unfold": the intruder is welcomed within a writing substantively redefined, the parasite turns guest, the unclenched creature an unlikely mascot for the unaccountable life-bearing properties of a home and a text. The last lines of the story read: "I called her Clémence. It was a girl, evidently, and she was getting stronger with each day" (153).

Through all of this, one is struck by the close affinity Darrieussecq's folding-unfolding, enveloping-developing ontology shares with Deleuze's Leibnizian imaginary in *The Fold*, after whose publication, incidentally, as Deleuze remarks in *L'abécédaire*, he had received the most meaningful letters ("Your story of the fold—it's us, its us"; "We are the fold") from two categories of persons: paper folders (practitioners of origami) and surfers, whose knowledge too proves richly relevant to Darrieussecq—portraitist of the sea and author of a short text, *Précisions sur les vagues* (2008; *Specifications on Waves*), that described different kinds of waves as so many distinct types of folds.[16] The Baroque imaginary, which *The Fold* revisits as a brief (and splendid) interlude during which "Some Thing [wa]s kept rather than nothing (92/68), was premised on a law of continuity: one could not say "*where the sensible ends and the intelligible begins*" (88/66). The problem of soul versus matter, human versus animal, world versus individual, inside versus outside was resolved by an intricate understanding of things being distinguished not by essence but rather, and only, by degree, manner, dimension, that is, by extent/intensity of folding. The world, for Leibniz and the Baroques, was contained and mirrored in the monad or individual subject, its folded forms of being anticipated and actualized in ideas: "Ideas are so folded [*pliées*] in the soul that we can't always unfold or develop them, just as things themselves are inextricably wrapped up [*pliées*] in nature" (66/49). The soul through its inner "pleats [*déplis*; translator Tom Conley would elsewhere write "unfolds"]" thus represents to itself the forms of the world (32/23). Foldedness, describing how the subject perceives and mirrors the world, is also understood by the Baroque imagination as an objective property of organic formation:

> The organism is defined by its ability to fold its own parts and to unfold them, not to infinity, but to a degree of development assigned to each species. Thus an organism is enveloped by organisms, one with another (interlocking of germinal matter), like Russian dolls. The first fly contains the seeds of all flies to come, each being called in its turn to unfold its own parts at the right time. And when an organism dies, it does not really vanish, but folds in upon itself, abruptly involuting into the again newly dormant seed by skipping all intermediate stages. The simplest way of stating the point is by saying that to unfold is to increase, to grow; whereas to fold is to diminish, to reduce, "to withdraw into the recesses of a world." (13/8–9; the last words quote a 1687 letter from Leibniz to Arnauld)

Some of these notions (the first fly containing within it all the flies to come, for instance)[17] had already informed Deleuze's concept of repetition in *Difference and Repetition*, written two decades earlier (1968), and others would continue to crucially underpin *A Thousand Plateaus*, where an extraordinary page described organic life as a vast "plane of plication" (255); but it is interesting to consider what essential impetus the notion of becoming-animal would owe to the encounter with Leibniz. *The Fold* recalls that what distinguished the organic from the inorganic in Baroque thought was that while the inorganic repeats itself from outside to inside as it were, each repetition distinguished from the last only in dimension, the property of the organic, which repeats itself from inside to outside, is to contain within it—*necessarily*—*other* kinds of living organisms: thus Leibniz wrote in *Monadology*: "The limbs of a living body are full of other living beings, plants, animals [*les membres d'un corps vivant sont pleins d'autres vivants, plantes, animaux*]" (quoted in *Le pli*, 13–14; left out in the English translation, 9). The furthest consequence of this is one that positions Leibniz the Baroque philosopher as exactly antipodean to Descartes, for the human as organism too is thus revealed to contain within itself multiple other species:

> With the union of the soul and the body, the other who now springs forth amid my belongings [*mes appartenances*]—in order to throw them topsy-turvy—is the animal, and first of all the little animals inseparable from the fluid parts of my body, insofar as they become as foreign to me as they had formerly been. "[. . .] our body is a type of world full of an infinity of creatures that are also worthy of life" [quote from a letter from Leibniz to Lady Masham in 1704]. The animals that I meet outdoors are nothing but an enlargement of the latter. [. . .] what my sphere of belongings essentially reveals to me are inverted, temporary or provisional belongings (even as a body always belongs to me). In fact it is very difficult for every one of us to make a list of our own belongings. (146/109; translation modified).

This passage (the last sentence of which I quoted in the last chapter), possibly the most visionary of *Le pli*, offers to my mind a theory of the animal even more richly poetic than the *becoming-animal* of *A Thousand Plateaus*, in whose blocks and intensities and *zones de voisinage* the animal would become in fact more estranged, less real, than the Leibnizian animal. With "the animal in me *as a concrete being*" (146/109; my emphasis), Baroque philosophy is deconstructive *avant la lettre*, substituting Having for Being (147/109) even as it ruins the idea of something "proper to" the human: "To have or to possess is to fold, in other words, to express what one contains 'to a certain power/with a certain potentiality [*dans une certaine puissance*].' If the Baroque has often been associated with capitalism, it is because the Baroque is linked to a crisis of property, a crisis that appears at once with the growth of new machines in the social field and the discovery of new living beings in the organism" (148/110; translation modified).

Darrieussecq proves most rigorously Leibnizian, one could say, when Jeanne in *A Brief Stay with the Living* discovers a new animal, the platypus: "Then, a box opened, with the typical 'pop' of bubble-wrap when pinched between two fingers: two neurones linked up, a synapse along which the platypus, *l'ornithorynque*, slid, duly labelled bilingually, recognized, opening out on to no other reality than what was there, vibrantly there, before her eyes. A new branch on the tree of animals in Jeanne's forest of representations. She clearly felt a bump forming on her brain, then sinking inside, assimilated at once. Thus do boxes in brains open" (151/108). The same could be said of the red dragon lizard of Australia in *Tom est mort* ("like a dragon from the Middle Ages, as if our myths had sensed the existence on the planet of such creatures"),[18] seen for the first time in the world while at the same time remembered and recognized in an inner, even innate, theater of representations. But going further, one could see Darrieussecq's embryonic, ill-formed, partially glimpsed creatures as exemplarily Baroque outgrowths and ingrowths, remembered and forgotten like phantom limbs.[19] A claw, a wing, teeth, a bit of an animal signifies, at the very least, a refusal of nothingness, at most, a real potentiality, the irreducible, prosthetic impropriety of a self whose parts add up to *more* than the whole. A dream in *Brief Stay with the Living*, in relating "inverted, temporary or provisional belongings" (*The Fold*, 146/109), offers a possible encrypted (or encysted? certainly baleened and barnacled) key to the workings of the waking diegesis: "Her thigh [. . .], when examined, turns out to be red and inflamed, covered with nodules, spots or jellyfish blisters, a whale's forehead pushing through just there and about to burst open, whalebones, flesh gnawed by parasites. [. . .]—if, in dreams, we're all the characters, then she's [. . .] everything all at the same time, herself, this body, and the atolls and arms and the whale's forehead, the animal forming a cyst in her leg" (51/32; translation modified). In *Le mal de mer* a subtle slippage has the little girl grow eight legs and merge indistinguishably with the insects burrowing under the sand: "Spiders, coleoptera, stag beetles, and earwigs are everywhere; the sand is so fluid you need only dig between two roots, let the warm grains shower down on you, and mingle your six or eight legs with the six or eight legs of your nest mates, in order to doze off lazily, conscious only—sweetly, erratically—that all the wing sheaths have begun to stir, without your knowing anymore whether it's you or one of your neighbors whirring like that, fast asleep" (24/16). Might one imagine that, in different conditions, the hedgehog of *Le mal de mer* would not have melted back into language but materialized in the sand? What is lost, what is gained, in these *mis*carried bodies?

DETOUR 1: WRITING WITH HEDGEHOG

Faced with the mystery of the missing hedgehog, I was left looking (following the usual method and rigor) to other hedgehogs for clues. Three years after Darrieussecq's bitsy specimen, Éric Chevillard's *Du hérisson* (2002) famously made of a hedgehog's intrusion the generative principle in a monumental exercise of constrained writing. The "naïve and globulous" intruder appears out of the blue on the desk of the narrator, also a writer, at the very moment at which he is preparing to embark on his magnum opus, an autobiographical work woven from childhood memories, sexual confessions, and morsels of ars poetica, to which, from the sound of it, we might well ascribe the words Darrieussecq's narrator used to describe her own just-completed project: "this enormous work [. . .] where I was settling my accounts with everyone, the living, the dead, sex, writing."[20] In both cases there is a writing project intended to account exhaustively for everything and in both an incongruous creature appears, as if it were what that projected economy had precisely left out. Here too, as with Darrieussecq's "Clémence," the inconvenient creature appears to embody the tight inextricability of the word and thing. Cited in every paragraph of the novel along with its dyadic epithet, the "hérisson naïf et globuleux" as fleshly obstacle and idée fixe constrains the movements of the writing hand as much as it waylays the content of the prose: "I am not writing what I had been planning to write. However shapeless it may be, this naïve and globulous hedgehog is insinuating itself into every one of my thoughts. People will end up believing I am taking interest in it. A terrible misunderstanding."[21] The misunderstanding will last as conceit the length of the novel, occupied and preoccupied as the text is till the end by the intruder, albeit with fluctuating intensity and in variable registers—realist, epic, trivial, naturalist, ecological, speculative, (il)logical, nebulous . . . In fact, this variance itself becomes the game, as the hedgehog repeatedly moves in and out of focus: from minimal satisfactions of the constraint (one *hérisson* per paragraph, at whatever cost) to verbose monographic elaborations on the species' popular history, behavior, or anatomy. And while the content, as always with Chevillard, is playfully generated and internally self-annulling, the play nonetheless produces a sort of hedgehog, a self-appointed now-inalienable (albeit apocryphal) element of the still life commemorating the millennial scene of writing—"on my table, in the midst of my writing in progress and my desk furnishings" (31–32), "huddled in that spot where in the olden days the writer would delicately place a scoured white skull" (114)—and which will no longer go away. So that there is something in the difficulty of writing away this remainder that recalls the limit-objects of Francis Ponge: Chevillard's attempt to exhaust "le hérisson naïf et globuleux" as thing and as word could just as well have been titled *Notes prises pour un hérisson* (*Notes Taken for a Hedgehog*) or *Le hérisson placé en abîme* (*The Hedgehog Placed in Abyss / en Abyme*).[22] In *The Table*, Ponge wrote: "The table, I just have the table to write to be absolutely done with it. The table [. . .] which enabled me to write my work, remains (very difficult to write) that which remains to write to be done with it [*pour en finir*]."[23] The difficulty (of being done with it) is demonstrated on one occasion when the writing hand knocks the creature off the edge of the table. The narrator picks it up and places it back on the table, only to then wonder why he did so. Would it not have been cleverer to observe the route it took to escape—likely the same as the one that it had taken *into* the room—and to block that passage? Or at least to be able to conclude firmly, if it didn't find a way out, that it had not entered the room through its own agency? The question of where the hedgehog could have come from and what porousness of boundaries such an infiltration might imply is a source of disquiet through the novel. But the path of the animal *into* the workspace and the text proves impossible to distinguish from the traces of writing itself. Examining a leg of the table for traces of the hedgehog's passage, so as to determine how it might have climbed up it if it did, the narrator does find fine scratches—but which he cannot be sure he did not make himself (with his foot): "In sum, it is impossible to tell which of us, the naïve and globulous hedgehog or I, left those marks while climbing the table" (95).

I expect that if Chevillard were to be asked about the hedgehog he would characterize it as he has certain other nebulous entities in his works (Palafox, Crab, the orangutan), as one of a class of "new personal pronouns that parasite language and profit from its extraordinary resources, from its terrible efficacy, to develop their own laws."[24] But as with the orangutan, here too, one should say, the particularity of the animal, even if initially incidental, or quaint, just a game, comes to accrue meaningfulness through the writing, so that retrospectively the novel is in content and form simply indissociable from the hedgehog (it is a veritable hedgehog machine), and no other animal could have done the job. So why a hedgehog? Because of how neatly and strikingly this species presents that primary enigma—the relation of inside to outside, of content to form, of (apparent) inanimateness to expression (and one could add: of having to being, of matter to time, of nothing to something . . .)—as ceaselessly dramatized and resolved by its own body, in the way it rolls up. "My naïve and globulous hedgehog rolls up in a ball. It retracts as much as it can" (109), writes the writer, and, further on: "I anticipate the moment when, rolling up ever more tightly onto itself, it will disappear" (139). The observation leads to a startling conjecture, namely that the hedgehog might have been there from the beginning, "in a spot on my desk, so self-enfolded [*replié sur lui-même*] (or should one say self-absorbed?) that I didn't notice its presence. Reassured by the apparent innocuousness of my activities and warmed little by little by the comforting heat of the hearth, it would have lowered its guard, and unfolded itself, relaxed, decompressed, suddenly entering the realm of the visible precisely within my field of view" (140). A hypothesis that elicits in turn the suspicion that there are countless hedgehogs invisibly inhabiting in precisely this way the cracks of the world, "imperceptible, bundled up in their anguish, that have made themselves so small that they have well and truly disappeared. Only conditions that would be particularly clement and rarely achieved in this world can incite them to reappear" (141). Might writing be what produces the rare and *clement* conditions that invite a hedgehog to unfold and emerge into view? We are led momentarily back to Ponge here, for whom the passion of the table was not unrelated to the fact that as a foundation and base for everything else, it could not itself be perceived and represented till everything else had been cleared and the right kind of conditions were thus met for it to emerge into view. So Ponge had decided his table was an "invisible table [*table sympathique*]," "the way one says invisible ink [*comme on dit l'encre sympathique*]" (916/11), that is, like invisible or disappearing ink, which reappears when exposed to a developer chemical or temperature or light that favorably interacts with it. So revealed by a thinking and writing that await and invoke it, Ponge's table returns to view from obscured recesses of the seen/said world ("it comes [elle *souvient*] to my elbow and the same time its notion comes to my mind" [915/9]). So it is with the animal wandering in, naively and globulously, as if plying the blind sympathetic paths opened up by narrative or language (which is why it may seem to appear unaccountably). Chevillard's and Darrieussecq's word "clément/ce" is something similar it would seem, not so much a property as an affective relation; as the former asks it of the world, the latter imputes it to the animal that wanders in ("I called it/her Clémence"). And it makes sense that if sympathy/clemency names a continuum between visibility and vanishing, with the animal traveling the length of that line, that in both Darrieussecq's and Chevillard's cases the animal should appear as something tentative, a clenched bundle of word and form, whose precise parameters remain undrawn, withdrawn. Undeveloped, *inexplicable*: that is, such animals may appear without completely unfolding, at least not to view nor to language, so that it is not inconceivable that before being figures for what irrupts or interrupts they are figures for what may be *interrupted* by *our* sight and speech. "In sum, they show themselves only when they have the assurance that no one is there to see them" (*Du hérisson*, 141).

In a 2006 *Guardian* essay titled "Where Have All Our Hedgehogs Gone?," the British novelist Adam Nicolson lamented the imminent disappearance of the "quiet, discreet and dignified" hedgehog, the very embodiment of Englishness, according to Nicolson, and moreover a valued ecological indicator: its "patient unobtrusiveness," the "generalism" of its feeding habits, "its happy existence at the bottom of hedges and in people's back gardens, [. . .] its fondness for the private, the scruffy and the marginal—all make it a measure of the state of the landscape's health as a whole."[25] The hedgehog, Nicolson concedes, is neither a modern beast nor a clever one: countless hedgehogs are found dead in tennis nets, in polystyrene cups, or "with yoghurt [. . .] or ice-cream containers clamped to their faces," knowing how to get into things only to find their spines getting treacherously caught when they try to get out. From Nicolson's piece transpires the hypothesis that the hedgehog is an indicator and casualty of another sort, that is, of the way space is carved up and apportioned, of the management of the relationship between discreteness and continuity, place and space, or even what Deleuze and Guattari would have called the plane of representation (or composition) and the plane of consistency (or flight). Specifically: because hedgehogs hug the hedges, their livelihood is threatened on the one hand by the tightness of closed-off enclosures with no gaps and on the other by increasingly large "chemically denuded" fields with no hedges. A community ecologist quoted in Nicolson's feature, recalling that "hedgehogs love the interstices [and] the rough brambly places, where they can hide," suggests that humans, if they want to save hedgehogs, "need to defragment the cities for these animals, leave more of the mess for them." The hedgehog's particular way of moving through and hiding in our spaces thus traces an alternate geography to our own, expressing (to no one in particular) the blind supplementary life-sustaining properties of human space. The word "unobtrusive" that Nicolson uses to describe the hedgehog comes from a 1979 Philip Larkin poem (cited in this chapter's epigraph) where a hedgehog is found "jammed up against the blades of a lawnmower." "It had been in the long grass," writes the poet, "I had seen it before, and even fed it, once. / Now I had mauled its unobtrusive world / Unmendably."

ROLLED UP IN A BALL

Then there was Derrida's hedgehog. Ten years before *Le mal de mer*, the philosopher had been invited by the Italian journal *Poesia* to write a few words in response to the question "Che cos'è la poesia?" (What is poetry?). Aware that his text would appear in Italian, he took the opportunity to reflect both on the nature of poetry and on the problem of translation, and he produced something between a poem and a hedgehog. Derrida's poem as hedgehog/hedgehog as poem is a wild thing that, attempting to prevent its own unraveling, folds in on itself. Yet, in seeking to hide, by bearing its bundled, bristling back in blind defense of its inside, it surrenders itself further to passivity and chance, as if only able to relate to the anticipated distress of its own accident (where it will be read, or missed, or misread) by precipitating it: "Rolled up in a ball, prickly with spines, vulnerable and dangerous, calculating and ill-adapted (because it makes itself into a ball, sensing the danger on the autoroute, it exposes itself to an accident). No poem without accident, no poem that does not open itself like a wound, but no poem that is not also just as wounding."[26] Curled up in a prickly ball on the highway, the hedgehog becomes the name for a specific relation between body and letter (i.e., a poem), that which protects itself only by "turn[ing] its pointed signs toward the outside" (299), that which cannot relate back to itself, that which can only be dictated by another, and never signed, but only learned by heart, and there too only as an initiation to the dispossession of heart: "That is the distress of the *hérisson*" (295).

If Derrida's essay was undoubtedly partly (mostly?) a provocation—where the name "hérisson," as the last page of the essay suggests, was chosen "for example" and, what is more, "arbitrarily" (237)—its inexhaustibility as a possible answer to what poetry is comes from its own poetic unity. One could say that it reproduces in its own way, in its vulnerable, retractile, bristling form, exactly what it describes (namely, "the poem as a hedgehog trying to cross the road"),[27] to the point of serving as its own best (and only, but irreducible) example. What I for one am inclined to take away from this difficult piece is this: that if a poem is like a hedgehog, it is because a hedgehog, like a poem, is a little like a Möbius strip, in that its outside and inside are continuous with each other, thing and name, flesh and language, life and meaning, and in that what separates them is a difference not of nature but of *time* and of *reading*, which are an *unfolding*. (I will return to this point.)

As was customary with every issue of *Poesia*, this one featured, as a last response to the assigned question, a text by a deceased writer (whose identity was withheld from the contributors till publication). As it happens—through an obscurely traced path where, like Chevillard's narrator, I am at pains to distinguish the marks of the hedgehog from my own remarks—it was in this case Kafka's "Cares of a Family Man," featuring, as we know, a most peculiar creature: "At first glance [this creature] looks like a flat star-shaped spool for thread, and indeed it does seem to have thread wound upon it; to be sure, they are only old, broken-off bits of thread, knotted and tangled together, of the most varied sorts and colors. But it is not only a spool, for a small wooden crossbar sticks out of the middle of the star, and another small rod is joined to that at a right angle. By means of this latter rod on one side and one of the points of the star on the other, the whole thing can stand upright as if on two legs."[28] Further on the troubled narrator adds, "The whole thing looks senseless enough, but in its own way perfectly finished. In any case, closer scrutiny is impossible, since Odradek is extraordinarily nimble and can never be laid hold of" (428). The very short story's haunting closing line reads: "[Odradek] does no harm to anyone that one can see; but the idea that he is likely to survive me I find most painful" (429).

Odradek has posed almost as much of a challenge to readers as Derrida's "Che cos'è la poesia?"—certainly a lovely essay by Joseph Lavery deems them "equally incomprehensible."[29] For Lavery, "Odradek is the gremlin in the house that disrupts its ability to be a home, but he is also the *animot* in language which mimics the postures of its epistemologies, razzes at its disavowals, purrs at its ignorance" (128). Bringing to an already substantial history of readings of Odradek dazzling turns of his own, Lavery is most careful to observe the critical externality to self of "the rebel-pet" (127) of "indeterminate address" (133) whose impropriety comes precisely from the fact that in him language and body refuse to be "deictically peg[ged]." "By allowing this other into our family, into our home," he writes ominously, "we have rendered irreversible a flaw that might have otherwise naturally eroded: there is an odradek *looking at us* in the home of our language" (133). Guided by the Derridean wager "to read Odradek as a hedgehog-poem" (130), and even a "hedgehog learned by heart" (140), Lavery considers Odradek as an "outward form [that] carries threads, lines of questioning that must be pursued into the object-creature's guts; to find his heart" (136). But these threads continually lead further out, it would seem, toward a shifting archive of ancient and new names, dead and live metaphors, a heart of "prior textuality." Ultimately, Lavery highlights Odradek's status as a deconstructive, queer, arabesque body in which "Kafka calls into question the limits of the domestic and inside, and pulls exteriority ever closer to the centre of being" (135).[30]

As if foretold by the opening of Kafka's story, where scholars struggle to decrypt the puzzle of his name—"Some say the word Odradek is of Slavonic origin [. . .]. Others believe it to be of German origin, only influenced by Slavonic [. . .] neither of them provides an intelligent meaning of the word"—much has been written on Odradek.[31] Eleanor Helms has proposed that this weird creature, as well as the "curious animal, half kitten, half lamb" from the story "A Crossbreed,"[32] are figures for a Kierkegaardian anxiety about continuity and isolation, and that "by having neither individuality nor history," they "each make conspicuous what is missing in a whole self" (90). Esther Bauer, reviewing German scholarship on Odradek, distinguishes those critics who see the creature as an intruder from the outside having infiltrated the domestic, familiar sphere and those who see him/it, rather, as the repressed forcing its way back from the unconscious (157–58). Of course, a Derridean reading such as Lavery's easily resolves this apparent dichotomy: Odradek would be the name for where the deepest inside connects directly with the outside, its gaps as if patched up with bits and pieces of outside. Still, I am interested in the uncertainty of direction, because it has consequences also for narrative/organic development or unfolding: Is a bit a whole on its way out or in? Is it the first fragment or the last? Here too Lavery offers an answer: taking issue with the Muirs' insertion of a "remnant" in the text where there isn't one, he nonetheless argues compellingly at the close of his essay for a Derridean sort of remnant, one that would not necessarily be the remnant of something with prior presence or wholeness (140). No doubt it is a consequence of this paradox that "his invisibility is no definite proof that he is not present."[33] For indeed, "often for months on end he is not to be seen; then he has presumably moved into other houses; but he always comes faithfully back to our house again" ("Odradek," 428). There is, in a word, a *sympathetic* principle at work here, in the French and Pongian sense of the word ("comme on dit l'encre sympathique"). Odradek is a *sympathetic* creature in that his appearances and disappearances in the nooks and crannies of diegetic space ("He lurks by turns in the garret, the stairway, the lobbies, the entrance hall") can seem to depend on inscrutable revelators and inhibitors of which the story is not itself cognizant. It is precisely because Odradek so fluidly inhabits that sympathy between presence and absence that there can never be "definite proof that he is not present" (whence the likelihood that he will outlive us all). But then, conversely, it is fair to wonder whether there is ever any sure evidence that he is not *absent*. Might this riddle bring us a step closer to Darrieussecq's bits of hedgehog? In Odradek is a parable of an entity behind whose hollow forms one may find nothing, yet in whose trace, once registered, can appear the trace of everything: "No one, of course, would occupy himself with such studies if there were not a creature called Odradek" (428).

Yet such inscriptions must owe their fragility to the fact that *sympathy* (understood in the sense proposed) as a theory for stories' or language's occasional porousness to animals may have to contend with recognition/misrecognition as its limit or peril. Palafox, that seemingly invincible metamorphic force of Chevillard's earlier novel, ultimately meets the fate of a common cockroach, crushed by a guest's slipper.[34] For Michaux too, the fixing of species identity was in those texts of the 1930s ("Encore des changements," "Naissance") equated with capture or destruction, so that freedom was in continuous flight from form. One might remember, on the other hand, Borges's words on animals that escape recognizable form in an essay where he cites among possible precursors to Kafka an apologue by ninth-century Chinese writer Han Yu:

> Even children and village women know that the unicorn constitutes a favorable presage. But this animal does not figure among the domestic beasts, it is not always easy to find, it does not lend itself to classification. It is not like the horse or the bull, the wolf or the deer. In such conditions, we could be face to face with a unicorn and not know for certain what it w as. We know that such and such an animal with a mane is a horse and that such and such an animal with horns is a bull. But we do not know what the unicorn is like.[35]

Borges adds in a footnote to this quote: "Non-recognition of the sacred animal and its opprobrious or accidental death at the hands of the people are traditional themes in Chinese literature." In other words, an animal's life in a text may be ensured only for as long as it can succeed in not being recognized (which is always *mis*recognized, if real animal life, as Heraclitus had known, is to hide and to flee).[36]

This knot of threads should lead us back to the Derridean hedgehog, as an emblem of the complicity between visibility and withdrawal, the tenuousness of a "sympathetic" relation preserved between name and thing. In a fascinating twist, Lavery notes that the "istrice" Derrida plays with in "Che cos'è la poesia?" (which appeared first, remember, in Italian) carries with it not only resonant paronomastic value (distress, restriction) but also a problem of *translation*. For "istrice" in Italian names a genus (the *Hystrix cristata*, or crested porcupine, i.e., not a hedgehog at all) quite different to the hedgehogs native to France (*Atelerix algirus*, literally the Algerian hedgehog, and oh, is there not here yet another fascinating expropriation?) and to Britain (*Erinaceus europaeus*, that embodiment of Englishness as established above), so that "the recognition of the animal is first and foremost, then, a misrecognition" (130). In this important sense too, then, the hedgehog cannot be identified once and for all with itself but is always beside itself, exempting itself from its holdings and unfoldings. Even Derrida would admit in a later interview, invoking the Grimm brothers' tale "The Hare and the Hedgehog" (where a hare, believing itself to be racing against a single hedgehog, is defeated by a second—the first's wife which, through a mistake of number and gender, it cannot distinguish from the first), that his own hedgehog in "Che cos'è la poesia?" was quite possibly more than one, indeed that it carried traces of others (that is, the hedgehogs of Grimm, Heidegger, and Schlegel, to which I shall return).[37] So it seems increasingly clear that to track bits of hedgehog, and yet to resist rounding them up or rounding them off, is to read with an eye not only to what the text carries but also to what it carries over or under its legible, signifying charge. A method if not a malady: since I first translated that Darrieussecq passage I have been reading for bits of hedgehog (divining their presence along edges or in cracks, sometimes, like Jean Rolin and his stray dogs,[38] with the sense that I have found a place where bits of hedgehog *should* have been and are somehow *missing*). The question remains as to what kind of conception of narrative, life, or meaning may accommodate, or arise from, these bits of hedgehog.

DETOUR 2: THE MOLLUSK AND THE HERMIT CRAB

Darrieussecq's seamless world or world "sans rupture" conceives of being as a continuum between inside and outside, self and other, human and animal, whole and part, so that it is a very particular sort of folding that is implied. In a moment of aroused somnolence, the narrator of *A Brief Stay with the Living* experiences a "luminous reassurance—her insides are also her outside. A continuity you can follow like a Möbius strip. Down a slide [*Dans un glissement de toboggan*]. She exists constantly, without a break [*sans rupture*] or gaps" (49/31). *Le pays* recalls the Native American origins of "toboggan," the name the Algonquin Indians of Canada give to their snow sleds (41). But Darrieussecq plausibly uses the word in the modern French sense of one of those elaborately twisting roller-coaster-like slides in an amusement park, which can be shaped very much like a Möbius strip.[39] The curious property of the Möbius strip—easily modeled with a long, thin strip of paper that you half-twist in one place before joining its ends—is that it has not two edges but a single surface which slides inside and outside alternately (so that to return to its starting point, once it has started following the length of the strip, a pencil—or an ant, as per the usual explanation—must travel a distance that is double the length of the strip itself). Like the circle, there is no end to the Möbius strip (an eternal march could not get the ant off the strip), but its poignancy—for which it was resorted to by Lacan during his "surface period" to describe the relationship between consciousness and the unconscious[40]—lies in its capacity to represent the paradoxical continuity of certain structures where, as it were, *there is no inside and outside*, only a single continual edge whose length time itself must stretch, and double up on itself, to measure. In this sense it is a topological paradox resolved only phenomenologically: commenting on Lacan's *envers-endroit* model, Jeanne Lafont thus makes clear that "the unconscious is not separated from the conscious except by the time it takes to go there."[41] The provocation of such a structure is in allowing that realms supposed *discontinuous*, separated by a bar—in the subject of psychoanalysis, the bar of repression; in theories of language, that of words and things—be in fact, by virtue of an irreducible fold, connected in perplexing but *seamless* continuity.

An intuition regarding just such a congruency between words and things in the works of Ponge had moved Gérard Genette to write, in *Mimologics*, that the poem "14 JUILLET," offering a motivating reading of its own title, in fact "loops the loop and joins the signifying with the signified face of language in a Möbius strip."[42] I would contend that one could say this about most if not all of Ponge's poems. Everywhere in Ponge the thing is revealed to be inseparable, inextricable from the word that names it, thus dramatizing the single inexhaustible boundary of signification itself. Thus is experienced structurally a certain "always already" paradox of human time, which is that there is no access to a world *before* language. In the words of Émile Benveniste, "We can never get back to man separated from language and we shall never see him inventing it."[43] Every *thing* is, conversely, a thing of language, a *leçon de chose* (object lesson). If we remember that Saussure had offered, by way of illustration for the double structure of the sign, the analogy of a sheet of paper (where signifier and signified would respectively form each side), Ponge's PPC = CTM poetics (*Parti pris des choses = Compte tenu des mots / taking sides with things = taking account of words*) turns the sheet of paper into something more like a strip,[44] half-twisted before joining back onto itself—a Möbius strip.

This in turn would explain why Ponge's pieces, even the shortest, most-finished pieces of *Le parti pris des choses*, are always, on some level, about writing itself, patiently, not to say obsessively, concerned with the surplus, in writing, that reveals each of its objects to be, in turn, inexhaustible. But also, in each object is sought a specific answer to the riddle of how whole and parts, function and expression, being and denomination are welded, in what sort of assemblage, and how this solution might mirror back to the human the secret of its own formative compact with language. Is this what Derrida meant—Derrida, who had read Ponge so closely—when he said "no poem that does not open itself like a wound, but no poem that is not also just as wounding"? In *Signéponge*, he would note that in Ponge causing to sign and to signify (*faire signer et se signifier*; "it is the other, the thing as other, that signs") was never all that far from a causing to bleed (*faire saigner*; recall the violence of "L'orange" or "L'huître").[45] Derrida's interest in Ponge's signature unlocks a meditation on his poem-objects as paradoxical bodies that try to absorb their own outer border, to fold in their outside ("the signature is both inside and outside, it overflows, flows over itself" [114–15]). In these texts that are so many *mises en abyme*, texts about their own writing, the abyssal invagination of a thing striving to account entirely for itself produces an ever-receding supplement, an unclosable gap between a presenting and a representing, a marking and a re-marking, the presence/absence of a ghostly signatory who, before being the writer, is *nature*, which, as Ponge never forgot (spelling it sometimes *gnature*), derives its name from the past participle of *nascere*, Latin for "to be born." Modeling his remark on what Ponge had said of the "éponge" or sponge—that it had "*every quality*, and hence *one quality the more* [*plus une*]: that of having them all" (72–73), Derrida described Ponge's poems as "texts which explain themselves very well, and in such a way that everything can be found there, in addition to that remainder [*plus ce reste*] which prevents an explanatory discourse from ever attaining saturation" (30–31).

Given all this, Ponge really should have written some notes for a hedgehog. Instead, the closest animal he wrote on was the mollusk, about which Elissa Marder has written insightfully in pages that argued far ahead of their time for the productive and critical work of nonhuman figures at the heart of concepts of the human.[46] I will be leaning heavily here on her reading of this poem; Marder is quite clear early on that "Le mollusque" ("The Mollusk") of *Le parti pris des choses*, which Bernard Beugnot has since deemed the heart and the hinge of the volume,[47] presents as its crucial proposition "the impossibility of distinguishing between creature/mollusk and poem/mollusk" (1:114) and that for such exemplarity (as a figure for the relationship between being and expression, and even of [ironized] authorship) it could well have carried the title "Poem" (recall that Ponge's "Fable" had through precisely such a logic inspired Derrida's *Signéponge* [116; 125]). To consider for a moment the poem in its entirety:

> Le mollusque est un *être—presque une—qualité*. Il n'a pas besoin de charpente mais seulement d'un rempart, quelque chose comme la couleur dans le tube.
>
> La nature renonce ici à la présentation du plasma en forme. Elle montre seulement qu'elle y tient en l'abritant soigneusement, dans un écrin dont la face intérieure est la plus belle.
>
> Ce n'est donc pas un simple crachat, mais une réalité des plus précieuses.
>
> Le mollusque est doué d'une énergie puissante à se renfermer. Ce n'est à vrai dire qu'un muscle, un gond, un blount et sa porte.
>
> Le blount ayant sécrété la porte. Deux portes légèrement concaves constituent sa demeure entière.
>
> Première et dernière demeure. Il y loge jusqu'après sa mort.

Rien à faire pour l'en tirer vivant.

La moindre cellule du corps de l'homme tient ainsi, et avec cette force, à la parole,—et réciproquement.

Mais parfois un autre être vient violer ce tombeau, lorsqu'il est bien fait, et s'y fixer à la place du constructeur défunt.

C'est le cas du pagure. (24)

The mollusk is a being—almost a *quality*. It doesn't need a skeleton, just a rampart; something like paint in a tube.

Nature has abandoned all hope here of shaping plasma. She merely shows her attachment by carefully sheltering it in a jewel case, more beautiful inside than out.

So it's not just a gob of spit; but a truly precious reality.

The mollusk is endowed with terrific energy for self-closure. Strictly speaking it's nothing but a muscle, a hinge, a door-closer and its door.

A door-closer that has secreted the door. Two slightly concave doors constitute its entire dwelling.

The first and last dwelling. It stays on even after it dies.

No getting it out alive.

The slightest cell in the human body clings just as tightly to language—and vice-versa.

But sometimes another being violates the tomb, if it's well-made, and takes the place of the deceased builder.

As is the case of the hermit crab.[48]

Ponge's mollusk-poem indeed forms a remarkable poem-mollusk. As Marder puts it, the mollusk "survives by means of its self-expression," "materially cling[ing] to its speech" in a reversal of the usual priority of inside and outside—for it is not here a case of an outer form reflecting an inner essence; rather, the shell, secreted over time by the amorphous creature, lends it "both form and figure," without which it is "unimaginable, unrepresentable," arguably unviable (121–22). The shell in turn outlives the creature as its death mask and "perfect autobiography."[49] Marder shows that "Le mollusque" is an exemplary instance of Ponge attempting to arrive at things "at the impossible point at which the thing and the word that expresses that thing cling together inseparably and without 'meaning'" (140). It is not difficult to see why the perfect model for the poem then (and for the ideal, essential adequation between the human and its expression for which the poem in turn serves as emblem), just as for Derrida it was the hedgehog (assuming we are to take that seriously), for Ponge must be the mollusk. The manner and force with which the mollusk remains beyond its death in its shell, its first abode and its last, in a Möbius-strip-like invagination of putative inside and outside, flesh and verb, would seem to illustrate with drama and pathos the tenacity with which the human inhabits language like an inseparable outer skin. An intriguing chiasmaticity, whereby "the slightest cell in the human body clings just as tightly to language—and vice-versa" suggests a topology in which the two are originarily tethered together: No body without language, and by the same logic, viewed from the other "inflection" of the strip, no language without body. Hence, perhaps, Derrida's no-poem-unlike-a-wound/-wounding. So many of Ponge's poems (one thinks here notably of the fragrant passion of "L'orange" [The Orange] and of the opinionatedly clammed-up and finally prized-open oyster of "L'huître" [The Oyster]) are about openings, that is, opening a thing, a thing opening, ex-pressed, pressed out of itself, unfolding progressively, to bare its innermost inviolable material/verbal fold ("that remainder which prevents an explanatory discourse from ever attaining saturation," as Derrida wrote), like a mollusk steadfastly refusing to leave its shell, like a human joined to language as by cartilage to its own outer shell.

Yet the last word of the last line of the poem-mollusk names a creature quite different, a posthumous interloper, and in a way so startling ("another being" violating the mollusk's abode and sepulture that is this text) as to recall Lewis Carroll's absurd "For the Snark *was* a Boojum, you see."[50] The *pagure*, more commonly known as the *bernard l'hermite*, or hermit crab, does not secrete its own shell like the mollusk but, rather, takes over the salvaged gastropod shell of other creatures, often sea snails, but also marine mollusks. I will have reason (yes) to return to the particular behavior of this species. The case of the *pagure* here ("As is the case of the hermit crab"), signifying as it does the end of the mollusk in both word and flesh, owes its supplementary disquiet to the fact that it annexes the careful analogy drawn between mollusk and man. For what human secretes its own language-armor like the mollusk its shell-doors? Once one starts to wonder whether the figure for the human in Ponge's intricate metaphor is not the hermit crab rather than the mollusk, the poem opens itself to a more suspicious reading. For is it not, well before the end, retroactively occupied, its meanings parasitically rerouted to the advantage of the *pagure*? Is it not the stubborn survival of the occupier in its borrowed abode (rather than that of the original mollusk in its secreted one) that inspires the evocation of the way every cell of the human body clutches onto language? In Marder's lucid words, "the viability of the mollusk's speech is confirmed only when this speech is violated—quoted and translated—by another. Perversely, the mollusk's self-expression comes to speak perfectly for another" (126). The model is in fact one of "expropriation," by which "speech is neither proper nor property" but always appropriation, usurpation, citation, of dead material which, reanimated, in turn can bestow life (127). The "perver[ted]" model certainly offers a more rigorous (Derridean *avant la lettre*) description of the human relationship to language, so that one must ask whether in the end the mollusk as original inhabitant is not quite a mythical entity. Not that there are no such things as mollusks (this would be a dreadful prospect for a hermit crab), but Ponge presents his amorphous object from the outset as something as hidden and inaccessible in the poem as in nature itself: "Nature has abandoned all hope here of shaping plasma. She merely shows her attachment by carefully sheltering it." To still be able to speak of "the mollusk" (as "paint in a tube") accordingly implies that the hermetic exteriority it presents in nature *has* been violated, that one has arrived at it, as per the natural law the poem itself cites ("No getting it out alive"), after its death, not to say *as* its death: "Authorship is merely the voice of death."[51]

Another text of the same period as "Le mollusque" confirms the terms of the captured analogy. In "Notes pour un coquillage" ("Notes toward a Shellfish") Ponge deems of writers and composers of measure and proportion (Bach, Rameau, Malherbe, Horace, Mallarmé . . .) that "their monument is made of the human mollusk's true secretion, the thing best proportioned and adapted to his body, and yet as different in form as one can conceive: I mean LANGUAGE."[52] But immediately after these lines Ponge looks far beyond the human to that time and place where "la PAROLE" (language) might be discovered and inhabited by other tenants: "Oh Louvre of language!—that may one day, after we're extinct, perhaps have other inhabitants, some kind of ape, for example, or bird, or a higher being, just as crustaceans, like the hermit crab, assume the place of the mollusk in the miter-shell." Marder's posthumanist reading of Ponge finds here its deepest reach.[53] Yet one might wonder whether ultimately there is not an irresolvable instability to the location of the human in all of this; almost as if Ponge couldn't quite decide which one, mollusk or hermit crab, human or posthuman carried the final truth regarding language and life. By this token the "case of the hermit crab" would seem to be a case of what Derrida would have called an originary supplementarity, that is, a ruining of unity and self-identity from the very beginning. From the moment that the "pagure" enters and makes the departed mollusk's shell its own, or more dramatically still, from the moment that this becomes possible (which is the very beginning, if there is such a thing), ownness or ownership itself is ousted from its usual place. In the end the one-to-one correspondence between mollusk and shell or human and language is preyed upon not so much temporally and from the outside by a third term (the hermit crab) as conceptually and internally by an openness that must always expose life to what in it outlives it and utterance to the "empty place" at its heart that can always be reoccupied.[54] Thus the poem on the mollusk attains its innermost material-verbal fold and place of truth only by substituting *itself* for the mollusk (and ink for the "paint in the tube"). And the poet writing his way into the mollusk's shell himself assumes the metaphorical features of a "pagure" that *writhes* into it. But my prose is parasited again by Lewis Carroll (to whom it is now time to turn), whose Mock Turtle, in *Alice's Adventures in Wonderland*, fondly recalls his early lessons in "Reeling and Writhing" . . .

GRIN WITHOUT A CAT

If all this makes for a "plane of plication" generally favorable to the grin of a Cheshire Cat, one dimension—or *unfold*—of this grin remains to be considered, and this has to do with words and things in Darrieussecq, and what animals have exactly to do with that relation, if anything. (But a converted Baroque myself now, I will be seeking *something rather than nothing*—and perhaps this is what is meant, in the end, by bits of hedgehog.) For this last movement I shall draw from the Deleuze not of *The Fold* but of *Logic of Sense*, where he turns to Stoic thought through the prism of the works of Lewis Carroll. Meaning, for the Stoics, writes Deleuze, in an early "series" of this work ("Sense"), is "the thin film at the limit of things and words," something that is independent of a given proposition, in fact its "neutralized double," its dry "phantom, and a phantasm without thickness."[55] Such a fantomatic immobilizing is the only way to resolve a double aporia concerning each of the series of terms (words and things, or metalanguage and object language)—"my impotence to state the sense of what I say, to say at the same time something and its meaning; but also the infinite power of language to speak about words" (41/29). Meaning, thus understood as the "evanescent double" of the proposition, is deemed, at this point, "[exactly] Carroll's smile without the cat" (45/32, though Deleuze's "exactement" vanishes in the English). And this grin *as meaning*, in turn, is "exactly the boundary between propositions and things," which by "turn[ing] one side towards things and one side toward propositions" (34/22) assures neither separation nor reunion but the "articulation of their difference," like a juncture or hinge (*la charnière*, writes Deleuze here—Ponge of "The Mollusk" called it *le gond* or *le blount*) between body and language (37/24). Meaning, then, is "this *aliquid* at once extra-Being and inherence [*insistance*], that is, this minimum of being which befits inherences" (34/22). It is fantomatic, both less than body and more than word, because indifferent to qualities, to contradiction, to possibility/impossibility. Its existence is inferred from the Stoics' observation that every proposition is caught between an "implies" and a "therefore," thus always gesturing toward something that it cannot itself contain (27/16; one cannot help remembering here Derrida's reading of Ponge and of what cannot ever attain saturation). But because things/body and word/language are separate, discontinuous series, and because meaning can be located in neither one, it is accessed only "by breaking open the circle, as in the case of the Möbius strip, by unfolding and untwisting it," in brief, by *undoing* the half-fold of the Möbius strip connecting along a single side words and things (31/20). In the Möbius strip is a figure for what Deleuze considers to be Lewis Carroll's lesson: that depth is an illusion, in fact produced by extending or following a surface to the place where it turns and becomes its own other side. Thus, commenting on the bipartite character of Carroll's *Alice books*, where the verticality of meaning sought in the first gives way to horizontality and surface in the second, he described a Möbius-like structure, this time centered on the motif of a curtain (we remember here the curtain where Darrieussecq's "thing" had appeared in the short story of *Zoo*): "If there is nothing to see behind the curtain, it is because everything that is visible, or rather all possible knowledge is along the length of the curtain. It suffices to follow it far enough, precisely enough, and superficially enough, in order to reverse sides and to make the right become the left or vice versa. It is not therefore a question of *the adventures* of Alice, but of Alice's *adventure*: her climb to the surface, her disavowal of false depth and her discovery that everything happens at the border" (19/9; translation modified). It is worth noting here that the narrator of *Naissance des fantômes*, halfway through the novel, sensing that her husband was "necessarily somewhere, vaporous perhaps and on the verge of exiting the universe, but necessarily somewhere, leaning over the edge (whatever edge we must suppose there is)," wondered if he might be lurking "behind doors" or "in a breath of air against the curtains on a perfectly still day" (96/87–88). And that, two pages earlier, remembering how, as a child, looking at one's reflection in two mirrors facing each other, "(you laugh in terror at seeing yourself multiplied; you are in the process of understanding that you will go no farther, and indeed your understanding of your whole life will go no further, you will do nothing but glimpse the absence of edges in the world)" (94/85–86). One of the "decisions" shaping Darrieussecq's work is indeed in the move from *My Phantom Husband*, still lured by the hope of recovering what is *behind* or *beneath* the surface, to *Le mal de mer*, whose fascination is directed largely toward the border itself, the "jointure du monde" (78/66)—where the world joins or the world's joint—between water and land (a place of folds and concealed organic life), the matricial figure for a border constitutive of and ceaselessly animating phenomenal reality. Whence the "bouts de hérissons": the boundary is no longer the shore nor the curtain but the more intimate one of skin and nails, sites of incrustation fleshly and poetic by creatures no longer really *inner* or *outer* vis-à-vis the self but laterally contiguous, coterminous, as if aligned along the same border—the single seam—of being.

But let me return to *The Logic of Sense*. In the sixth series, titled "Serialization," Deleuze notes the perpetual slippage and imbalance between the series of the signifier and the signified, the fact that the signifying series is always *in excess* relative to that of the signified. Recalling Lacan's famous analysis of Poe's *Purloined Letter*, he calls the letter, by which Lacan assures the meaningful articulation of the two series, "a very special and paradoxical [entity]," which ceaselessly circulates between the two series, thereby enabling them to communicate: "It is a two-sided entity, equally present in the signifying and the signified series. It is the mirror. Thus it is at once word and thing, name and object, sense and *denotatum*, expression and designation, etc. It guarantees, therefore, the convergence of the two series which it traverses, but precisely on the condition that it makes them endlessly diverge. It has the property of being always displaced in relation to itself" (55/40). "We must say," adds Deleuze here, "that the paradoxical entity is never where we look for it, and conversely that we never find it where it is. As Lacan says, *it fails to observe its place* (*elle manque à sa place*)"—so that Deleuze proposes to baptize the paradox "Lacan's paradox" (55/41, see 55/338n6: "A Carrollian inspiration is often in evidence in Lacan's writings"). It will become clear in the progression of *Logic of Sense* that the "paradoxical entity" is nothing other than the very condition of production of meaning (88/70, 91/73). As what articulates together the signifying and signified series, the "paradoxical element" is constitutive of meaning, perhaps indistinguishable from the fantomatic production and effect of meaning (99/81). But its terrible paradoxicality lies in what appears to be, again, a Möbius-strip-like property, the fact that while it theoretically has two sides, each is always missing the other, yet inseparable from it: "Its excess always refers to its own lack, and conversely, its lack always refers to its excess. But even these determinations are still relative. For that which is in excess in one case is nothing but an extremely mobile *empty place*; and that which is lacking in another case is a rapidly moving object, an *occupant without a place*, always supernumerary and [always] displaced" (56/41).

This paradox is illustrated easily by the episode in the sheep's shop in *Through the Looking-Glass*, wherein Alice is faced with "the complementarity of 'the empty shelf' and of the 'bright thing always in the shelf next above,'" a noncongruency of excess and lack which in the final analysis must ruin the calculus—"the *thing*" ends up passing right "through the ceiling" (56/41). But it is also something at work through all of language; as such it is renamed "Robinson's paradox" in the eighth series ("Structure"). The signifying series in Robinson Crusoe's case is the totality of laws, rules, and terms that he gives himself in a single move, even though they may not yet all have corresponding objects in the signified series formed by the things and possible relations on his island. The "paradoxical element" is here the gap between the totalness of the signifier on the one hand, and the incompleteness of the signified on the other. Deleuze quotes Lévi-Strauss: "'The Universe signified long before we began to know what it was signifying . . . Man, since his origin, has had at his disposal a completeness of signifier which he is [hard pressed to allocate] to a signified, given as such without being any better known. There is always an inadequacy between the two'" (63/48). It is as if, in the relationship between language and world, seen as two discontinuous, heteronomous series, there were always a continually moving empty place and a continually floating placeless element and that the *possibility of meaning* were always premised on the fact that the two are never joined, so that "whatever totalizations knowledge may perform, they remain asymptotic to the virtual totality of language."

The *asymptote* was notably also Lacan's word, in his description of the mirror stage as a model for the constitution of the subject, for the relationship between the self—as uncoordinated inchoate body—and its unified, signifying, even "fictional" image—as reflected in the mirror.[56] The gap between thing/body and its symbolization is precisely what is at stake here, so that one could be forgiven for imagining, when reading these moments of Deleuze's demonstration in *Logic of Sense*, that something like *an incomplete creature*, or maybe something like *creaturely incompleteness*, stands at this place of variance—as a leftover of that peculiar enfoldedness of excess (of signifier) and poverty (of signified) otherwise known as meaning.

Or is it just that the grin without a cat, as it moves through *Logic of Sense* as a "paradoxical element," seems to have to imply on some irrecoverable other—or same, single, *un*otherable—side a cat without a grin? By the time we reach the thirty-third series ("of Alice's adventures") Deleuze is distractedly calling Carroll's cat "le chat de Chester" (duly corrected in the English by Lester) and equating it with "the good penis" and the idealized "voice of the heights" (274/235). The equation makes some sense in the case of *Naissance des fantômes*, and is one to which, given her knowledge of Lacan, Darrieussecq would moreover likely not object altogether.[57] The Chester cat, says Deleuze, requires of Alice that she choose between being a child and being a pig (the Duchess's baby having turned into a pig, as Alice reports to the cat), and more generally, between depth and height. Choosing correctly, she succeeds in learning the lesson of surface, and in *Through the Looking-Glass*, will no longer need the identification with cats (on which she will look down rather patronizingly). Even if Deleuze goes on to qualify such a reading, noting that there is little profit in reading Oedipally and that in any case the interest of the Alice adventures is that psychic regression is supplanted by speculative investment (279), it seems likely that—as Derrida suggests in passing in one of the seminars of *La bête et le souverain II* (regarding specifically Deleuze's text on Michel Tournier's *Vendredi ou les limbes du Pacifique*)—Deleuze was at this time excessively influenced by Lacan.[58] As for me, I will confess to being more intrigued by the Cheshire Cat than by its reterritorialized Chester version (Chester is a city in Cheshire county but it is not mentioned in *Alice*) and rather inclined to take seriously the work a bit of animal could do in all those places where Lacan gave paradoxical elements another name: letter, penis (good or bad), Real or *objet petit a* (unless of course this secretly stands for *petit objet animal . . .*).

YOU CAN'T BE CERTAIN THAT I HAVEN'T DONE IT

In a interview following the publication of "Che cos'è la poesia?,"[59] Derrida confessed to a curious anamnesis—the ghostly return, behind his singular hedgehog, of other possible hedgehogs:

> In "*Che cos'è la poesia?*" the figure of [the hedgehog] seems to herald, as if in silence, something about the "by heart" and memory. Well, quite a bit later after publishing this text, I had to give in to a strange certainty: if this hedgehog had appeared to rise up before me, unique, young as on the first day of creation, but also given secretly for the first time, an incomparable present, in truth I must have come across it at least two times before. In two texts that mean a lot to me. But I didn't recall this for a single instant at the moment of writing. I didn't even have the distant feeling of other possible hedgehogs—in my memory or in literature. Before the depth of this forgetting, which effaced even the support of the message, I wonder if I even noticed during my reading, which was perhaps distracted, the two other hedgehogs that now come back like ghosts, or if instead an operation of effective censoring had not already imposed in me the accident that that text talks about. It little matters. And it is true that although they have the same name, these two hedgehogs don't have much relation to "mine"; they don't belong to the same family, the same species, or the same genre, even though this non-relation says something about a deep genealogical affinity, but in antagonism, in counter-genealogy. Compared to these two hedgehogs, which turn out to be German hedgehogs, bearing therefore a German name (*Igel*), the one that occurred to me is a solitary counter-hedgehog, first of all Italian [*istrice*] or French [*hérisson*]. (*Points* 311/301–2)

The German hedgehogs in question, Derrida would go on to tell Maurizio Ferraris, were hedgehogs invoked by German philosophers, in both instances as emblems for things quite different, not to say inimical, to what Derrida himself had in mind with his "counter-hedgehog." First there was Schlegel's famous fragment 206, which Derrida had "read or reread" in Philippe Lacoue-Labarthe and Jean-Luc Nancy's *The Literary Absolute*: "Like a little work of art, a fragment must be totally detached from the surrounding world and closed on itself like a hedgehog." Lacoue-Labarthe and Nancy had drawn from this axiom a logic of "fragmentary totality" which they baptized "the logic of the hedgehog": "Each fragment is valid for itself and for that from which it is detached" (quoted on 302). In the interview, Derrida is loathe to locate such individualized integrity or integrality, or even any "logic" in his "counter-hedgehog." Produced by "the chance of a language and of signifiers that play the role of temporary proper name"—*istrice, hérisson*—his is a "'catachrestic' *hérisson*," he insists, "neither a concept nor a thing"; also, "it has no relation to itself—that is, no totalizing individuality—that does not expose it even more to death and to being-torn-apart. Another logic. Or rather: this very young hedgehog is older than 'logic.' The 'logic of the hedgehog' is one of the possible traps in the adventure of this other hedgehog, of its name and of its dispatch" (303). Indeed, at the end of "Che cos'è la poesia?" he had written clearly: "'What is . . . [*Qu'est-ce que* . . .]?' laments the disappearance of the poem—another catastrophe. By announcing that which is just as it is, a question salutes the birth of prose" (298/299). In a sense the unreadability—and the obscure drama—of that piece had been precisely this: that you could say what a hedgehog/poem was only by saying how it was not what it was and thereby abolishing it. The "accident" being something like this twist in the road, in the ribbon of thinking or being (a Möbius strip), which has the hedgehog continually walking toward its own vanishing. Derrida makes clear that there is nothing destinal, sacrificial, or sublimatable about such an accident; it is something far more humble. Yet such accidents are regularly given magnified meanings, and that is when they become disastrous, catastrophic, and the hedgehog is frozen, on its way to its humble disappearance, into a logic. This is what occurs also in the second case, a passage at the end of Heidegger's *Identity and Difference*, where "the silhouette of an *Igel* ["hedgehog" in German] passes by still more quickly." Heidegger there had formulated a possible objection to his thinking on the difference between Being and being, as being a distance or an arriving that only pretends to be one: "It is as in Grimm's fairytale 'The Hedgehog and the Hare': 'I'm here already'" (quoted on 303). The Grimm (if certainly not grim) Hedgehog had won the race against the Hare by "send[ing] his female hedgehog ahead to the finish line"—so that "the concept, the figure, the sense of the hedgehog, in this case, whatever its language may be and whatever its name may be, mean the 'always-already-there,' the structure or the logic of the 'always already' (303).[60] First inserting within this structure the unresolvable uncertainty of who it is that in fact calls out the "I'm here already" or "Ick bünn all hier/da" (using the German word for both gender and genus, he asks, "What is the *Geschlecht* of this triumphal voice?"), Derrida goes on to except his hedgehog from this fable too: "The *istrice* that came to me can barely say '*Ich*' and certainly not '*bünn*,' still less '*hier*' and '*da*.' It is still waiting and is not assured of any 'always already.' [. . .] It is barely a hedgehog, strictly speaking; it is neither a work, nor poetry, nor truth, only a letter and a few syllables destined to die by accident" (304). Still, later in the interview Derrida would concede a little ominously: "But it's true, it is truth itself, that one can always bring this hedgehog back into the Heideggerian logic. As we have already seen, this can always happen to it as one of its accidents. As its loss. Its salvation is its loss. There is no longer anything fortuitous about this and the consequences of this strange proposition remain to be drawn" (325).

There are several terms and turns of phrase in the interview that merit more puzzling through, not least, in what I have just quoted, the "it is the *truth itself*" and the "there is *no longer* anything fortuitous about this." For these are places where the hedgehog itself "turns," one might say, from a creature humble, aleatory, stubbornly insignificant into a figure for the event of deconstruction itself. Thus in a response to a question from Ferraris about the politics of his philosophical preferences (hedgehog over phoenix, writing over voice, history's rejects over its victors . . .), Derrida describes his concern always to reach for "that point at which a formalization [and especially one given as a couple or binary] remains necessarily incomplete, open to what may come." Here he says simply: "A hedgehog may always arrive, it may always be given to me. There is something non-formalizable and the concern comes from there, precisely," "perhaps an 'ethical' concern, in fact." Ultimately, he grants, this nonformalizable something or possible arrival of a hedgehog is the "very thing" that preoccupies him, as a "place that no longer belongs either to the couple or to the circle" (323). But if we have learned anything from Derrida, it is that an object of such unobtrusiveness and modesty (what may arrive/happen pared down to the size of a little hedgehog) is no place of transparency or rest—quite the contrary, for in this unassuming creature the world itself stands to be faced with its non-self-identity (and Western thinking with its inconsistency), and to unravel. In fact, the unraveling power of the hedgehog (as of anything that might have been in its place—this being the point) reveals itself to be overdetermined—or as Derrida might have said, originarily complicated. First, it is an entity which stands before (or rolls into) itself in a relationship of non-self-sameness. This is in turn more complicated than it seems: the hedgehog's rolling up into a ball is itself only a metaphor for the fact that the hedgehog is catachrestic; and that it is a catachresis (sometimes called a dead metaphor) because, like a catachresis, it "borrows" part or even most of its being from another realm, but in this case that other realm is language *tout court*, for which there is no other, and the borrowed part is its name, without which there would be nothing to think it by, perhaps because that is all there is to it.[61] Which is why Derrida likens the hedgehog to the "aleatory factor" of the mark or the trace (305), and why he is pointedly reluctant to "re-semanticize this letter," insisting that "it must remain of little meaning. Without secret but sealed. It is also better not to stuff polysemic vitamins down the throat of a humble little mammal. Let's not entrust it with any message" (311). Because it is "barely a hedgehog, strictly speaking [*c'est à peine un hérisson, à proprement parler*]" (314/304), and precisely in this "barely," in this trace that it registers, (at least) three important disrupting or resignifying capacities are encrypted, or rather, left delicately unforeclosed. The first is that as a living creature, "even if it is a catachrestic one," this hedgehog introduces a humble note of unsettlement in the Heideggerian "dominant discourse" that the animal is poor in world and that being-for-death—and therefore Being accessed "as such" (that term by which the animal is repeatedly denied Being in *Fundamental Concepts of Metaphysics*)—is reserved for humans (311). For, on the one hand, if the hedgehog is not aware of the possibility of death "as such," it is no easier to claim that the human Dasein can stand in such a relation to its own death ("What is the 'as such' in the case of death?"); besides, the hedgehog's rolling up into a ball constitutes a sign of an apprehension of death, if ill seen and ill said (312). On the other hand, if "the hedgehog is poor in world since it is very low, close to the earth," well, "so is man," who is "also more or less rich, thus more or less poor in world" (325). We thus see here well in place, rolled up in Derrida's humble hedgehog, all the moves, soundly rehearsed in part VII of *De l'esprit* (1987) that had first addressed some of "the difficulties [Heidegger] encounters with animality," that would lead more than a decade later to the critique of Western philosophy's historical occlusion of the animal in *L'animal que donc je suis*.

The second way in which Derrida's hedgehog is infinitely more than itself is one that I shall derive less directly from what Derrida says and more from some of the fascinating perspectives suggested by Ferraris as a close reader of the philosopher's work (who at times, it is true, speaks at such great length that the interviewee is left uncharacteristically speechless). At various points in the conversation, Derrida has made it clear that his hedgehog is catachrestic also because it "doesn't belong to the species or the genre" (302), that it is "indissolubly linked" to a tentative, temporary assemblage of letters, perhaps secretly to that "dead letter come from the other; before any living act, and even before any position of the cogito" (320). Ferraris in turn receives Derrida's insistence on the letter as confirmation of a historical difference between German and Romanic philosophical thinking, where the former, idealist and classical in its thrust, has traditionally treated the letter as subordinate to the spirit which gathers, resolves, and transcends it (316), while the latter has tended to privilege the work "of 'close reading' and of faithfulness to the letter" (315). The hypothesis concerns not national essences or inclinations, but rather an epochal German investment in a Classical Greek scene (as described by Plato), where "the living and still current spirit" is eternally young and vitally and seriously present to itself, whereas "a repetition of letters, citations and elements not present to spirit"—as in the case of Egyptian/Oriental civilization and later Roman (and then Italian and French), where "everything is written down"—would weigh the spirit down and deprive it of its actuality (317–18). Ferraris, continually responding through this elaboration to Derrida's own work (on Heidegger, Husserl, De Man, etc.), states that "the paradigm of the classical and the metaphysical [in which he quickly bunches together Plato, Heidegger, Husserl and even Nietzsche in spite of Derrida's note of caution] is consciousness present to itself, monologically self-conscious, which nothing—neither letters, traditions, indexes, nor lists, that is, anything that is of the order of the letter written on paper and not on the soul—can carry away from itself" (318). The animal, Ferraris notes at this point, plays here "a non-peripheral role," for "in Greece, the animal is infinitely inferior to self-conscious man, which was not the case in Egypt, where it made no difference whether one buried an ox or a sovereign in a pyramid" (319). In other words, the history of Western philosophy according to Ferraris-reading-Derrida-reading-Western-philosophers can be recounted pithily as "the formation of two series: on the one side, there is spirit, youth, humanity, life, Greece; on the other, there is letter, old age, animality, death, and Egypt as *realm of death*" (319).

All of this is thoroughly fascinating (the animal-letter adjacency particularly would merit fruitful reflection),[62] and I do not infer from

Derrida's very terse response ("But let's be careful. Let's not construct between us a Franco-Italian axis or a southern highway . . ." [319]) that he was in substantive disagreement with it. Rather, I should think, he abstained from further comment at this point both because in pursuing that path further lay yet another risk of turning the hedgehog into a logic, into an element in a couple (the two series, German/French, Classical/Oriental, spirit/letter), *and* because the scene Ferraris had described was no doubt precisely the reason (or one way of describing the reason) for the hedgehog and for why it had to be catachrestic, "barely a hedgehog"—so that it could straddle the epistemic divide between life and letter, human and animal, or continually confound it. So that Ferraris was perhaps not even expecting a response but simply providing what he saw as being (in its most ambitious scope) the backstory, a footnote to the hedgehog. It is a very rich moment especially, then, because it illustrates the sense in which nothing less than the most comprehensive or dramatized account of the history of Western thought is at stake in the footnote to the sudden, unaccountable arrival of what is barely a hedgehog. And that this is also, even more dizzyingly, why Derrida's hedgehog is an über-catachresis, because it is without intrinsic content or life but, once named, can come to carry inexhaustible traces of language, philosophy, history, of other possible hedgehogs, and because without these letters—without this endless work of the letter, of reading and writing—it dissolves into nothing. The second limitless property of Derrida's hedgehog, then, is this: once named (so it "arrives"), it prevents any possible closing off of the distribution of matter and letter, human and animal, "I" and "it," because it keeps excepting itself from each accounting, which therefore is never an accounting of everything. As Derrida would say a little further, in describing his "'ethical' concern": "none of the names would be apt any longer, writing no more than the voice, Egypt no more than Greece" (323).

The third abyssal property of the hedgehog arrives with delay. Just as two other possible hedgehogs return as ghosts soon after "Che cos'è la poesia?," the shadow of yet other hedgehogs would pass many years later, distinguished equally by ellipsis or belatedness, or, rather, indissociable from the suggestion that there was not time enough to fold everything back into a hedgehog as with infinite time one might or should have done. It is toward the beginning of the first seminar of *L'animal que donc je suis*, when Derrida is still distinguishing his cat from other cats—Baudelaire's, Montaigne's, Alice's (Carla Freccero has tracked this cat community richly):[63] "'My' pussycat [*"ma" chatte*] (but a pussycat never belongs) is not even the one *who speaks* in *Alice in Wonderland*" (23/7). It is a movement riddled with citation, digression, false leads, ambiguities, equivocation (the sure signs of catachrestic labor, we now understand) as Derrida both yields to and resists the seduction of literary cats: he cannot forbid us, for instance, from reading in his insistence on the realness of his cat a citation from the penultimate one-line chapter (titled "Waking") of *Through the Looking-Glass*, "*—and it really was a kitten after all*" (quoted in *L'animal que donc je suis*, 23/7). Then, after quoting this line both in English and in two different French translations (to no apparent ends; but there is fascination at work here with the letter, with the cat as letter, with the letter as cat), Derrida says the following, worth quoting at some length:

> Although I don't have time to do so, I would of course have liked to inscribe my whole talk within a reading of Lewis Carroll. In fact you can't be certain that I am not doing that, for better or for worse, silently, unconsciously, or without your knowing. You can't be certain that I didn't already do it one day when, ten years ago, I let speak or let pass a little hedgehog, a suckling hedgehog [*un nourisson hérisson*] perhaps, before the question "What is Poetry?" For thinking concerning the animal, if there is such a thing, derives from poetry. There you have a thesis: it is what philosophy has, essentially, had to deprive itself of. It is the difference between philosophical knowledge and poetic thinking. The hedgehog of "What is Poetry?" not only inherited a piece of my name [*Le hérisson de "Qu'est-ce que la poésie?" n'héritait pas seulement d'un morceau de mon nom*] but also responded, in its own way, to the appeal [*appel*] of Alice's hedgehog. Remember the croquet ground where the "balls were live hedgehogs" ("The Queen's Croquet Ground"). Alice wanted to give the hedgehog a blow with the head of the flamingo she held under her arm, and it would "twist itself round and look up in her face," until she burst out laughing.
>
> How can an animal look you in the face? That will be one of our concerns. Alice noticed next that "the hedgehog had unrolled itself and was in the act of crawling away: besides all this, there was generally a ridge or a furrow in the way wherever she wanted to send the hedgehog to." It was a field on which "the players all played at once, without waiting for

> turns, quarreling all the while, and fighting for the hedgehogs" [*s'arrachaient les hérissons*]. (23–24/7)

It is a passage critics turn to often, especially—not to say exclusively—for the critical pronouncement on literature and philosophy's respective relations to the animal. But what of Carroll and the hedgehogs amid which these lines are nestled? Derrida does not comment as such on the hedgehogs, limiting himself to the *strict speech* of quotes and paraphrase. In what follows immediately, he would express astonishment at Alice's humanistic credulity, that is, her conviction on waking that a cat doesn't ever respond or speak (but only purrs undifferentiatedly), implying, conversely, that it is possible to distinguish in humans between yes and no. If this particular move seems a bit easy (for surely there are texts far more guilty than Carroll's of precluding animals from speech and thought), Derrida goes on to quickly correct Alice's humanist bias from the inside of her own story by recalling the Cheshire Cat's proclamation that everyone is mad, and the polemic it provokes on the meanings of words and ultimately on what the word "word" means: "'Call it what you like,' the Cat ends up saying about the difference between growling and purring, before announcing that he will be present at the Queen's croquet game, where my poor hedgehogs will be badly treated [*là où mes pauvres hérissons seront mis à mal*]" (26/9). Catachresis: Derrida is moving here in and out of Carroll's text, proceeding seamlessly from the Cheshire Cat's dismantling of the signification of purring (and by implication of the decidability of human signifiers) to the croquet game featuring "my poor hedgehogs," in a move which, pretending to be intradiegetic and proleptic ("before announcing . . . where . . ."), is in fact on another level analeptic, not to say *meta*leptic, for it is a move to a moment in *Alice* already invoked by Derrida and invested in ("*my* poor hedgehogs") as seminal, abstracted out of diegetic time, and perhaps precisely because (or with the result that) no amount of deconstructing of words and meanings by the Cheshire Cat "before" the croquet game can have the power to save the hedgehogs (whence their poorness) from being "badly treated." Yet one may also note that "badly treated [*mis à mal*]" seems excessive, since everyone is equally buffeted about in "The Queen's Croquet Ground" (chapter 8 of *Alice*), and if anything the hedgehogs have not too bad a time, in the last instances fighting each other and running away before they can be croqueted ("By the time she had caught the flamingo and brought it back, the fight was over, and both the hedgehogs were out of sight" [54]); and also that Derrida having said just a few paragraphs earlier that one should not say "'my' pussycat [*ma* chatte]" ("a pussycat never belongs" [23/7]), the "my poor hedgehogs" without emphasis nor further comment (and so doleful as to hardly mount a protest against Heidegger's thesis that animals are poor in world) is a possible sign that these are in fact *barely hedgehogs*, but rather things so bristlingly intertextual—responding to each other from text to text (Grimm, Heidegger, Schlegel, Lacoue-Labarthe/Nancy, Carroll, Derrida)—that even within the same text they seem to only cite and echo each other to no end. And if this is the last we will hear really of the hedgehogs of *Alice* (indeed, Derrida would not do much more at all with Carroll in the seminars, which is itself curiouser and curiouser), it is because the effect of the hedgehog *as tracked letter*—but also as a sort of *crawling*, not to say a sort of *rolling up onto itself*, of the text itself—at this moment is to make the end of the passage simply feed back into the beginning ("where my poor hedgehogs [that is: *the very ones I started out with, hence now mine; already "poor" because I know how this ends*] will be badly treated"). Hedgehogs as signals and (moving!) signposts then, between Carroll and Derrida, of the way a text is exceeded, preceded, blindsided by its reading and re-membering, an "iterability" (whose secret indifference to direction the ant on the half-twisted strip knows) that is not a surface effect but a foldedness ("without secret but sealed") which the text would carry close to its heart or as its heart, like its first graft. If this is in keeping with the paradox of every signature so often addressed by Derrida, here it so happens that the hedgehog carries at/as its heart a very particular signature. For as we learn in passing in *L'animal* (although it easily escapes notice in the earlier essay and interview), the *hérisson* had *also* been from the very beginning (like the *éponge* for Ponge in *Signéponge*, only even more subtly, in a prising apart of the syllables) an encrypted bit of the name of D*erri*da : "Le *hérisson* de 'Qu'est-ce que la poésie?' n'*héritait* pas seulement d'*un morceau de mon nom* [The *hérisson* of "What Is Poetry?" not only in*her*ited *a piece of my name*]." So subtle a bit-of-name (*eri*) hardly risked being detected, even less in Italian, where it was to be encrypted beyond recognition (*istrice*). It is also this secret signature (barely a secret, barely a signature) that is sealed, that disappears to view when the h*éri*sson rolls up in a ball, or crawls away, and which may account for a certain *pudeur* in Derrida when he insisted to Ferraris in 1989: "But I must not overburden this *letter on the letter in istrice* with too much significance: it must remain elliptical, just barely serious, poematic in some respects, in the manner of the poem about which it *converses with itself*, by means of which it *maintains itself* [*dont* elle s'entretient d'elle-même], that is to say, blindly (like the hedgehog that Homer recalls), deprived of meaning and responsibility" (304).

Of the two hedgehogs that escape the croquet ground (note that the end of this chapter 8 sees also the last appearance of the Cheshire Cat), one would walk into Derrida's text ("You can't be certain that I didn't already do it [inscribe my whole talk in a reading of Lewis Carroll] one day when, ten years ago, I let speak or let pass a little hedgehog, a suckling hedgehog [*un nourisson hérisson*] perhaps . . ."). It is not clear to me at what point Derrida in fact "read or reread" *Alice*, whether he was already quite familiar with it before reading *Logic of Sense* on its publication in 1969, or whether it was Deleuze's book that prompted him to (re)turn to the Carroll classic—assuming he did. In any case it is *L'animal que donc je suis* that to my knowledge carries the only explicit reference within Derrida's writings to the *Alice* books, and the retroactive, spectral, doubly disinhibited return of "Alice's hedgehog," so that it appears in *L'animal* only by preceding itself there, is precisely the third inexhaustible property of Derrida's hedgehog ("You can't be certain that I didn't already do it"—one is reminded of Odradrek, whose "invisibility is no definite proof that he is not present" [Bauer 160]). Not through a Heideggerian *always-already-there*, but rather—its ghostly inverse?—by the supplementary work of a return of what was never provably there in the first place (a *never-there-to-begin-with*), because the first hedgehog had been neither Grimm/Heidegger's nor Schlegel/Lacoue-Labarthe/Nancy's nor Carroll's nor any other (even as Darrieussecq might like to claim it as hers) but a trace, a catachresis, just about enough of a hedgehog to stand in and make visible an empty first place, itself barely a place, strictly speaking. (This is of course also the paradox of the "first time" of the signature . . .) Early on in the "Che cos'è la poesia?" piece, Derrida had admitted his discomfort with whole, countable hedgehogs, as figures of integrity or cunning: "Whether in Schlegel or Heidegger, it is always a matter of this gathering together, of this being-one with oneself, in all these stories of the hedgehog, of indivisible individuality or of being always already with oneself, from the origin or the finish line of some *Bestimmung* [destination/determination—the reference is clearly to the race in the Grimms' fairy tale]" (305). Taking up some of Heidegger's key terms, he then presented the hedgehog as what remains when all is spoken for: "There where the *Versammlung* [gathering] doesn't win out, where the force, the *Verwalten* [governance, administering] of the *Versammlung* doesn't win out, there is some hedgehog [*il y a du hérisson*] and a solitary hedgehog that no longer belongs to Grimms', Schlegel's, or Heidegger's family."

THE CAT AND THE HEDGEHOG

All this to say that it is worth being attentive to what is barely a hedgehog, strictly speaking, and which, no less than a cat's grin, may mark what falls out of the usual count of bodies within a gathering, a story, or a life. Precisely such a property links the hedgehogs and the Cheshire Cat in *Alice*: for both seem disinclined to stay in place or in shape, or should I say, more simply, disinclined to stay. Of course the Cheshire Cat's technique of materializing and dematerializing gradually around its grin is a considered concession to Alice, who at the end of chapter 6 requests that it "wouldn't keep appearing and vanishing so suddenly," for it was making her "quite giddy" (41). This micro–plot element matters, for not only does the Cat's slower modulation of its visibility—from the grin slowly outward, over several minutes—receive thereby its motivation (and supposedly young readers' affection, rather than fright), but it is also specifically what produces the grin, as the first and last feature, itself paradoxical, perhaps untenable (a gap, a gaping, this grin "from ear to ear," a tear, a hole): "She noticed a curious appearance in the air: it puzzled her very much at first, but after watching it a minute or two she made it out to be a grin" (53). (What did this grin—and, even more puzzlingly, the pre-grin—look like?) Alice's first encounter with her hedgehog on the croquet ground is likewise something "provoking": the creature has "unrolled itself" from the ball it was supposed to be, and is already "in the act of crawling away" (52). The Queen's hedgehog, which Alice is about to croquet, is the next to run away (54); soon thereafter, having secured her flamingo mallet, she finds that "both the hedgehogs were out of sight." By the end of chapter 8, the hedgehogs and the Cheshire Cat are both decidedly out of sight; they have fallen out of the story, in which they will no more appear. Of course, there is nothing so very peculiar about that, in this episodically structured tale through which so many animal characters pass. This said, these two occupy rather particular positions within *Alice*'s bestiary. The Cat, because it is knowledgeable, a master of paradox but also a friend, and present in two nonconsecutive chapters (this being a rare distinction), clearly enjoys the most privileged place among them. Conversely, the hedgehogs (along with the flamingos, admittedly, but the latter's size [originally they were ostriches], wings, and speed make them particularly unsuited to use, and less able to disappear) are the apparently least privileged—mute, turned into croquet balls, without any other known home or purpose. Does the Cat stand in a secret correspondence and even *respondence* or response to the hedgehogs? Does it arrive to somehow compensate for them, to distract from them or to watch over them? Henri Bué, the very first French translator of Carroll, in 1869 seemed to insinuate as much, by renaming the Cheshire Cat "Grimaçon" (whose American equivalent today might be *Grimacello* or *Grinnola*—though for my point to work here it would have to be *Grin-hog*), thus pressing it into phonemic and syllabic homology with "hérisson" ("'Pourquoi votre chat grimace ainsi?' / 'C'est un Grimaçon,' dit la Duchese, 'voilà pourquoi.' ['Why does your cat grimace/grin like that?' / 'It's a Grimacello/Grinnola/Grin-hog,' said the Duchess, 'that is why.']").[64] We do know that the Cheshire Cat, the most memorable of the characters in *Alice*, was added to the book *a posteriori*, not featured

Figure 4.1. John Tenniel, Alice and the Cheshire Cat, illustration from the original edition of *Alice's Adventures in Wonderland* (Lewis Carroll, 1865).

in the original edition. It is a supplementary cat (possibly the projected/phantasmatic double of a real cat), and therefore its place—where it performs its apparent prescience or omniscience, its way of hovering, perhaps presiding, its friendship, its grin—in some ways is not a place, or is not its place at first (for *it* wasn't *there* in the first place). Perhaps this is why it must repeatedly vanish and reappear, and not at all always in the same place (41). And why it appears and vanishes around its grin, which is not a solid material form or a place but an emptiness. So its possible link with the hedgehogs is that it too, like the hedgehogs, folds and unfolds around *nothing*, "without secret but sealed." Both the cat and the hedgehogs mark thus in different ways the vanishing points of the story, points where the text gathers together and disperses around a temporary arrangement of sorts—between a place that is repeatedly deserted by its creature and a creature that repeatedly disappears as if its place were being pulled from under it. And what better name than "catachresis" for such paradoxical elements, for those things named poorly, barely, yet which can be named in no other way, and always risk being mistaken for something else: the hedgehog for a ball or a burr, the Cheshire Cat for a Chester Cat or a "Grimaçon," its grin for a passing thickness in the sky.

And perhaps this obscure complicity accounts for why Derrida seemed to slide secretly in his signatory sympathies between the hedgehog and the cat, and why while he announced his thinking on the animal to be a response to the "poor hedgehogs" of *Alice* and a reading of Lewis Carroll, it is not about hedgehogs that he speaks in this last seminar, nor about Carroll, really, but about a cat—which in turn is not the Cheshire Cat and not even or not only his own cat but also a catachresis of a cat, a ghostly signature. Jean-Luc Nancy, in *À plus d'un titre*, a posthumous tribute, recalls a note Derrida had intended for reading at his funeral: "*I smile at you from wherever I am* [*Je vous souris d'où que je sois*]."[65] Musing on these words, Nancy asks: "*(Would he have withdrawn like Alice's cat, that vanishes slowly from her sight, its face erasing itself bit by bit, leaving in the end only its smile, its only feature still remaining, pending the last erasure? [. . .])*" (37; emphasis in original; my translation). For Nancy, this was Derrida's way of imagining "a completely other *survival* [*une survie tout autre*] [. . .] which would survive survival itself, a survivance [*une survivance*] which he would finally inscribe like a smile [*un sourire*], in a smile appearing from nowhere" (36–37; emphasis in original). In "Survivre, sourire" (survive/smile—playing on the literal breakdown "over-live" and "under-laugh")

Figure 4.2. John Tenniel, Alice and the flamingo (and hedgehog), illustration from the original edition of *Alice's Adventures in Wonderland* (Lewis Carroll, 1865).

Nancy notes a field of complicity and tension both in sound and in meaning: "a very fine difference/notch just over or just under, just above life and just under laughter [*au-dessus de la vie et au-dessous du rire*]" (38). Marie-Dominique Garnier, at the end of an inspired essay that tracks the work of animal phonemes (or "faunemes") *k* and *che* through Derrida's prose, by which a network of key words constellate around the cat—*que*, *donc*, *pharmakon*, *cas*, *cache*, *chasse*, *castration*, and let me add *catachrèse*—notes in counterpoint that "built into the melancholy of the sentence" *Je vous souris d'où que je sois* (I smile at you from wherever I am), Derrida's surviving words, between the *je* and the *a* of the outer ends of the name of *Ja*cques Derrid*a*, hides a possible "souris," an undeclared or feigned mouse (*une souris*), which is also Hamlet's "not-a-mouse [stirring]."[66] It is a neat and devastating proposition, and the sort of thing Derrida would have favored: a mouse hidden within the grinning riddle/riddled grin of a cat. Still, stubbornly, I will maintain, because this has from the beginning been all I have been counting, and because when present they are always apt to disappear, and because even when recognized they barely seem to fit the place or the argument, that yes, this time too, if we were to count or speak improperly, we should rather find a hedgehog.

Carroll is without a doubt important to Darrieussecq—remember the Cheshire Cat grin moment in *My Phantom Husband*. The narrator of *Le pays*, a writer, when forced to decide what essential books to take with her on a big move, is very definite about taking "all of [. . .] Carroll" (33). So perhaps, to conclude, I could offer three tentative Carroll-like riddles to account for the hedgehog lost in translation in *Le mal de mer.* The first we could call the Chester Cat effect. For it turns out that Derrida too, like Deleuze, had consulted, plausibly among other translations, that of Jacques Papy in 1961, where the Cheshire Cat is called "le chat du Comté de Chester."[67] Chester is indeed the main town of Cheshire county, archaically called the County Palatine of Chester but not, as far as I understand, since 1830. So that Jacques Papy's preference for Chester over Cheshire in 1961, if justified by phonetic convenience, has the odd consequence of dislocating the referential axis of Alice's adventures from the Northwest of England to Pennsylvania, where indeed there is still today a Chester County, and where, as in the rest of America, there are no native hedgehogs in the wild. The Chester Cat hypothesis then is one that foretells the disappearance of hedgehogs by the work of the letter.

The second riddle may be of interest to scholars of Derrida. It proceeds from the observation that the only other place where Derrida mentions Carroll, albeit very briefly (as part of a list of writers/subjects that Deleuze had treated), is in an obituary he wrote in *Libération* three days after the death of Deleuze in November 1995, and republished in *The Work of Mourning*. In this piece, he writes of the deep agreement that had united them, and starts the final paragraph with the lines: "I am going to continue—or begin again—to read Gilles Deleuze in order to learn, and I'm going to have to wander all alone in that long discussion that we should have had together."[68] And so it is just possible that when in Cerisy in 1997, in the seminar that would come to be later known as *L'animal que donc je suis*, Derrida retroactively puts Alice's hedgehogs *back* into the "Che cos'è . . . ?" piece of 1990, in a *second* supplement to it (the first being the interview *Istrice 2*), what is in fact happening is that he is *rereading Carroll*, and that perhaps it is *rereading Deleuze* that led him there, and that perhaps it is this particular mourning and this particular wandering alone that is at work in this rereading that is also a writing. One may imagine Derrida in this way being led to chapter 8 of *Alice*, that croquet ground in whose hedgehogs he would have recognized—or invested—his own trace, for Deleuze to find, had he returned to the scene like a Cheshire Cat. For would this not explain why Derrida so strongly suggests that he might have been speaking of Alice's hedgehogs and of Carroll all the while, even when he was not? The croquet ground forms a phantasmatic ground, where hedgehogs are both mistreated (*mis à mal*) and run away, where they continually appear and disappear, marking the ground with their criss-crossing traces, as the secret scene of all symbolic transactions, and the place which Derrida would in turn come to haunt from the other side as a grinning cat.

The third riddle presents itself in the hedgehog census method used in the United Kingdom some years ago and which Adam Nicolson deems paradoxical: essentially, one counts the number of dead hedgehogs found per twenty miles of motorway. What is thereby measured, he notes, is not "how many hedgehogs have been killed by cars but how many hedgehogs there are for cars to kill. The more dead hedgehogs on the roads, the better the health of the hedgehog population." Now this sounds like something the Cheshire Cat would say to Alice, logic taken to its provocative limit. But it is precisely at its nonsensical limit that logic is truly logical, and the secretly scandalous relationship between things (or between words and things) becomes legible. In Derrida's words, "The poematic hedgehog crosses the highway at the risk of being run over by a great discourse that it cannot resist . . ." (*Points*, 312). The U.K. census was compiled over four years by coordinating "reports of many thousands of drivers who ha[d] been looking out for squashed hedgehogs," and it was found that the population had dropped by 50 percent in fifteen years. Imagine a world measured in terms of hedgehog miles (i.e., the distance that must be traveled before finding a dead hedgehog)—it is this distance that is getting longer and longer, according to the census, which predicts that by 2025 the hedgehog will have altogether disappeared from Britain. Yet if there is a lesson to learn from Carroll, teacher of Darrieussecq, Deleuze, and Derrida, it is that there is no such thing as nothing, for something always remains. Take the hedgehog from a story or from the world, what remains? Remains the hedgehog, as the name for a missing hedgehog, or for the length of the story or of the world itself, that is, as the distance that would have to be exhaustively traveled before finding or losing the next hedgehog. Just as a hedgehog "may always arrive," the word "hedgehog" may always name one that is no longer there or not yet there, or one which, as in a Möbius strip, may always be walking on (what is and is not) the other side.

Epilogue: The Case of the Hermit Crab

Darrieussecq would offer her own singular illustration of the paradox of the *place sans occupant* and the *occupant sans place* (or of the discontinuity of the series) which, in Deleuze's account of the Carrollian/Stoic theory of meaning, generally conditions symbolic structures (65–66). Here is her "cas du pagure," or case of the hermit crab:

> The story about the hermit crab who grows and grows, until its shell is too small, then the other crabs, lobsters and creepy things with feet, claws and snappers are on the lookout: he'll be out soon, just has to be, he's a smothered, soft, transparent little thing, I'd have liked to see one bare [. . .] [We the Johnson daughters were] haunted by a hermit crab suffocating in its shell but refusing to come out, no way . . . [. . .] The hermit-crab knight without his helmet, lying pathetically at the bottom of the pool. Soft, defenceless and pitiful. We tried to pull them out of their shells, but they [*ça*] resisted, preferring to let themselves get torn in two rather than give up, disgusting, translucent, soft flesh . . . (*Brief Stay*, 59–61/39–40)

The *bernard-l'ermite* here manifestly clasps as tenaciously onto its borrowed shell as Ponge's more rightful mollusk. But then since there is no poem on *le pagure*, which can only appear as shadowy interloper at the end of "Le mollusque," Ponge does not dwell on what happens when the hermit crab has grown too large for its scavenged shell and must in turn abandon it for another.[1] Darrieussecq, for her part, is haunted by that moment, which in the life of a hermit crab cannot be avoided but conceptually, as intermittent vacation from place and form, can hardly bear thinking. In fact, the hermit crab, evoked in at least three of her novels, seems to be invested with a rare symbolic charge—a sort of threshold function—whenever it appears, so that it may just exceed the texts' explicit "knowledge."[2]

So what does the hermit crab do when it has overgrown its shell? Filmmaker Jean Painlevé in a short 1930 documentary on the species "experimental[ly]" called this chapter "Housing Crisis" and presents us with hermit crabs fighting over available shells,[3] and, even once a new shell has been secured, acting all the more wary of their lurking, shell-less, defense-less brethren. In another instance we see "A Hermit Crab in a Tight Spot," a crab grown too large for its shell and trying another, which proves to be too heavy to haul. "Return to reason and to the small shell." Eventually it finds a shell of the right size and weight and slips in, "saluting in its own way" (with a slap of its tail). Darrieussecq presents an almost identical scenario in *Le pays*, wedged in perfect non sequitur fashion within a stream of consciousness:

> The hermit crab out of its shell, naked, was looking for a new abode. The first shell was so large that its back legs could not get a grip in it, and the front legs couldn't drag it. The second shell was so small that none of its legs, front or rear, could fit in it. The third shell was perfectly sized for the front and back legs, and the hermit crab slid inside happily. (*Le pays*, 183; my translation)

Four years earlier, this Tale of the Three Shells had seen a more elaborate telling in *A Brief Stay with the Living*, in fact therein lie the roots of the imperfect tense of the scene in *Le pays*—for it is a story remembered from childhood in *Brief Stay*, told often by the three sisters' mother, and what is more (if one reads carefully!—the clues are scattered wide) the favorite story of Jeanne, whose death in Buenos Aires (itself split open by the Buenos Aires / Paris time difference) frames the novel (52/33):

> When we were little, the hermit crab out of his shell looking for a new one. The first shell (a font as resonant as a

> church) was as heavy as a stone and so huge that its rear legs couldn't get a purchase on it, nor its front legs drag it across the sand. The second one (a winkle in which nothing could be heard) was so narrow that, once inside, it couldn't move its feelers and its feet, a real corset. The third one (a lovely shine, as spotted as a sea leopard) was the right side for both its front and its back feet. Inside, you hear the sea . . .
>
> There were wanderings between these three shells, whose names varied according to Mum's conchological vocabulary . . . The struggle with the crab, the storm, man overboard, the equinoctial tide and the little naked foot . . . Which belonged, according to the maternal mood, to Jeanne, to Anne and later to Nore . . . Nonore . . . Ronron . . . Momo . . . And her unbearable tickles and her fits of euphoria as hard to put up with as her fits of rage, or her silence . . . (214/155)

Here too, as in *Le pays*, the hermit crab story arrives as if unintended, unauthored, an orphan tale rising from some subterranean place; it is an involuntary memory as Anne of the roving consciousness drinks herself to a stupor in a bar. Animal subplots consistently appear to well up from somewhere else in Darrieussecq's oeuvre, though this exogeny takes different forms: most often it is a television documentary sequence (or something gleaned from another educational or informational source) that is remembered or which through some other mediation infiltrates the prose, often not as content alone (the behavior of elephants in mourning, the particularity of giraffe births, the symbiotic arrangement between hippopotamuses and ibises, etc.) but also as a block of text composed in a perceptibly different narrative style, verb tense, or sometimes even font. It is as if a vast mass of prose were submerged—a buried dimension, everything that is not human and that most novels wall out—and were resurfacing (in bits) from time to time. I would go so far as to say that this animal "memory," or this animal "outside" as it were, is what uniquely haunts Darrieussecq's world, pressing in at its borders and in the gaps, hallucinatory knowledge of lives in the wild swarming just beneath the skin of the text. Occasionally, from one novel to the next, a "bit" of this material reappears in slightly modified form, as if to confirm the sense of a submerged archive that the text can at any time "dip" into. This is technically the case of the hermit crab story, except that its fairy-tale- or game-like character distinguishes it from virtually all others and lends it foundational qualities: it is in truth a story about how certain first notions—about what it means to have a body, to be alive, and to die—had from the very beginning been borrowed *seamlessly* (*before* being perceiv-ed/-able as trans-species analogy or allegory) from an animal phenomenology. As children the sisters had themselves "played" the hermit crab seeking its shell (this projection accounting in turn for some of the enunciatory/point-of-view strangeness of the passage), they had intimately reanimated the "scene," filling it out with their own emotions and their own protruding feet. True, the hermit crab may not be the most common mascot among children, or an animal one generally knows a great deal about; it is rare, even on TV, to see a hermit crab ponderously trying to decide between three shells; and no doubt for the very reason that preoccupies Darrieussecq: because a hermit crab out of its shell is an extremely vulnerable thing. Its exposure can mean its death. Hence its fast clinging to its shell when under pressure—a fact corroborated in Pongian tones by Painlevé: "No getting a hermit crab out of its shell without tearing it [the shell] apart, given the way it rolls itself up." Painlevé's signature microcinematography finds in "le Bernard" (as he keeps calling it) its worthy subject, one might say, for even as such technology exploits the fantasy of seeing what (because too small or submerged too deep) had thus far eluded human vision, the hermit crab with its leery, tenacious hedgehog-like behavior (coiled up and fastened fast to "its" shell) by definition strives not to be seen. In fact, Painlevé so much wants to see with what "manner and force" (to use Ponge's terms) the creature clings to the inside of the shell that at one point he effects a cross section of the shell, which he presents in characteristic elision of the slicer-scholar: "The shell sectioned longitudinally offers several openings. The Bernard enters and thinks itself safe. One can see how its body rolls up. If one pulls the Bernard, one only makes it press its body harder against the shell." Alas, this is not where the interventions end, as just moments earlier, in support of the theory that the hermit crab is guided principally by the tactile sense, we are shown a specimen "whose eyes have been removed." As an early animal documentary and because it appears riveted to this very particular drama of hermit crab life—the equation (which turns into a paradox only once a camera or an eye enters the scene) of aliveness with successful coiled-up-ness and retreat from view—Painlevé's short film anticipates Darrieussecq (and accompanies Ponge—who was writing about his hermit crabs at exactly the same time) quaintly and richly. Still, its occasional aquarium trick limits its capacity as poetic (not to speak of scientific) truth about "le cas du pagure." In a particularly astonishing moment at the end, hermit crabs seem to be playing football (the pitch is set up neatly and apparently "the umpire's decision is non-negotiable"). They play with a closed spherical ball, which we see them turn over and over again, manifestly perplexed, as the voice-over intones (it is the last line of the film): "This ball represents for them a shell without an opening, a baffling matter, of course . . ."

Current-day research on the question of what a hermit crab does between shells can seem in some ways no less improbable (or deserving of a musical score) than Painlevé's scenarios.[4] If we are to believe recent studies, shell redistribution among this species is performed collectively, following the principle of a *vacancy chain*:

> Several hermit crab species, both terrestrial and marine, use vacancy chains to find new shells. When an individual crab finds a new empty shell it will leave its own shell and inspect the vacant shell for size. If the shell is found to be too large, the crab goes back to its own shell and then waits by the vacant shell for anything up to 8 hours. As new crabs arrive they also inspect the shell and, if it is too big, wait with the others, forming a group of up to 20 individuals, holding onto each other in a line from the largest to the smallest crab. As soon as a crab arrives that is the right size for the vacant shell and claims it, leaving its old shell vacant, then all the crabs in the queue swiftly exchange shells in sequence, each one moving up to the next size. Hermit crabs often "gang up" on one of their species with what they perceive to be a better shell, and pry its shell away from it before competing for it until one takes it over.[5]

I quote here in fact the Wikipedia entry, where a hyperlink to "vacancy chain" leads to a description, in the language of labor and sociology, of a dynamic structure for distribution of resources: "In a vacancy chain, a new resource unit that arrives into a population is taken by the first individual in line, who then leaves his/her old unit behind, this old unit is taken by a second individual, leaving his/her old unit behind, and so forth."[6] A few lines later the page offers examples of what a vacancy chain would mean in concrete social terms:

> Vacancy chains are started when an initial vacancy enters a population, such as when a new house is built, a new car

> is manufactured, or a new job is created. It can also begin when an existing unit is vacated by someone leaving the system under consideration, such as an employee retiring, or a home owner goes to a nursing home. Eventually a chain will come to an end, usually with a new entrant into the system or when the last unit in a chain is abandoned, merged, or destroyed. This can involve a new employee recruit or a housing unit on market for the first time, or when a house in the chain is torn down, left empty, or the duties of a vacant job are distributed among other employees. A vacancy chain is simply the sequence of moves that a vacancy makes from initial entry into a system to final termination.

The vacancy chain, in other words, is about how a system of circulation processes its outermost terms—newness and obsolescence, entries and exits, births and deaths. Behind the dry technical term is in fact a drama that every structure articulating two discontinuous and mobile series of properties/positions and occupants must reckon with, at those points where it joins the gestational and mortal reality of the world—its points of making and unmaking. Darrieussecq's fascination with the hermit crab forced to leave its shell, an occupant glimpsed in the brief placelessness between places, if not in a final loss of place, is thus in line with a thinking about vulnerability and the idea/body threshold that underpins all her fiction. In this matter too *My Phantom Husband* carried an anticipatory imprint of what was to follow, for it is in this novel that, as the narrator reels from the disappearance of her husband and yields with emotion to the embrace of her friend Jacqueline, she first resorts to a hermit crab–inspired "image of ourselves": "If we consider physical love to break through some of these dams [skin, muscles, membranes . . .] until it succeeds [. . .] in coaxing the hermit crab out of its shell a tiny bit, to go with its little elytra or whatever they're called, feeling its way forward toward the tip of the antennae of the beloved hermit crab across the way, then something comparable happens when a friend [. . .] takes you in her arms" (80–81/71). If the Tale of the Three Shells three years later in *A Brief Stay with the Living* fills out in more detail the components and essential drama of hermit crab survival (which would then loom again briefly in *Le pays*), it more gravely links the species with a scene or a logic (compared in passing to that of Goldilocks and the three bears; we may also think of the glass slipper tried on in *Cinderella* by the three sisters) involving fewer spots to fill than contenders to fill them, thus giving its cruelest explanation for the death of the protagonist's young brother (214–15/155), even while foreshadowing that of the sister. But the soft pink transparency of the exposed crab, that "defenceless and pitiful" flesh," is in its furthest threshold function an intolerable approximation of what happens to life as it is forced out of representation: "the inside of [the] brain colonized by hermit crabs, thoughts snapping their tiny pincers and, more stubborn than ever, panicking (so they say) at the moment of death" (*Bref séjour chez les vivants*, 65/43; translation modified). The direction of the severance here is in fact undecidable: it is as much life evicted from representation as it is representation that is forced to quit life. Perhaps this is why Ponge had insisted in "Le mollusque" on the chiasmic reversibility of the relation ("The slightest cell in the human body clings just as tightly to language—*and vice-versa*"), each of the terms having no reality without the other. But to account for all this—the pact of life and representation, body and thinking, things and words—by way of the vacancy chain is to consider that the two "series" can be articulated (or "engaged," in the mechanistic sense) together dynamically only because there is a two-sided vacancy (a missing place on the one hand, a missing occupant on the other) that continually exacts its work at either end of the chain, and that this vacancy stands, on the one hand, for all that in life exceeds representation, and on the other, for all that in representation exceeds life. An odd two-faced "paradoxical element" which the system can hardly tolerate but which in fact founds it as its working principle. I should think that this bifid vacancy quite precisely accounts for the ghost/animal pair in Darrieussecq. Both gather on the edges of these stories, half-glimpsed or half-realized forms, below or beyond whole representation, continual reminders of what is yet nameless and of which names name nothing, and if the two are sometimes blurred into indistinction (or correspondence), these are perhaps merely two ways (viewed in inseparable alternation, as in a Möbius strip: catless grin and grinless cat) of saying the same thing, that the *joint* between the two spheres is a place of continuous production of excesses and remainders and missings—a secretly devastating asymmetry cleaving shells away from crabs: "My mother believed in the inadequacy of language. There was on one side the realm of words, on the other the realm of things. Their correspondence was impossible. Since words were not things, they were necessarily disappointing and inappropriate. At their joint, too much meaning leaked/escaped [*fuyait*]" (*Le pays*, 239).

FOR THE BITS OF HEDGEHOG WERE BITS OF HERMIT CRAB, YOU SEE

Perhaps we should not be surprised that the bits of hedgehog vanish when examined too closely in *Breathing Underwater* (nor that the hedgehog has largely disappeared from my own meditations here). Darrieussecq presents a case, in sum, for a hermit crab theory of what fiction is, and more essentially of what conscious life is, its most difficult-to-bear proposition being that a shell is not occupied by the occupant one thinks—or, to formulate it as the paradox it is: the shell is not occupied by who/what the occupant might think they are. In *A Brief Stay with the Living* which, as I have said, attempts the furthest putting-to-test of a certain conviction regarding the power of narration as metamorphosis and self-expropriation, Anne the telepath makes sense of her parasitic mission—inhabiting a succession of "cranial boxes"—via a fleeting analogy with the hermit crab: "to slip into the shell of the world like a hermit crab or, rather, given that [this] space isn't empty, to slip over from one consciousness to another, like an egret ridding a hippopotamus of its parasites, and thus, in hopping along with them, helping them in their work" (30/17; translation modified). The hasty revising of the hermit crab analogy here seems a red herring; it too easily assures us of the existence, "before" any interloping occurs, of a legitimate order of correspondence between places and occupants, and that the hermit crab can only enter a shell once it is empty. True, there are several empty shells scattered through and even structuring these novels, and they are more often than not linked to death. We may remember most vividly the "empty shell" of the dead child in *Tom Is Dead* (an image whose species rigor is then immediately compromised: "A slough like animals leave behind, that you find curled up on a path or clinging to trees, useless, translucid, a little disgusting" [74/50]) and the more complicated, ghoulish way that marine death turns the corpse of the child brother in *A Brief Stay* into both shell and mollusk-flesh of itself: "He smelt of the sea, one side of his head was a huge mollusc, his own flesh transformed by the sea into a shell of himself . . . / An incrusted red tumour, black stripes, exactly like the limpets which you know have soft pink skins beneath the shells, clinging on to the rock, burnt in the sun . . ." (161/115). It is true also that many motifs conspire to suggest that this oeuvre's deepest imaginational impulse follows two obscurely connected (and usually censored) pathways: the ability to think one's way into animal livingness is possible and even irrepressible in the same way that the possible/unavoidable sliding into the vacated consciousness of a corpse is: "If they transplant dead people's eyes, what do we then see, what ghosts, what waking dreams?" (*Brief Stay*, 40/24). And that this may have to do with the fact that a certain sort of afterlife of the human—as what happens after death to the place (our skulls, our flesh) that our consciousness once filled—is imagined most *realistically* in fact in the terms of the sort of processes—incrustation, parasitism, molting, scavenging, necrophilic growths—that have long been understood as productive facts about animal lives or the scientific/proverbial "cycle of life," but less easily admitted as facts coproducing the human real. Still, it seems to me that such macabre *lignes de fuite* only exploit what is a more vital poetico-ontological principle embedded in all these works, and most explicitly thematized in *A Brief Stay with the Living*, which is the disquiet intrinsic to the occupation of one's place, the murky fact that this uncontested occupation may not entirely resolve a larger or older question of "who" or "what" it is that sees and thinks and speaks in and from one's place. In *Tom Is Dead*, it is suggested that the dead may be thinking and speaking through those who mourn them (171/123). In *Brief Stay*, a recurrent preoccupation with what one might see on the brink of death culminates in what is both a troubling ontological question and what one might call an inescapable narratological conundrum: "And if your entire life does pass before your eyes, what do you see? An objective, panoramic overview? Or a rewind of everything you've seen? Who does the choosing? Who's the narrator?" (238/173). I should add that pregnancy as a theme in some of these works (*Le pays*, *Le bébé*, more negatively *Naissance des fantômes* through the theme of miscarriages) supplies in turn a structuring metaphor for how one can carry something that is other than oneself, where it is unclear where one ends and the other begins: "A continuity you can follow like a Möbius strip. Down a slide. She exists constantly, without a break or gaps. And if a child was growing inside her and multiplying, she would be nursing a being outside her straight from the start [*un être dès l'origine hors d'elle*] . . ." (*Brief Stay*, 49/31).

And what if the mollusk were a myth? Darrieussecq's most provocative claim is not the license to be the hermit crab to others' mollusks but rather that we are all hermit crabs. Suit (or fit) ourselves as we might, our relationship to what we see, think, speak, write, is infected with a lingering bit of outside(r)ness or besideness (or anteriority or posterity) to self, a lag, a disquiet that won't go away, the sense that there was or is or could be/have been perhaps someone or something else where one stands. Perhaps another way to say that there is a sense of borrowedness to it all, a title of ownership claimable only on the condition of suspending deeper scrutiny of what "own" means. Certain pages of Robert Harvey's *Witnessness* offer as searing a theorization as one is likely ever to find of this sort of conception of self and irreducible other. Such is the tightening field in which all the motifs here have been circling that I am not altogether surprised to find Harvey's account too resorting early on to images of the hermit crab (11, 31), a figure not of imposter or interloper but of "a consciousness that decided one day to call itself 'I' and dwell in my head" (46)—the shortest and uncanniest definition of the *I* (or, shall I say, of the *j/e*) since Benveniste. Through a grammar and a scene intimately dictated by Beckett's late text *Worstward Ho*, Harvey assembles a grave model of subject responsibility predicated on what is most paradoxical about the event: that one is not present at it, that it is precisely what happens to one in one's absence: "When the event befalls you, your wits fail you. [. . .] But when things calm down, [. . .] you work with the martyr within you, from now on perceiving the world through those jaded, haggard eyes" (49). This may be a description of one's relationship to one's birth or one's early childhood as events at which one was absent, which one has "forgotten before forgetting exists"; or it can be an ethics of how to live and bear witness to the trauma or destruction that has affected another who may or may not have been oneself. Beckett's insight (but also Dante's and Primo Levi's), in Harvey's devastating reading, is that of "a vicariousness intrinsic to one's consciousness" (50), so that thinking is a "feel[ing] one's way around" (90) "the skull of another, occupied by me" (26). We could say that the hermit crab emerges by force of such metaphorics, produced irrepressibly by (and for) the empty shell the skull comes to resemble and which it must share (as metaphoric vehicle) with the corpse. Interesting to find Harvey recalling, here, Primo Levi's initial speculation, in "poignant blind[ness] to the obvious connection of Muslim to Jew," that *Musselman* meant shell-man or shell of a man (68). Harvey notes the fact twice—such is the metaphoric force, indeed, exerted by empty shells. The first time he follows it with a concession: "As absurd as that origin is, however, there is some poignant truth-value in the image of entering another as if he were hollow" (32)—and for Harvey this "as if" describes the operation of witnessness, a reimagining of life against the inescapable odds of death, and the self on the model of the (dead, forever dying) other. It is also a theory of the imagination, which must continually supplement what in the event happened to another who was excessively present at it (that is, did not survive it)—or what in the event did not fully take place because one was insufficiently present at it (that is, blind to it or not in full presence of mind) because it was intolerable. In the end the two amount to the same, and we are faced with the gravest version of the Möbius-strip duo of *occupant sans place* and the *place sans occupant*, an arithmetic, conceptual, cruel riddle that can be resolved only (and is resolved continually) in flesh and in time, and in "poignant truth-value," here signified, it is only right, by a nervous hermit crab: "Activating the -ness of witness requires the unmitigated re-affirmation that nothing escapes the 'sights' of the skull, the full mobilization of the skull's skills when it is full of life, even if blindness affects the hermit crab occupying the dwelling" (11).

The gravity of Harvey's material (Purgatory, the concentration camps, trauma theory) is only apparently at thematic or tonal odds with Darrieussecq. In fact, one finds in *Rapport de police*, the extraordinary work that charges of plagiarism seemed to force out of her in 2010, a crystalline theory of subjecthood assimilating Lacanian psychoanalysis, poststructuralist theory, and certain somber lessons of literary-political history, wherein the slightest "bits" of her fiction are raised to their potentially most serious theoretical (metafictional) coherence and stakes. The book happens to offer a singularly powerful and refined conceptualization of literary imagination as a freedom and as an ethics; had this not been so one might be saddened to see Darrieussecq having to slough off the multiple, experimental, masked voices of fiction for the earnest, "serious," naked language of scholarship and critical commentary—indeed, not unlike a hermit crab forced to leave its shell.[7] In truth it is *Rapport de police* which gives its deepest coherence and "poignant truth-value" to the hermit crab motif, and takes it even further—through a supplementary conceptual fold—than where common naturalist faith in a metaphor might lead. "What thinks, in our cranial boxes?," Darrieussecq writes, "What thinks, at mouth-level, perched between my two ears, between my beating temples, what thinks when I think that I think?" (238/239). Where by now even you may be prepared to find the hermit crab—perched, watchful, its antennae groping—is an "emptiness that thinks," an essential nothingness prior to identity for which Darrieussecq finds names in the works of many writers and thinkers, from Lacan to Mandelstam:

> At the heart of writing there is an empty place [*axe*], where the world gives way [*s'engouffre*]. To find the path toward

> this absence that gives access to worlds: this is how I conceive of the process of writing. There is much to be known in the emptiness that is neither nothingness nor death. In that place, there is no one. Naming/proclaiming oneself in/at the place of this emptiness [*Se nommer à la place de ce vide*] is ridiculous. Rather, one can accept its dizziness, without names, without prayers, without glory [*sacre*]. And turn oneself into a chamber of echos and metamorphoses. (378)

We have arrived at the (empty) heart of the matter, and the reason why even mollusks are only hermit crabs with shells—because not even a mollusk ever perfectly replaces or erases that originary void, the shell's true first occupant (yet who was never there in the first place, only [emerging retrospectively and theoretically] in its superseding). *To name oneself in that place is ridiculous* . . . and yet that is perhaps the only sort of naming there is.

It is not a problem as much as it is a curious solution: at an undetermined place, shall we say, of the reading of the hermit crab—as a rigorous, ethical figure for consciousness and for the "I"—it may imperceptibly twist like a Möbius strip to lead us to what is in fact a "béance" or gap(ing) (238) that precedes and survives the I—but is given so seamlessly the name and properties of the hermit crab as to be indistinguishable from it (as Darrieussecq keeps making clear in *Brief Stay with the Living*, it is very very hard to think of nothing). Of course, this means that "nothing" can never be named completely nor once and for all, for it is precisely its property to continually subtract itself from what is thought and named, so that naming it "hermit crab" may be said to have only the rueful consequence of producing more hermit crabs. Nonetheless, such a conjuring of hermit crabs is the closest one gets to thinking nothing,[8] and that—nothing—is a serious question, ultimately the most serious question, the most difficult to think, as Darrieussecq knows, for it risks undoing the very thinker:

> I knew: the forest, the continents, the sea, could've done without humans. The air would've been breathed only by animal gills and lungs, the ground trodden only by paws, the sea would've been traversed only by flippers, the sky by feathers. Or nothing. An empty planet. Nothing to breathe it. Nothing to roam over it. Thought about by nobody. Whirling alone, absurd, absurd anyway. (*Tom Is Dead*, 213/154–55)

It is Jean Baudrillard in *Impossible Exchange* who to my mind best succeeds in thinking "nothing" in its scandal and its paradox, as what ruins every economy precisely because it forms the first truth about everything—that is, the fact that even as within our inhabitable reality everything is exchangeable, reality itself can be exchanged only for nothing, given that the only equivalent of (or alternative to) the world, life, consciousness, is, simply, nothing. This is impossible exchange, a radical uncertainty that haunts the reality principle, and whose result is that "behind the exchange of Something, we have, then, always, the exchange of the Nothing,"[9] a place where the production of meaning and value must implode, for it reaches its outside. This nothing is both prehistoric—in the sense of there actually being a vacuum (pre–Big Bang, prehuman, or prelanguage) that frames (precedes and perhaps follows) reality—*and* (it is an inextricable alternative, a sort of and/or, a Möbius strip) what is produced (as a prehistory *effect*) *by* the fact of *something*. Whence its ambiguous, doubly negative or always-disappearing quality: "The Nothing does not cease to exist as soon as there is something. The Nothing continues (not) to exist [*continue de (ne pas) exister*] just beneath the surface of things" (17/8). According to Baudrillard, human economies and systems share as their ultimate drive the hunt to exterminate this Nothing—which he also calls the Inhuman (26/16)—but it is indelible, like the very shadow of the real. In fact it is a logical postulate that cannot be done away with, only pushed further back into a receding theoretical time-space, for if we concede, as we must, that reality starts/started somewhere, at some place and time, then we must by the same move grant that there was/is a place and time (words failing here, for the nothing names something preexisting even space and time) where there was/is nothing, and the shadow is also the absence of a shadow, for there is nothing for reality to cast its shadow *on*. Baudrillard thus speaks of the suddenness of the world's emergence, like language or the cosmos, following the sorts of paradoxes theorized by Gosse and Russell: "This emergence out of the void, *this non-anteriority of things to themselves* continue[s] to affect the event of the world at the very heart of its historical unfolding" (20/10; my emphasis).

The last short section of *Impossible Exchange*, titled "Shadowing the World," offers an arresting, riddle-like summary of what it means to be human, that is to say, to stand in an essential relation with such nothingness: "The world lacks nothing before being thought, but, thereafter, it can be explained only on that basis. It is something like that 'nothing' which theory simultaneously reveals and supplants, an absence that it both makes visible and masks. One may say also that the world indeed lacks 'nothing' [*le monde manque effectivement de "rien"*], and that thought is the shadow cast by that Nothing on the surface of the real world" (187/150).

In the course of writing this book I came to think of animals as marking gaps, thresholds, tricks, twists, vanishing points that stories or thought might usually cover up or leave unthought, not *because* animals stood there but, I like to think, *with the consequence that* animals appeared there. Placeholders for bits of thought and life difficult to think, they were perhaps figures for our relationship with nothing, and, by that impossible measure, with everything.

Notes

PROLOGUE

1. Roland Barthes, *The Rustle of Language*, trans. Richard Howard (New York: Hill and Wang, 1986), 148.

2. The phrase comes from Jean de La Fontaine's fable "Le loup, la chèvre et le chevreau" [The wolf, the goat and the kid], where the wolf poses as the kid goat's mother and knocks at the door. Instead of falling into the trap, the kid asks the wolf first to show "patte blanche," i.e., a white paw, which the wolf cannot. The phrase has come to be synonymous with showing one's credentials, proving one's identity or one's good intentions.

3. Roland Barthes, *Critical Essays*, trans. Richard Howard (Evanston, Ill.: Northwestern University Press, 1972), 160.

4. Friedrich Nietzsche, "On Truth and Lying in an Extra-Moral Sense," in *The Birth of Tragedy and Other Writings*, ed. Raymond Geuss and Ronald Speirs, trans. Ronald Speirs (Cambridge: Cambridge University Press, 1999), 147.

5. Nicole Shukin, *Animal Capital: Rendering Life in Biopolitical Times* (Minneapolis: University of Minnesota Press, 2009). See chapter 1, note 10.

6. Tiphaine Samoyault, "Littéralité des rats," in *La question animale: Entre science, littérature et philosophie*, ed. Georges Chapoutier, Catherine Coquio, Lucie Campos, and Georges Engélibert (Rennes: Presses Universitaires de Rennes, 2011), 231 (my translations throughout).

7. To cite an important essay by Cary Wolfe, "Flesh and Finitude: Thinking Animals in (Post)Humanist Philosophy," *SubStance* 37 (2008): 8–36.

8. Cary Wolfe, *What Is Posthumanism?* (Minneapolis: University of Minnesota Press, 2010), 119. See also his essays "Exposures," in Stanley Cavell et al., eds. *Philosophy and Animal Life* (New York: Columbia University Press, 2008), 1–41; and "In the Shadow of Wittgenstein's Lion: Language, Ethics and the

Question of the Animal," in Cary Wolfe, ed. *Zoontologies: The Question of the Animal* (Minneapolis: University of Minnesota Press, 2003); 1–57. Wolfe is to my mind the commentator who makes the most rigorous and elucidating case for the *necessity* of deconstructive thought for any serious ethical treatment of the question of the animal.

9. See Jean-Christophe Bailly, *Le parti pris des animaux* (Paris: Christian Bourgeois, 2013).

10. Gérard Farasse, *Déplier Ponge: Entretien de Jacques Derrida avec Gérard Farasse* (Villeneuve d'Ascq: Presses Universitaires du Septentrion, 2005), 75; my translation.

11. In *Thinking Animals: Why Animal Studies Now?* Kari Weil maintains that "animal studies is coming of age in conjunction with theory's ethical turn," notably in response to the inability of poststructuralist theories "to deal with the concerns of live animals" (New York: Columbia University Press, 2012), 16.

CHAPTER 1

1. Patrick Modiano, *Des inconnues* (Paris: Gallimard, 1999), 117. This text has yet to appear in English. All translations that follow are my own.

2. The Prize was awarded to Modiano "for the art of memory with which he has evoked the most ungraspable human destinies and uncovered the life-world of the occupation." See NobelPrize.org, accessed August 18, 2019, https://www.nobelprize.org/prizes/literature/2014/summary/.

3. Francis Bacon, *The Brutality of Fact: Interviews with Francis Bacon*, ed. David Sylvester (Oxford: Alden, 1975), 23.

4. And from literary memory, where they so regularly featured alongside men in war narratives. Here we might think of Claude Simon's work, most notably *La route des Flandres* (Paris: Minuit, 1982) / *The Flanders Road*, trans. Richard Howard (New York: George Braziller, 1961), which features a haunting subtext involving horses, "the long line of horses that had apparently been walking forever extended interminably [. . .] those shadows advancing since the night of time" (35/36–37); see also the reference to "the sound, the monotonous and multiple hammering of the hoofs on the road increasing (hundreds, thousands of hoofs now)" (28/29), "animal and armor united, combined" (29/30), the "interminable horse ride [*chevauchée*]" (39/41, translation modified), and the "ghostly cavalcade" (125/133). Another obvious intertext here is Louis-Ferdinand Céline's *Voyage au bout de la nuit* (Paris: Gallimard, 1962) / *Journey to the End of the Night*, trans. Ralph Manheim (New York: New Directions, 2006), featuring allusions both to warhorses and, as in Simon's novel, to horse racing as the war's prehistory: "But up ahead of us there was nothing we could be sure of but the echo that came and went, the echo of our horses' hoof beats, a horrendous sound you wanted so bad not to hear that it stopped your breath. Those horses seemed to be trotting to high heaven, to be calling everybody on earth to come and massacre us" (29/20). Modiano's story would seem to complete this fatal march, whereby horses are led beyond the frame of the story. On the historic and poetic end of horses, see Tiphaine Samoyault's essay "Achever le cheval" (http://www.crlc.paris-sorbonne.fr/colsem/pdf/Tiphaine-Samoyault-Achever_cheval.pdf).

5. Jean-Louis Aragon, "Le cheval, un patrimoine," *Le Monde*, May 13, 2010; my translation here and below.

6. Étienne Souriau, "L'univers filmique et l'art animalier," *Revue internationale de filmologie* 7, no. 25 (January–March 1956): 51–62; my translation. I shall return to why the coincidence of the development of cinema and the disappearance of horses is particularly noteworthy.

7. John Berger, "Why Look at Animals?," in *On Looking* (New York: Pantheon, 1980), 12.

8. Akira Mizuta Lippit, *Electric Animal: Toward a Rhetoric of Wildlife* (Minneapolis: University of Minnesota Press, 2000), 187.

9. Rebecca Solnit, *Motion Studies: Time, Space and Eadweard Muybridge* (London: Bloomsbury, 2004), 22–24.

10. For Raymond Bellour (see more below), Lippit considers the animal "always already dead" (436). For Nicole Shukin, Lippit's "brilliant recapitulation of discourses of the 'undying' animal in Western philosophical, psychoanalytic, and technological discourses" is at the cost of "idealistically speculating in the animal as a rhetorical currency transcending its material body" (41). As long as animals are treated as specters, Shukin cautions, they are "never fully subject to histories of violence and exploitation" (37). Her *Animal Capital* is to date the most powerful complement and counterpoint to *Electric Animal* as well as to Bellour's study, arguing as it does (by means of a rigorous material-cultural history of the abattoir and of gelatin) for the historical contingency of automobility and cinema on mass animal slaughter. Shukin's analysis faces us with the astounding extent to which technological and aesthetic modernity, even as it speculated in animals' spectrality, was from the beginning critically implicated in a mass "rendering" of animal flesh—that is to say, their industrial death and disassembly. (See chapter 2, "Automobility: The Animal Capital of Cars, Films, and Abattoirs," 87–130).

11. Raymond Bellour, *Le corps du cinéma: Hypnoses, émotions, animalités* (Paris: POL, 2009), 34; translations are my own.

12. Eadweard Muybridge, *Animals in Motion*, ed. Lewis S. Brown (New York: Dover, 1957), 13.

13. And these do not seem to reflect the shortest exposures, which at Palo Alto reached "the one six-thousandth part of a second," as Muybridge specifies in the introduction to *Animals in Motion* (23).

14. The unnamed artist may have been Jean-Louis-Ernest Meissonier. This prominent academic painter, who specialized in battlefields, historical scenes, and horses, seems to have been driven to despair by the results of the Stanford-Muybridge experiments: "After thirty years of absorbing and concentrated study, I find I have been wrong. Never again shall I touch a brush!" (quoted in Solnit, *Motion Studies*, 197).

15. Roland Barthes, *Camera Lucida*, trans. Richard Howard (New York: Hill and Wang, 1981), 5–6.

16. Henri Michaux, *Passages (1937–1950)* (Paris: Gallimard, 1950), 54–55; my translation.

17. A logic no doubt taken to its furthest point by Werner Herzog's film *Grizzly Man* (2005).

18. I transcribe these terms from the table of contents.

19. Excerpted here from the back cover of Jean-Philippe Toussaint, *La vérité sur Marie* (Paris: Minuit, 2009); my translation.

20. Toussaint, *La vérité sur Marie*, 77 / *The Truth about Marie*, trans. Matthew B. Smith (Champaign, Ill.: Dalkey Archive, 2011), 61. Here and throughout, whenever possible, quotations from primary texts are followed by two page numbers. The first refers to the original French text, and the second to the English translation (when there is one).

21. Presumably historians with a better understanding of horse breeding and racing concerns—and of the horse's place (technological and symbolic) in the history of an unprecedented shift in speed and scale at the end of the nineteenth century—would not find this connection as mysterious as I do. Solnit, for instance, writes that "understanding the gaits of a horse in a mechanical way enhanced the possibility of tinkering with it, through breeding, training, and other forms of management. For Stanford, the experiment would allow him to further shift the essence of the horse from the mysteries of nature to the manageable mechanics of industrialism" (*Motion Studies*, 183). Later she writes of the divergent legacies of Muybridge's motion studies: "[Stanford] expected the pictures to be useful in breeding and training horses, in managing them yet more precisely for yet faster results. Almost the first use of watches that recorded fractions of seconds was horse racing, and though racing was a sport, not an industry, it came to have many affinities with the development of industrial work in the late nineteenth century [e.g. Taylorism]" (211).

22. Jean-Louis Aragon of *Le Monde* notes that horses' nerves are much harder than bovines', so that a horse slaughtered for meat must be systematically denerved ("Le cheval, un patrimoine"). An unseemly detail to recall here, but it serves to account for the specificity of this body in the text (its "nervosité" denoting its *resistance* within a human narrative), and helps us not lose sight of the troubling intersections of representations at which an animal must stand.

23. Jorge Luis Borges, *Collected Fictions*, trans. Andrew Hurley (New York: Penguin, 1998), 242–49.

24. André Bazin, "Ontology of the Photographic Image," in *What Is Cinema?*, vol. 1, trans. Hugh Gray (Berkeley: University of California Press, 1971), 9.

25. It memorably becomes Zidane's paradox in Toussaint's *La mélancolie de Zidane* [The melancholy of Zidane] (Paris: Minuit, 2006).

26. Worth pursuing here are the associations, significant or fleeting, suggested in contemporary literature and film between animals and certain vehicles, whether, like in *The Truth about Marie*, to portray a mighty animal inside a vehicle navigating a milieu utterly unnatural to it—Yann Martel's *Life of Pi* (2001) does something analogous by placing a Bengal tiger in a boat adrift at sea—or to feature an animal *galloping parallel* to a motorized vehicle: Claire Denis favors such "subliminal" scenes, both in *35 Rhums* (2009), where the train driver protagonist imagines for an instant his daughter on a black horse moving in the same direction as his suburban train, and in *White Material* (2010), where, before Maria's son jumps off a truck to madness, a dog is seen fleetingly running in the forest parallel to said truck. A similar scene figures in Jacques Audiard's *Un prophète* [A prophet] (2009), where the only instance of prophesy, as it were, is preceded by the flash sighting of a small herd of deer running on the road in front of a car (and, like a caption in a dream, the pres-

ence of a road sign with an icon warning of deer). Jean-Christophe Bailly opens his beautiful book *Le versant animal* (Paris: Bayard, 2007) with a scene very much like the one in *A Prophet*, but set at night. The vision of the back of a deer running on the road, illuminated by the car's headlights, allows Bailly to build his ensuing reflection on a chance intersection of his and the animal's nights. A short film in Iranian director Narzieh Meshkini's triptych *The Day I Became a Woman* (2000) includes incredible footage of men on horses trying to catch up with a group of women on bicycles. Such scenes are effective in capturing animal movement as phantasmatically, phantomatically written over by, and folded into the interstices of, enhanced human locomotion.

27. I claim improbable support for this configuration from a chapter titled "The Intertwining—the Chiasm" in Maurice Merleau-Ponty's *The Visible and the Invisible*, where an author's insertion (presented as a footnote by the editor) reads: "One can say that we perceive the things themselves, that we are the world that thinks itself—or that the world is at the heart of our flesh. In any case, once a body-world relationship is recognized, there is a ramification of my body and a ramification of the world." *Le visible et l'invisible*, ed. Claude Lefort (Paris: Gallimard, 1964), 177 / *The Visible and the Invisible*, trans. Alphonso Lingis (Evanston, Ill.: Northwestern University Press, 1968), 136.

28. Jean-Philippe Toussaint, "Zidane's Melancholy," trans. Timothy Bewes and Thangam Ravindranathan, in *Best European Fiction 2010*, ed. Aleksandar Hemon (Champaign, Ill.: Dalkey Archive, 2010), 35. I should note that the vomiting scene is discussed at some length by Toussaint and Pierre Bayard in a dialogue that accompanies the second edition of *The Truth About Marie*. Bayard, ever the literary sleuth, suggests that the vomiting may indicate that the narrator is autonomous (and jealous) enough to have poisoned the horse without the author's knowing; Toussaint, defending the innocence of his narrator, grants at most that it is a metaleptic moment wherein he *as author* may have done the "poisoning." He admits then that the horse vomiting in the Boeing aloft in the dark sky was the original image that had inspired the whole novel, and that its violation of earthly laws—and the realist pact—ultimately only served to further demonstrate "that we are not in a plane in flight, but in literature" ("L'auteur, le narrateur et le pur-sang. Une enquête de Pierre Bayard et Jean-Philippe Toussaint," *La vérité sur Marie* (Paris : Minuit, 2013) 207–19; my translation).

29. See on this point the beautiful introduction to Laurent Jenny's *L'expérience de la chute: De Montaigne à Michaux* (Paris: PUF, 1997).

30. Incidentally, Souriau attributes the privileged presence of animals in cinema in part to their extraordinary "cinetic" properties, that is, the specific movements they introduce into filmic "language." He evokes a documentary on deep sea life where a shark, entering the screen from the top left, moved downward and to the right in a curved and irregular movement ("en boomerang") to finally exit the screen at the top in the second third of the frame, to then comment on it as something without precedent: "And from a filmological point of view one simply had to note that such an eloquent, beautifully traced, 'musical' arabesque of movement [*arabesque cinétique*] had *never* featured on a screen before the filmic study of marine fauna" (Souriau, "L'univers filmique et l'art animalier," 58–59; my translation).

31. See, notably, Marey's chronophotographic and filmic work on birds in flight from the late 1880s and 1890s.

32. The other end of this vertical unconscious brings us to the depth of the sea, another region that has fascinated cinema from its very beginnings—witness the numerous "microscopic" films Jean Painlevé devoted to deep sea creatures: *La pieuvre* [The octopus] (1928), *Les oursins* [The sea urchins] (1929), *L'œuf d'épinoche* [The stickleback's egg] (1929), *Hyas et stenorinques* [Hyas and Stenorrynchus] (1929), *La daphnie* [The daphnia] (1929), *Les crabes* [Crabs] (1930), *Bernard-l'hermite* [The hermit crab] (1930), *L'hippocampe* [The seahorse] (1934), etc. More recently, Perrin and Cluzaud, the makers of *Winged Migration*, likewise followed the verticality downward in *Océans* (2009).

33. I do find this idea most beautifully melancholic and would myself have opted for it.

34. Julia Kristeva, *Powers of Horror: An Essay on Abjection* (New York: Columbia University Press, 1982), 3.

35. Years before his horse motion studies, Muybridge had achieved some measure of fame traveling through San Francisco, in the 1860s and into the 1870s, with a horse-drawn darkroom on wheels that could capture 360-degree panoramic views of the city. Unaccountably, he had named this contraption Helios Flying Studio. I cannot help seeing in this fact confirmation of Muybridge's long fascination with the theme of the flying horse and in its association with Helios (or the sun) a prophesy of the trembling line, seen here, between Pegasus and Icarus.

36. The coincidence carries more weight, naturally, in the French. See Franz Kafka, *La métamorphose*, trans. Marthe Robert, in *Oeuvres complètes* (Paris: Cercle du Livre Précieux, 1963), 65.

37. Marina Warner, *Fantastic Metamorphoses, Other Worlds: Ways of Telling the Self* (Oxford: Oxford University Press, 2002), 115.

CHAPTER 2

1. Éric Chevillard, *Sans l'orang-outan* (Paris: Minuit, 2007), 31 for the preceding quote. All translations from this text are my own.

2. "Remarkable dysfunctionings, the chain of links is severed, the bucket no longer arrives at the fire, the fiancée awaits her ring, we search everywhere for the sponge and the salt that are not in the kitchen yet no longer in the sea. We are going to pay a high price for our flippancy, I anticipate deep upheavals. // For instance, we observe this already, the length of the meter has changed. It is increasing. Forgotten, the formidable span of the orangutan that moved among the trees by brachiation, making sure of its next grasp before releasing the first, then throwing itself into the void hanging from the hooks of its fingers, no more, that prodigious locomotion among the heights" (Chevillard 16–17).

3. Recall the character Crab in *La nébuleuse du crabe* [The crab nebula] (1993) and *Un fantôme* [A ghost] (1995), along with the logic of *Palafox* (1990), *Du hérisson* [The hedgehog] (2002), *Démolir Nisard* [Demolishing Nisard] (2006), and *Dino Egger* (2011), all published by Minuit, Paris.

4. Marc Escola, *Lupus in fabula: Six façons d'affabuler La Fontaine* (Paris: Presses Universitaires de Vincennes, 2003), chap. 1, "Brèves histoires de loups." In this section I summarize and sometimes translate the terms of Escola's analysis.

5. See here, among other essays where Paul de Man has written on allegory, irony, and their crossed temporal operations, "Pascal's Allegory of Persuasion," in *Allegory and Representation*, ed. Stephen Greenblatt (Baltimore: Johns Hopkins University Press, 1969).

6. Susan McHugh, "Literary Animal Agents," *PMLA* 124, no. 2 (2009): 488.

7. Thomas Keenan, *Fables of Responsibility: Aberrations and Predicaments in Ethics and Politics* (Stanford, Calif.: Stanford University Press, 1997).

8. Indeed, Butler in these seminars, revisiting Adorno, Laplanche, Althusser, Lacan, Lévinas, etc., proceeds very much from and in line with Keenan's insights regarding the "fabulous" structure by which the "I" cannot tell the story of its own emergence, even if citations are rare. See Judith Butler, *Giving an Account of Oneself* (New York: Fordham University Press, 2005).

9. David Wills, *Dorsality: Thinking Back through Technology and Politics* (Minneapolis: University of Minnesota Press, 2008). The seriousness with which Wills follows Derrida in understanding the human as technological, prosthetic, from the beginning, not to say preceded by the technological (whence the "technological *turn*," which he calls "dorsality"), means that *Dorsality* finds many ways to suggest that "the ethical relation may not be a human relation at all but a relation to the nonhuman other" (54). In complicating human self-coincidence on every level—revealing all the places of long-supposed identity (body, home, friendship, country, etc.) to be affected by exile, exteriority, expropriation—Wills is powerfully pursuing Derrida's work in deconstructing a long history of deep-seated notions of *le propre de l'humain*. If this necessarily clears a crucial space for the animal, Wills seems more often than not reluctant to give it this (only) name. Perhaps because the notion of "animal" is burdened with too much, risks exerting its own properties or propriety. His interest seems to be, rather, in locations at which animality might be indistinguishable from technology. Still, even "clandestinely" present, the animal seems to be almost *breathing* in this strange and beautiful work.

10. *Depuis le temps*: This adverbial locution serves in *L'animal que donc je suis* to mark the time of the animal, its existence not just since time immemorial, so to speak, but *since time* itself, that is, ever since such a thing like time came to be (an event that, for Derrida in the first seminar, finds its fable in the book of Genesis). The leitmotiv inscribes the complicity of time itself—historical, human time—in obscuring the view of the animal, and thus makes somehow readable (*as* something unreadable, as it were) the irony by which time *was precisely*, among other things, this work of obscuring. The expropriating structure to which the phrase points (implying a time somehow outside time, thus ruining the wholeness/closure of the latter while at the same time conferring on the former the character of a shadow, a specter) is that of a series of fundamental moves in Derrida's work, indeed it describes the very movement of the famous supplement. This, by way of an attempt to explain why it is extremely difficult, in fact, to distinguish or extricate the question of the animal, in Derrida's writ-

ing, from the movement of deconstruction itself. In his later years, remarks suggesting that his work had from the beginning been, in an important sense, about the animal (see, for example, the first seminar of *The Beast and the Sovereign: La bête et le souverain I (2001–2002)*, ed. Michel Lisse, Marie-Louise Mallet, and Ginette Michaud [Paris: Galilée, 2008] / *The Beast and the Sovereign*, vol. 1, trans. Geoffrey Bennington [Chicago: University of Chicago Press, 2009]), both confirm what has since become increasingly clear in rereadings and make one wonder whether Derrida himself, analyst of unregulatable economies, could control the extent to which deconstruction in deconstructing the human along various fault lines was, one could say, *following the work of the animal* (*following*, in the exactly complicated sense of the "suis"—both *follow* and *be*, and in following, both *precede* and *succeed*—as per the polysemy so important to the seminar. *L'animal que donc je suis*, ed. Marie-Louise Mallet (Paris: Galilée, 2006) / *The Animal That Therefore I Am*, trans. David Wills (New York: Fordham University Press, 2008). Hélène Cixous says as much when she notes that "with the first trace of the thinking of the trace in *Of Grammatology*, the whole machine that tends to replace the word 'writing' in the ordinary sense by 'trace' or the word 'speech' by trace had as its final purpose that writing, speech, trace are *not the proper characteristic of the human*. There is animal trace, animals write." "Jacques Derrida: Co-Responding Voix You," in *Derrida and the Time of the Political*, ed. Pheng Cheah and Suzanne Guerlac (Durham, N.C.: Duke University Press, 2009), 43.

11. Emmanuel Levinas, *Totality and Infinity: An Essay on Exteriority*, trans. Alphonso Lingis (Pittsburgh: Duquesne University Press, 1969), 131–32.

12. See "Le bestiaire des fables de La Fontaine (1668–1694)," in *Les Animaux célèbres*, ed. Michel Pastoureau (Paris: Arléa, 2008), 204–11.

13. Emmanuel Levinas, "Nom d'un chien ou le droit naturel," in *Difficile liberté* (Paris: Albin Michel, 1976), 231–35. See chapter 3 for a detailed discussion of that essay.

14. See Derrida, *La bête et le souverain I*, 316–17 / *The Beast and the Sovereign*, 1:237; see also *L'animal que donc je suis*, 148–49 / *The Animal That Therefore I Am*, 107–9.

15. Derrida would comment at length on the open-ended infinity, through history, of this boundary, made of a continuing addition of properties that the human in ascribing to itself in the same movement deprives the animal of (see first seminar of *The Animal That Therefore I Am*); Giorgio Agamben, in showing this boundary to be a "mobile border" passing "*within*" the human, accounts with poignant simplicity for both the politics and the anxiety continually accompanying its various locatings. See Agamben, *The Open: Man and Animal*, trans. Kevin Attell (Stanford, Calif.: Stanford University Press, 2002), 15.

16. I refer here to Gilles Deleuze's *The Fold: Leibniz and the Baroque*, trans. Tom Conley (Minneapolis: University of Minnesota Press, 1993), where the differently vectored double-fold is quite clearly suggested to be a formal solution, in the Baroque imagination, to the problem of the relation between the human and the animal. Making thinkable moreover a formation wherein "justly what is expressed does not exist outside of its expressions" (35), the Baroque fold is certainly, if uncannily, inflecting a certain poststructuralist thinking of the sub-

ject (Derrida, de Man, Keenan, Wills) engaged with here. I engage more directly with Deleuze's thinking in chapters 3 and 4. In the meantime, I take liberal license in playing, in my thinking of the animal, on the etymology of duplicity, complicity, multiplicity, complicate, etc., all derived from the Latin *plicare*, "to fold"—indeed, an extraordinary page of *A Thousand Plateaus* presents creaturely life as a vast plane of "plication." Gilles Deleuze and Félix Guattari, *A Thousand Plateaus: Capitalism and Schizophrenia*, trans. Brian Massumi (Minneapolis: University of Minnesota Press, 1987), 255.

17. "The Murders in the Rue Morgue," in *The Portable Edgar Allan Poe*, ed. J. Gerald Kennedy (New York: Penguin, 2006), 239.

18. Nietzsche famously considered "the doer" to be "merely a fiction added to the deed." *The Birth of Tragedy / The Genealogy of Morals*, trans. Francis Golffing (New York: Anchor Books, 1956), 179. If Dupin here appears distinctly un-Nietzschean, my proposition with this reading is that Poe's text may itself, strictly and red herrings aside, be retaining a measure of skepticism vis-à-vis such retroactive subject effects. That this should not strike most readers, nor be architextually receivable (i.e., a genre and a whole epistemology stand to be threatened), then works as a paradox not dissimilar to that of Poe's "The Purloined Letter," as analyzed by Lacan, Derrida, Johnson, and others: too obvious, too depthless a surface, to behold. But more anon . . .

19. Manifestly because they suggest the work of nonopposable thumbs, though this is an error, we now know, in Poe's understanding of the anatomy of the orangutan, genetically even closer to the human than he thought.

20. For a reflection on the ways in which the animal is here a site of possible displacement of the figure of the Black slave, I refer to Christopher Peterson's extraordinarily insightful essay "The Aping Apes of Poe and Wright: Race, Animality, and Mimicry in 'Murders in the Rue Morgue' and *Native Son*," *New Literary History* 41, no. 1 (Winter 2010): 151–71. In dialogue with Lacan, Derrida, and Steve Baker on the animal, Peterson argues in highly nuanced terms that while such a displacement (slave to animal) *can be* imputed to such a text, recovering it as the text's stable truth (as a critic such as Ed White does) risks performing a more dangerous displacement yet, and one endemic to literary interpretation, where the animal is reduced to a "transparent signifier" of the human, and the ultimate referential logic of dehumanization of certain humans—which operates precisely and crucially via subtextual historical discourses and representational treatments *of the animal*—is lost to view. By attending to the "fabulist" logic of Poe's story here, I have chosen not to assume that dehumanizing or animalizing is itself a simple or stable operation.

21. Thus merging with the ape *in the* human, we might add; for Agamben, who notes the significance of Linnaeus's decision to ascribe to the human the classification *Anthropomorpha*, or "manlike," the human's relationship to itself was that of a "lack of a face of his own," the difference of degree ("his being always more or less than himself"), then, rescued by the "anthropological machine" that converted resemblance to self-recognition (see *The Open*, 29–30).

22. And here the orangutan's movement arguably mimes that of the *oikos* itself, to quote Wills as he discusses, precisely, Homer's *Odyssey*: "There is no

undisturbed domestic space from which to set out and to which to return [. . .]. There cannot be any direct route back to a space of the proper or the contained, the native or the natural" (*Dorsality*, 73).

23. See Akira Mizuta Lippit, *Electric Animal: Toward a Rhetoric of Wildlife* (Minneapolis: University of Minnesota Press, 2000), chaps. 2–4; quote on 127. Lippit in fact discusses Poe's story in the first few pages of his first chapter, but focusing ultimately on the orangutan's inarticulate cry that had so troubled its witnesses, uses it to frame the question of the animal in terms of its complicated position vis-à-vis the *logos*. Reviewing quickly the positions of Aristotle, Rousseau, and Derrida on this question, he summarizes at the close of this section: "The phantasm of a primordial unity continues to haunt the dialectics of *logos* and *zoon*, writing and speech, human and animal being, even as the proximity of speech to its other, the affective cry of the animal, establishes the spaces and temporalities that regulate the opening of worlds—the human and animal worlds that form apart from one another" (33).

24. Here too the text—Homer's—does not literally make a mystery of this question, ascribing words to the song, and here too this proves a finer point, the going beyond of which proves more interesting. E. V. Rieu's translation of the passage reads as follows: "'Draw near,' they sang, 'illustrious Odysseus, flower of Achaean chivalry, and bring your ship to rest so that you may hear our voices. No seaman ever sailed his black ship past this spot without listening to the sweet tones that flow from our lips, and none that listened has not been delighted and gone on a wiser man. For we know all that the Argives and Trojans suffered on the broad plain of Troy by the will of the gods, and we have foreknowledge of all that is going to happen on this fruitful earth.'" Homer, *The Odyssey*, trans. E. V. Rieu (Harmondsworth: Penguin, 1946), 194.

25. Theodor Adorno and Max Horkheimer, *Dialectic of Enlightenment*, trans. John Cumming (London: Verso, 1997), 58.

26. Quoted from *The Sirens' Song: Selected Essays by Maurice Blanchot*, ed. Gabriel Josipovici, trans. Sacha Rabinovitch (Bloomington: Indiana University Press, 1982), 59; my emphasis.

27. See Deleuze and Guattari, *A Thousand Plateaus*, 304–6. But this aspect of *Moby-Dick* is mentioned also, briefly, in their book on Kafka.

28. "The Silence of the Sirens," trans. Willa and Edwin Muir, in Franz Kafka, *The Complete Stories* (New York: Schocken Books, 1995), 431.

29. I deliberately use this word (also in what follows), rather than the more common "inequality," in order to maintain the trace of Poe's unequal animal.

30. On the orangutan's status as endangered, see IUCN (International Union for the Conservation of Nature) Red List of Threatened Species, accessed August 17, 2018, www.iucnredlist.org. And the story of exotic animals' transfer to European collections is well documented and poignantly retold in Nigel Rothfel's *Savages and Beasts: The Birth of the Modern Zoo* (Baltimore: Johns Hopkins University Press, 2002).

31. The rarely used infinitive ending that sentence may be the germ from which Chevillard's subsequent novel *Choir* (Paris: Minuit, 2010) grew. For I like to think that in its ruminating account of a dystopic island of collapsed dimensions, of swamps and despair, that near-unreadable text amplifies (or zooms in on) the bleak middle section of *Sans l'orang-outan*, devoted to

the crawling, writhing wretchedness of the human world abandoned by the orangutan.

32. Éric Chevillard, "Questions de préhistoire," interview by André Benhaïm, in *Écrivains de la préhistoire*, ed. André Benhaïm and Michel Lantelme (Toulouse: Presses Universitaires du Mirail, 2004), 183; my translation.

33. *Du hérisson* [The hedgehog] is about a hedgehog that unaccountably appears on the narrator's desk just at the moment at which the latter has decided to commence the writing of his autobiography, and parasitically proceeds to occupy and thereby hijack every one of his—and the novel's—paragraphs. See chapter 4 for a discussion of this text.

34. See Thangam Ravindranathan, "'Je fus toutes choses': L'innommé animal," in *Poétiques de la liste et imaginaire sériel dans les lettres (XXe et XXIe siècles)*, ed. Nathalie Dupont and Éric Trudel (Montreal: Nota Bene, 2019), 39–64, as well as two earlier essays in which I consider Chevillard's oeuvre in relation to that of Michaux: "Du *scarabée aptère* (Kafka, Michaux, Chevillard)," *French Forum* 36, no. 1 (2011): 75–94, and "Pour voir: L'animal, le nom, la distance," in *Histoires naturelles des animaux, XXe–XXIe siècles*, ed. Alain Romestaing and Alain Schaffner (Paris: Presses de la Sorbonne Nouvelle, 2016), 91–102.

35. Henri Michaux, *Œuvres complètes*, vol. 1, ed. Raymond Bellour and Ysé Tran (Paris: Gallimard, 1998), 663; my translation and emphasis.

36. Mathieu Larnaudie, "Des crabes, des anges et des monstres" (interview with Éric Chevillard), in *Devenirs du roman*, ed. François Bégaudeau et al. (Paris: Inculte/Naïve, 2007), 103; my translation and emphasis.

37. Éric Chevillard, *Oreille rouge* (Paris: Minuit, 2005).

38. Walter Putnam, "Can the Subaltern Growl?," in *Remembering Africa*, ed. Elisabeth Mudimbe-Boyi (Portsmouth, N.H.: Heinemann, 2002), 136.

39. See notably Wills, *Dorsality*, 27; David Wills, *Prosthesis* (Stanford, Calif.: Stanford University Press, 1995).

40. Indeed, Chevillard's novel *Préhistoire* (Paris: Minuit, 1994) most ambitiously exploits this notion.

41. Chevillard admits as much in the 2007 interview cited above: "History starts when the outcomes are sealed. [. . .] Prehistory is, on the contrary, the age when everything was possible. A writer able to transport himself there would suddenly enjoy absolute freedom to dream of things other than what was, than what is. Because nothing was written, everything remains to be written, starting from the origins, everything, except what has occurred" (Larnaudie, "Des crabes," 96–97; my translation).

42. Derrida uses the term "fabulous complication" to describe the impossible inaugurality/originary supplementarity in the performative, metafabulist "Par" that opens Francis Ponge's "Fable"—and that one understands would apply equally to every fable, name the paradox of every signature, and so on. Jacques Derrida, *Psyché: Inventions de l'autre* (Paris: Gallimard, 1987), 58.

CHAPTER 3

1. Homer, *The Odyssey*, E.V. Rieu's translation, 216.

2. Lewis Carroll, *The Complete, Fully Illustrated Works* (New York: Gramercy, 1995), 162.

3. Homer, *The Odyssey*, 266. Rieu opts for the Latinized spelling of Argos.

4. Max Horkheimer and Theodor W. Adorno, *Dialectic of Enlightenment: Philosophical Fragments*, trans. Edmund Jephcott (Stanford, Calif.: Stanford University Press, 2002), 45.

5. As poet Henri Michaux, visiting the Madras aquarium in 1932, had suspected of fish: "Une brosse à dents, un fiacre, un lapin peut être un poisson, tout dépend de son intérieur [A toothbrush, a carriage, a rabbit, anything can be a fish, it all depends on its inside]." *Œuvres complètes*, vol. 1, ed. Raymond Bellour and Ysé Tran (Paris: Gallimard, 1998), 407–8.

6. Here and in all quotes that follow, the first page number refers to the original French text, the second to the English translation: Marie NDiaye, *En famille* (Paris: Minuit, 1990) / *Among Family*, trans. Heather Doyal (Kent: Angela Royal, 1997).

7. "Whose longing and for what? Whose loneliness? Above all, whose muteness?" asks Kuzniar poignantly, commenting on Derrida's melancholy in *The Animal That Therefore I Am*. A little further on, she recalls the nineteenth-century German writer Jean Paul Richter's answer to these questions—"Language. In the impossibility of bringing the animal voice into words I see the poverty of the letter"—to argue that it is "the human response to animals that needs to be assessed in terms of melancholy." Alice A. Kuzniar, *Melancholia's Dog* (Chicago: University of Chicago Press, 2000), 27, 35.

8. Dominique Rabaté interestingly compares Fanny's not being recognized by the dogs to a child at its birth not being "recognized" by the family dog; see *Marie NDiaye* (Paris: CulturesFrance / Éditions Textuel, 2008), 27.

9. See: "Often, inside, a dog would bark threateningly" (94/75); in the Village M. "nasty little dogs rushed out and howled for a long time as Fanny passed" (66/53); later, entering a villager's house, she is faced with three big, chained, growling dogs, which try to bite her foot, then catch her boot: "Now they were howling, as if Fanny's unexpected and remarkable presence had aroused an old hatred" (95–96/76).

10. See Gérard Genette, *Figures III* (Paris: Éditions du Seuil, 1972), 192 / *Narrative Discourse: An Essay in Method*, trans. Jane E. Lewin (Ithaca, N.Y.: Cornell University Press, 1983), 172.

11. See on this question the lucid piece by Lydie Moudileno, "Délits, détours et affabulation: L'écriture de l'anathème dans *En famille* de Marie NDiaye," *French Review* 71, no. 3 (February 1998): 442–53.

12. Nadia's first encounter with the dog is in her son's car: "A warm, heavy breath mists my ear. I feel a hairy tickle on the back of my neck. I snap my head to one side. A dog's gaping maw has just appeared by my face, as if threatening to rip me apart should I say one more word." Marie NDiaye, *Mon cœur à l'étroit* (Paris: Gallimard, 2007), 230 / *My Heart Hemmed In*, trans. Jordan Stump (San Francisco: Two Lines, 2017), 213.

13. Michèle Clément, *Le cynisme à la Renaissance d'Erasme à Montaigne, suivi de, Les epistres de Diogenes (1546)* (Geneva: Droz, 2005), 137–38; my translation.

14. Peter Sloterdijk, *Critique of Cynical Reason*, trans. Michael Eldred (Minneapolis: University of Minnesota Press, 1987), 164, 168.

15. Michel Foucault, *The Courage of Truth (The Government of Self and Others II): Lectures at the Collège de France 1983–1984*, trans. Graham Burchell, ed. Frédéric Gros and Arnold I. Davidson (New York: Palgrave Macmillan, 2011), 224.

16. Foucault, *The Courage of Truth*, 201; for the French see Michel Foucault, *Le courage de la vérité: Le gouvernement de soi et des autres II: Cours au Collège de France (1983–1984)*, ed. Frédéric Gros and A. Gallimard (Paris: Seuil, 2009), 186–87.

17. Marie NDiaye, "Une journée de Brulard," in *Tous mes amis* (Paris: Minuit, 2004), 121, 130 / "Brulard's Day," in *All My Friends*, trans. Jordan Stump (San Francisco: Two Lines, 2013), 96, 103.

18. Michael Sheringham, "Ambivalences de l'animalité chez Marie NDiaye," in *Une femme puissante: L'œuvre de Marie NDiaye*, ed. Daniel Bengsch and Cornelia Ruhe (Amsterdam: Rodopi, 2013), 51–70; see esp. 57–64.

19. Lydie Moudileno notes astutely that "this character, who is perhaps the most African of the (female) characters in NDiaye, represents through her very stability a presence that I would say is eerie [*insolite*] in the oeuvre at large, like a statue in the midst of human beings." "Puissance insolite de la femme africaine chez Marie NDiaye," in *Marie NDiaye's Worlds / Mondes de Marie NDiaye*, ed. Lydie Moudileno and Warren Motte, *L'Esprit Créateur* 53, no. 2 (Summer 2013): 74; my translation.

20. Cited in Jean Rolin, *Un chien mort après lui* (Paris: POL, 2009), 246–47. All translations of quotes from this work are mine.

21. Donna Haraway, *The Companion Species Manifesto: Dogs, People, and Significant Otherness* (Chicago: Prickly Paradigm, 2003), 28.

22. Bridgett M. vonHoldt, Emily Shuldiner, et al., "Structural Variants in Genes associated with Human Williams-Beuren Syndrome Underlie Stereotypical Hypersociability in Domestic Dogs," *Science Advances* 19, no. 3.7 (July 2007), http://advances.sciencemag.org/content/3/7/e1700398.

23. One place to learn this history is the "Salle des espèces menacées et disparues" (Hall of Disappeared Species) at the Muséum d'Histoire Naturelle of the Paris Jardin des Plantes. There, in a glass case, stands a taxidermied specimen of the extinct French wolf—replaced today in the wild by the Italian subspecies. The "runneth yet" of La Fontaine's fable assumes sad irony in front of that glass case.

24. From Allan Stoekl, "Urban Ecology," a beautiful paper read at the Modern Languages Association annual convention in Chicago, January 2014, unpublished. For another recent hypothesis of a historic alliance between early humans and the first domesticated wolf-dogs, see Pat Shipman, *The Invaders: How Humans and Their Dogs Drove Neanderthals to Extinction* (Cambridge, Mass.: Harvard University Press, 2017).

25. Other accounts would have dogs play an unknowing but decisive role in the decline of other species (thereby clearing the way for a human world)—whether by carrying illnesses that decimated early American megafauna (see Alan Weisman, *The World without Us* [New York: Thomas Dunne Books / St. Martin's, 2007]) or because, to be able to feed their canine assistants, colonizers killed critical numbers of animals such as the fearless blue antelope in Africa

(whose taxidermied relics may also be seen in the Hall of Disappeared Species at the Museum of Natural History in Paris).

26. Michel Serres, *Biogée* (Brest: Éditions-dialogues.fr, 2010), 120; my translation.

27. To recall certain operative terms in Donna Haraway, *When Species Meet* (Minneapolis: University of Minnesota Press, 2008).

28. Carla Freccero, "Carnivorous Virility; or, Becoming-Dog," *Social Text* 106, no. 29.1 (Spring 2011): 178. I admit to this being an idiosyncratic reading, with which Freccero may well not agree. See also on the overdetermined intersections of race and species, Bénédicte Boisseron's remarkable *Afro-Dog: Blackness and the Animal Question* (New York: Columbia University Press, 2018).

29. Mark Neocleous and others, studying policing practices in Western societies, have also noted the logic by which which a sniffer dog comes to be understood as the extension of the police, indeed the nose and teeth of the state. See Neocleous, "The Smell of Power: A Contributon to the Critique of the Sniffer Dog," *Radical Philosophy* 167 (May/June 2011): 13–14.

30. Colin Dayan, *The Law Is a White Dog: How Legal Rituals Make and Unmake Persons* (Princeton, N.J.: Princeton University Press, 2011), 248.

31. Emmanuel Levinas, *Difficult Freedom: Essays on Judaism*, trans. Sean Hand (Baltimore: Johns Hopkins University Press, 1990), 152.

32. Emmanuel Levinas, *Difficile liberté* (Paris: Albin Michel, 1976), 232. I translate these locutions directly from the original text: because they are idiomatic, many of them do not survive Sean Hand's translation.

33. Including Derrida, *The Animal That Therefore I Am*, trans. David Wills (New York: Fordham University Press, 2008), 147–62/106–18; John Llewyn, "Am I Obsessed by Bobby? (Humanism of the Other Animal)," in *Re-reading Levinas*, ed. R. Bernasconi and S. Critchley (Bloomington: Indiana University Press, 1991), 234–45; Max Hantel, "Bobby between Deleuze and Levinas, or Ethics Becoming-Animal," *Angelaki: A Journal of the Theoretical Humanities* 18, no. 2 (June 2013): 105–26; Karalyn Kendall, "The Face of a Dog: Levinasian Ethics and Human/Dog Co-evolution," in *Queering the Non/Human*, ed. Noreen Giffney and Myra Hird (London: Ashgate, 2008), 185–204; Deborah Bird Rose, *Wild Dog Dreaming: Love and Extinction* (Charlottesville: University of Virginia Press, 2013), 29–41; David Clark, "On Being 'the Last Kantian in Nazi Germany': Dwelling with Animals after Levinas," in *Postmodernism and the Ethical Subject*, ed. Barbara Gabriel and Suzan Ilcan (Montreal: McGill-Queen's University Press, 2004), 41–74, and "Towards a Prehistory of the Postanimal: Kant, Levinas and the Regard of Brutes" (seminar paper, Center for Cultural Analysis, Rutgers University, n.d.); and Alain David, "Cynesthèse: Autoportrait au chien," in *L'animal autobiographique: Autour de Jacques Derrida*, ed. Marie-Louise Mallet (Paris: Galilée, 1999) 303–18.

34. Clark, "On Being 'the Last Kantian in Nazi Germany,' " 64, 66, 55–56.

35. For example: "It is via the face that one understands, for example, a dog. Yet the priority here is not found in the animal, but in the human face. We understand the animal, the face of the animal in accordance with *Dasein*. The phenomenon of the face is not in its purest form in the dog. In the dog, in the animal, there are other phenomena. For example, the force of nature is

pure vitality. It is more this which characterizes the dog. But it also has a face." "The Paradox of Morality: An Interview with Emmanuel Levinas," interview by Alison Ainley, Peter Hughes, and Tamra Wright, trans. Andrew Benjamin and Tamra Wright, in *The Provocation of Levinas: Rethinking the Other*, ed. Robert Bernasconi and David Wood, Warwick Studies in Philosophy and Literature (London: Routledge, 1988), 169.

36. David Clark, "Towards a Prehistory of the Postanimal," 32–33.

37. Clark's reading bears out a larger argument for reading Enlightenment and post-Enlightenment philosophy's "symptomatically incomplete denials" of the animal, "expressed in the form of ongoing foreclosures and erasures of the imagined animal, acts of renunciation whose repetitiveness and whose axiomatic nature puts to us that philosophy cannot have done with animals but *cannot have done with having done with them either*." "In other words," writes Clark, philosophical modernity is prey to an "interminable *anthropological melancholia*"; it "*mourns* animality, suffering interminably the ungrieved loss that it is responsible for having created in the first place" ("Towards a Prehistory of the Postanimal," 8).

38. As commented on a little ungenerously by Derrida in *The Animal That Therefore I Am*, 159–61/115–17.

39. Immanuel Kant, *Critique of the Power of Judgement*, ed. Paul Guyer (Cambridge: Cambridge University Press, 2000), 114. (Guyer also uses the English adjective "vague" a couple of times; see 117.)

40. Eva Schaper, "Free and Dependent Beauty," in *Kant's Critique of the Power of Judgement: Critical Essays*, ed. Paul Guyer (Oxford: Rowman & Littlefield, 2003), 113.

41. David, "Cynesthèse," 307; my translation.

42. I bring these two concepts together despite Deleuze and Guattari's protests against "mere" metaphor. Cf. "La métamorphose est le contraire de la métaphore [Metamorphosis is the contrary of metaphor]": Gilles Deleuze and Félix Guattari, *Kafka: Pour une littérature mineure* (Paris: Minuit, 1975), 40 / *Kafka: Toward a Minor Literature*, trans. Dana Polan (Minneapolis: University of Minnesota Press, 1986), 22. I would contend, rather, that Ricoeur's "métaphore vive," read radically, describes nothing less than becomings.

43. Clément Rosset, *The Real and Its Double*, trans. Chris Turner (London: Seagull Books, 2012), 77.

44. See here Jean-Louis Hippolyte's interesting book on the conceptual importance of vagueness or fuzziness in contemporary French literature, *Fuzzy Fiction* (Lincoln: University of Nebraska Press, 2006).

45. See Gilles Deleuze, *Logique du sens* (Paris: Minuit, 1969), 9 / *The Logic of Sense*, trans. Mark Lester (New York: Columbia University Press, 1990), 1–2.

46. I owe this account principally to Roy Sorensen's most instructive entry on vagueness in the Stanford Encyclopedia of Philosophy: s.v. "Vagueness," accessed August 13, 2015, http://plato.stanford.edu/entries/vagueness/.

47. Indeed, for H. G. Wells it was logic itself which, too literally or stubbornly applied, produced vagueness, as attested by the striking passage from *First and Last Things* (1908) quoted by Sorensen in his presentation of vagueness in philosophy: "Every species is vague, every term goes cloudy at its edges, and so in

my way of thinking, relentless logic is only another name for stupidity—for a sort of intellectual pigheadedness. If you push a philosophical or metaphysical enquiry through a series of valid syllogisms—never committing any generally recognized fallacy—you nevertheless leave behind you at each step a certain rubbing and marginal loss of objective truth and you get deflections that are difficult to trace, at each phase in the process. Every species waggles about in its definition, every tool is a little loose in its handle, every scale has its individual" (quoted in Sorensen, "Vagueness").

48. Therein following, it would appear, Wilhelm Windelband, one of his two principal sources; see Peter Fifield, "'Of being—or remaining': Beckett and Early Greek Philosophy," in *Beckett/Philosophy*, ed. Matthew Feldman and Karim Mamdani (Stuttgart: Ibidem, 2015), 142; Matthew Feldman, "Samuel Beckett, Wilhelm Windelband and Nominalist Philosophy," in *Beckett/Philosophy*, 151–84.

49. See the departing Arsene's verbose speech on the day of Watt's arrival at Mr. Knott's homestead: "There is a great alp of sand, one hundred metres high, between the pines and the ocean, and there in the warm moonless night, when no one is looking, no one listening, in tiny packets of two or three millions the grains slip, all together, a little slip of one or two lines maybe, and then stop, all together, not one missing, and that is all, that is all for that night, and perhaps for ever that is all, for in the morning with the sun a little wind from the sea may come, and blow them one from another far apart, or a pedestrian scatter them with his foot, though that is less likely. It was a slip like that I felt, that Tuesday afternoon, millions of little things moving all together out of their old place, into a new one nearby, and furtively, as though it were forbidden." Samuel Beckett, *Watt* (New York: Grove, 1994), 43. "Arsene's glissando," writes Chris Ackerley, "is not just an expression of the *sorites* paradox, the noise of the falling grains of sand, but equally one of apperception, of the mind's incapacity to register the impossible process, the 'change of degree.'" Chris Ackerley, *Obscure Locks, Simple Keys: The Annotated "Watt"* (Edinburgh: Edinburgh University Press, 2010), 63–64.

50. Chris Ackerley, "Monadology: Samuel Beckett and Gottfried Wilhelm Leibniz," in Feldman and Mamdani, *Beckett/Philosophy*, 189.

51. G. W. Leibniz, *Philosophical Writings*, ed. G. H. R. Parkinson, trans. Mary Morris and G. H. R. Parkinson (London: J. M. Dent & Sons, 1973), 187.

52. Wilhelm Windelband, *A History of Philosophy*, vol. 2: *Renaissance, Enlightenment and Modern* (New York: Harper & Brothers, 1958), 483.

53. Windelband would note that "in the language of to-day the *petites perceptions* would be *unconscious mental states*" (*A History of Philosophy*, 2:424).

54. Leibniz, *Philosophical Writings*, 180–81, 197.

55. Beckett had noted in his reading of Leibniz this feature of monads: "Each monad is, with reference to the rest, perfectly independent, unable to exercise or experience influence. Their 'windowlessness' is expression of their 'metaphysical impenetrability.'" Philosophical Notes TCD 10967/191; Windelband, *A History of Philosophy*, 2:423, quoted in Ackerley, *Obscure Locks*, 147.

56. See Arnaud Pelletier, "Une dissection du chien de Bayle: La dernière lettre de Leibniz à Bayle ou l'origine de l'exposé monadologique," in *Leibniz et Bayle:*

Confrontation et dialogue, ed. Christian Leduc, Paul Rateau, and Jean-Luc Solère (Stuttgart: Franz Steiner Verlag, 2015), 165–95.

57. Donald Rutherford, "Bayle's Dog and the Dynamics of the Soul," in Leduc, Rateau, and Solère, *Leibniz et Bayle*, 197–98; Pelletier, "Une dissection du chien de Bayle," 167–71, 187.

58. *Die Philosophischen Schriften von Gottfried Wilhelm Leibniz*, ed. C. I. Gerhardt (Berlin: Weidman, 1875–1890, Reprint, Hildesheim: Georg Olms, 1965); 4:532, quoted in Robert Merrihew Adams, *Leibniz: Determinist, Theist, Idealist* (New York: Oxford University Press, 1994), 291. Subsequent references to the complete edition of the *Philosophischen Schriften* will follow the custom within Leibniz studies of giving the acronym *GP* followed by the volume and page numbers.

59. Leibniz, GP 4:532–33/*Leibniz's "New System" and Associated Contemporary Texts*, ed. and trans. R. S. Woolhouse and Richard Francks (Oxford: Clarendon Press, 1997), 78.

60. Franklin Perkins, *Leibniz: A Guide for the Perplexed* (London: Bloomsbury, 2010), 152.

61. Gilles Deleuze, *The Fold: Leibniz and the Baroque*, trans. Tom Conley (Minneapolis: University of Minnesota, 1993), 56.

62. "No philosophy has ever pushed to such an extreme the affirmation of a one and same world, and of an infinite difference or variety in this world" (Deleuze, *The Fold*, 58).

63. See also: "Il faut considérer aussi que l'âme, toute simple qu'elle est, a tousjours un sentiment composé de plusieurs perceptions à la fois [One must consider also that the soul, simple as it is, always has a sentiment composed of several perceptions at the same time]" (*GP* 4:522, quoted in Rutherford, "Bayle's Dog," 205).

64. In this sentence "expressive work" refers to the following passage: "Tout cela n'est qu'une conséquence de la nature représentative de l'âme, qui doit exprimer ce qui se passe, et même ce qui se passera dans son corps, et en quelque façon dans tous les autres, par la connexion ou correspondance de toutes les parties du monde [All this is but a consequence of the representative nature of the soul, which must express what is happening, and even what will happen in its body, and in a sense in all other bodies, by the connection or correspondence of all the parts of the world]" (*GP* 4:523, quoted in Rutherford, "Bayle's Dog," 206).

65. Rutherford, "Bayle's Dog," 206.

66. Gilles Deleuze (with Claire Parnet), *Gilles Deleuze's ABC Primer*, trans. Andrew Shurtz et al. (credited as "We Have Photoshop"), (New York: The Supplement Number One, 2010), 29.

67. I take care to note this because, given that *L'abécédaire*, released posthumously, is seen/read more than *Le pli*, the genesis of this term in Deleuze's thinking gets lost in current citations.

68. Interestingly, Beckett is one of two writers (along with Henri Michaux) briefly mentioned by Deleuze in the "Animal" entry of *L'abécédaire*. See also Germaine Brée, "Beckett's Abstractors of Quintessence," *French Review* 36 (1963): 572. Ackerley more recently described *Watt* as "a tragedy of the monad"

(190). Since Brée's piece, both Garin Dowd and Naoya Mori have continued to track Leibnizian themes in Beckett's oeuvre. See Dowd, "Nomadology: Reading the Beckettian Baroque," *Journal of Beckett Studies* 8, no. 1 (1998): 15–49; and Mori, "Beckett's Windows and 'the Windowless Self,'" *Samuel Beckett Today/ Aujourd'hui* 14 (2004): 357–70, among others.

69. For the quotation, see Feldman, "Samuel Beckett, Wilhelm Windelband and Nominalist Philosophy," 152. For the biographical background, see *The Letters of Samuel Beckett: 1941–1956,* ed. George Craig, Martha Dow Fehsenfield, Dan Gunn, and Lois More Overbeck (Cambridge: Cambridge University Press, 2011), lxv–lxvi, 3–8.

70. Ackerley, *Obscure Locks*, 14.

71. Thus, in any case, goes my reading of the novel. The only other place (a paragraph) where one finds horror more intense, though without the emphasis on the *logical* dimension, is a description of Watt and Sam's taste for pursuing and destroying "in great numbers" birds, birds' nests, and eggs and in luring rats into eating each other (155–56)—rare and troubling content when one thinks of the curiosity, tenderness, or "elegiac calm" marking the encounters with animals in so much of Beckett's fiction. See among others Mary Bryden, ed., *Beckett and Animals* (Cambridge: Cambridge University Press, 2013); Steven Connor, "Beckett's Animals," *Journal of Beckett Studies* 8 (1982): 29–42; and Beckett, *Nouvelles et Textes pour Rien* (Paris: Minuit, 1958), 51–52 / *The Expelled and Other Novellas* (Harmondsworth: Penguin, 1980), 57: "Poor dear dumb beasts, how you will have helped me."

72. Gilles Deleuze, *Essays Critical and Clinical*, trans. Daniel W. Smith and Michael A. Greco (London: Verso, 1998), 153–54.

73. For a discussion of other more exhaustive or near-exhaustive enumerations, see François Martel, "Jeux formels dans *Watt*," *Poétique* 10 (1972): 153–75.

74. Martel, "Jeux formels," 169–70; see *Watt*, 89–90.

75. Ackerley, "Monadology," 190.

76. Chris Ackerley, "'Despised for Their Obviousness': Samuel Beckett's Dogs," in Bryden, *Beckett and Animals*, 186.

77. The early drafts read "lurcher" (as in "in the lurch") here, and the French would use *son fidèle sac d'os*, "his faithful sack of bones" (see Ackerley, *Obscure Locks*, 111).

78. Ackerley, *Obscure Locks*, 29.

79. Deleuze, *The Fold*, 87.

80. See Brée (who thus describes the novel's parody of monadology at large), "Beckett's Abstractors of Quintessence," 572.

81. "The Baroque Leibniz does not believe in the void. For him it always seems to be filled with a folded matter, because binary arithmetic superimposes folds that both the decimal system—and Nature itself—conceal in apparent voids. For Leibniz, and in the Baroque, folds are always full" (Deleuze, *The Fold*, 36).

82. See Tom Conley's introduction to *The Fold*, xii.

83. The two poles Knott/dog can of course also be understood as god/dog—that palindromic play never too far beneath the surface. See Ackerley, "'De-

spised for Their Obviousness,'" 177–87; Rolf Breuer, "Paradox in Beckett," *Modern Language Review* 88, no. 3 (1993): 573. The possible wrath of god, an intolerable possibility, thus makes unthinkable the possible misery of a dog.

84. See both the French and the English: "Un chien vint dans l'office / et prit une andouillette. / Alors à coups de louche / Le chef le mit en miettes. / Les autres chiens ce voyant / Vite vite l'ensevelirent [. . .] / Au pied d'une croix en bois blanc / Où le passant pouvait lire: / Un chien vint dans l'office . . ."; "A dog came in the kitchen / And stole a crust of bread. / Then cook up with a ladle / And beat him till he was dead. / Then all the dogs came running / And dug the dog a tomb—[. . .] / And wrote upon the tombstone / For the eyes of dogs to come: / A dog came in the kitchen . . ." Samuel Beckett, *En attendant Godot* (Paris: Minuit, 1952), 79–80 / *The Complete Dramatic Works* (London: Faber and Faber, 1986), 53–54.

85. See Ackerley, "'Despised for Their Obviousness,'" for more on Beckett's dogs. Ackerley's title refers to a sentence in *Dream of Fair to Middling Women:* "Dogs, for their obviousness, he [Belacqua] despised and rejected, and cats he disliked, but cats less than dogs or children." Samuel Beckett, *Dream of Fair to Middling Women* (Dublin: Black Cat, 1992), 127.

86. After the war, Beckett had nursed his mother, afflicted with Parkinson's disease, until her death.

87. Samuel Beckett, *The Complete Dramatic Works* (London: Faber and Faber, 1986), 219–21.

88. See, for example, paragraph 21 of the *Monadalogy*; *Philosophical Writings*, 182n1.

89. Dowd, "Nomadology," 37; Leibniz quoted in Dowd, "Nomadology," 36–37.

90. Leibniz, *Monadology* para. 30, quoted in Dowd, "Nomadology," 37.

91. Samuel Beckett, *Three Novels: Molloy, Malone Dies, The Unnamable* (New York: Grove, 1994), 185.

92. Samuel Beckett, *Company* (London: John Calder, 1996), 32.

93. Samuel Beckett, *Three Novels*, 404.

94. Jean-Paul Sartre, "Bad Faith," in *Being and Nothingness: An Essay on Phenomenological Ontology*, trans. Hazel E. Barnes (London: Routledge, 2002), 47–70.

95. Beckett, *Company*, 32.

96. Derrida, *The Animal That Therefore I Am*, 83–84/56–57.

97. Derrida, *The Animal That Therefore I Am*, 130/93.

98. Samuel Beckett, *Nouvelles et Textes pour rien*, 140 / *Texts for Nothing and Other Shorter Prose, 1950–1976* (London: Faber and Faber, 2010), 17.

99. Breuer, "Paradox in Beckett," 575–76.

100. See on these questions (language and the animal; passivity/finitude shared with animals) much of Derrida, *The Animal That Therefore I Am*, esp. 48–50/27–29, 120–32/86–94. See also Cary Wolfe, "Flesh and Finitude: Thinking Animals in (Post)Humanist Philosophy," *SubStance* 37 (2008): 8–36.

101. Derrida's riposte to Lacan on this point is by now well known. See "And Say the Animal Responded?," in *The Animal That Therefore I Am*, 163–91/119–40.

102. See here Michael Sheringham's luminous analysis, "La figure de l'enseignant chez Marie NDiaye," in Moudileno and Motte, *Marie NDiaye's Worlds / Mondes de Marie NDiaye*, 105–6.

103. César Aira, *The Musical Brain and Other Stories*, trans. Chris Andrews (New York: New Directions, 2015), 46.

104. What is it about dogs? While Aira's story is a particularly chilling example of what a dog may "express," there are others that suggest in more ordinary (and thereby even more disquieting) terms that for the I (even one without past crimes, even for one about which hardly anything is known) to continue to bear its own existence requires wishing any dogs back out of it. So seems to suggest the opening of a Kafka story about an elderly bachelor who imagines in all its vivid details a dog that would keep him company through the years—only to abort the vision when it leads ineluctably to the time where the dog will, in turn, unbearably, fall ill ("Blumfeld, an Elderly Bachelor," in Franz Kafka, *The Complete Stories* [New York: Schocken Books, 1995]). This is also the subject of a story by Jeanette Winterson, where a day spent in exhilaration with a lively, adorable puppy leads to the decision to return it. "The 24 Hour Dog," in *The World and Other Places* (New York: Knopf, 1999). For other writers, like Raymond Queneau, one of whose characters is accompanied by an invisible (or perhaps inexistent) dog who eventually abandons him (Queneau, "Dino," in *Stories and Remarks*, trans. Marc Lowenthal [Lincoln: University of Nebraska Press, 2000]), and Modiano, for whom also a dog appears only as easily as it disappears (in *Chien de printemps* [Paris: Points, 1995]), it would seem that a dog bears beholding only as a thing that flickers or fades.

105. Vicki Hearne, *Adam's Task: Calling Animals by Name* (1986; repr., New York: Skyhorse, 2007), 59.

106. I have reflected at greater length on this Rolin passage and on missing dogs—and missing's dog(s)—in "Missing," *Political Concepts: A Critical Lexicon* 3, no. 5 (Fall 2016).

107. Alan Beck, *The Ecology of Stray Dogs: A Study of Free-Ranging Urban Animals* (Baltimore: York, 1971), 13. Today, nearly fifty years later, free-ranging dogs are as rare in the streets of Baltimore as in any other American city.

108. Colin Dayan, *With Dogs at the Edge of Life* (New York: Columbia University Press, 2016), 148.

109. Hearne, *Adam's Task*, 59.

110. And of course nothing to do with eggs. See entry for "egg" (verb) in Robert Hendrickson, *The Facts on File Encyclopedia of Word and Phrase Origins*, 4th ed. (New York: Facts on File, 2008).

111. Marie NDiaye, *Rosie Carpe* (Paris: Minuit, 2001), 227–28 / *Rosie Carpe*, trans. Tamsin Black (Lincoln: University of Nebraska Press, 2004), 201–2.

112. See also Marie NDiaye, *Y penser sans cesse* (Talence: Éditions de l'Arbre Vengeur, 2011).

113. See interview with Catherine Argand, *Lire*, April 2001, republished in *L'Express*, accessed November 28, 2016, http://www.lexpress.fr/culture/livre/marie-ndiaye_804357.html. As for Asibong's most original study, it follows the theories of British psychoanalysts such as Donald Winnicott, André Green, and

Wilfred Bion—who, as it happens, was also Beckett's young psychoanalyst for two years. See Andrew Asibong, *Marie NDiaye: Blankness and Recognition* (Liverpool: Liverpool University Press, 2013). Asibong, of the opinion that links between NDiaye and Beckett are significant but "should not be overstated," does note interestingly that Jung's phrase describing certain individuals' feeling of "having *never been properly born*," known to have made a great impact on Beckett, applies equally to a host of small creatures and "pre-babies" in NDiaye's oeuvre, hapless, undeveloped figures, spectral and ghostly (144, 210n3, 221n2).

114. Rabaté, *Marie NDiaye*, 77; my translation.

115. See Genette, *Figures III*, 192/172. Equally remarkable (and intriguing for its potential connection with the dog) is the occasional instability of voice/perspective—and precisely a slippage between internal monologue and free indirect discourse—in "Une journée de Brulard" [Brulard's day], which I do not have the space to discuss further here (see pages 132, 151, 155).

116. See interview with Catherine Argand, *Lire*; my translation.

117. Elisabeth Arnould-Bloomfield, "Rosie Carpe et le récit désastreux," in Moudileno and Motte, *Marie NDiaye's Worlds / Mondes de Marie NDiaye*, 25; my translation. On the relationship between narrator and character in this novel see also Lydie Moudileno's most interesting analyses in "Marie NDiaye's Discombobulated Subject," *SubStance* 35, no. 3 (2006): 83–94, and "L'excellent français de Marie NDiaye," in *Marie NDiaye: L'étrangeté à l'oeuvre*, ed. Andrew Asibong and Shirley Jordan (Villeneuve d'Ascq: Presses Universitaires du Septentrion, 2009), 25–38.

118. Elissa Marder, *The Mother in the Age of Mechanical Reproduction: Psychoanalysis, Photography, Deconstruction* (New York: Fordham University Press, 2012), 230. Marder is writing here, strictly speaking, about the primal scene, but the formulation offers an eloquent description of trauma more generally.

119. Michel Foucault and Maurice Blanchot, *Maurice Blanchot: The Thought from Outside/Michel Foucault as I Imagine Him* (New York: Zone Books, 1990), 12, 25, 31.

120. See opening of "What Is an Author?," where Foucault quotes those lines and then notes: "In this indifference [of who is speaking] appears one of the fundamental ethical principles of contemporary writing." *The Foucault Reader*, ed. Paul Rabinow (London: Penguin, 1984), 101. See also Blanchot on Beckett in "Où maintenant? Qui maintenant?," in *Le livre à venir* (Paris: Gallimard, 1959), 286–95 / "Where Now? Who Now?," in *The Sirens' Song*, 192–98.

121. On NDiaye's reluctance to write explicitly about race, see Moudileno, "L'excellent français de Marie NDiaye."

122. A mere speculation, this. Asked by Claire Devarrieux of *Libération* what influence the film project with Claire Denis had on *Ladivine*, NDiaye admitted that the ten days in Ghana had naturally interested her (*ça m'a évidemment intéressée*) and no doubt shaped "the vacation" in *Ladivine*, the core scene around which the whole novel had been composed (NDiaye, "J'aime cette période de vacances," interview with Claire Devarrieux, *Libération*, February 13, 2013). In the course of the film *White Material*, whose scenario NDiaye would cowrite

and whose opening scene would feature dogs running across the frame, the protagonist's son would jump off a truck (abandoning the attacked plantation) and "become" a running dog in order not to leave: is this essentially what gets reimagined from the inside in *Ladivine*? This novel was written between July 2010 and June 2012. I have not been able to date the ten-day stay in Ghana (work on *White Material* would have started at some point following the completion of *L'intrus* in 2005; it was submitted to its first festival at the end of 2009 and released commercially in the spring of 2010). In another interview published on the blog site of Pmalgachie/Pierre Maury, NDiaye is asked, "Why dogs?," and answers: "In the family holiday part, with the dog watching Ladivine whenever she goes out, I asked myself the question of the choice of the animal that would keep an eye on her or protect her. It seemed obvious that it was [to be] a dog because, in a way, it was impossible for it to be anything else. In the streets of a big city, only a dog can be there without it seeming strange." Pmalgachie/Pierre Maury, interview of NDiaye, *Le journal d'un lecteur* (blog), accessed August 5, 2017, http://journallecteur.blogspot.com/2014/10/marie-ndiaye-trois-generations-de-femmes.html; my translation.

123. "No country kills more dogs or imprisons more people than the United States," notes Dayan (*The Law*, 217–18); conservative estimates suggest that 1.2 million dogs are euthanized in the United States every year.

124. In another short book, Antoine Traisnel and I have thought at some length about the imaginary history/metaphorics by which the "truth" of being (philosophical knowledge, human meaning, and world) has, since Plato, been something flushed out from the depths of the forest, or something for which forests have been cleared. See Ravindranathan and Traisnel, *Donner le change: L'impensé animal* (Paris: Hermann, 2016).

125. Marie NDiaye, *Ladivine* (Paris: Gallimard, 2013), 80 / *Ladivine*, trans. Jordan Stump (New York: Knopf, 2016), 53.

126. Examples abound, particularly in the first pages of the novel, of sentences featuring both "Malinka" and "Clarisse Rivière," as if the very (all-consuming) task of language had become to keep these apart: "Of Clarisse Rivière, Malinka's mother knew nothing" (13/6); "Where Malinka's mother was born, a place Clarisse Rivière had never been and would never go [. . .] everyone had those same delicate features" (15/7); "Malinka's mother was not to insert herself into Clarisse Rivière's life in any way, and she alone, Clarisse Rivière, was permitted to eat the food she prepared [. . .]. She alone, Clarisse Rivière, for the bitterness passed through her without swelling inside her" (22/12).

127. *Ladivine*, as Asibong has noted, presents an ambitiously condensed and intensified replay of the drama running through all of NDiaye's novels: each of the female protagonists of the four generations that this novel spans must experience "what it means to have [their] life split into non-cohering sections; to be repeatedly stripped of the complexity of [their] 'true' self, but to be actively complicit in that stripping; to be constantly 'blanking out' humiliating experiences that demand to be spoken" (*Marie NDiaye*, 13, 171). In the case of the younger Ladivine, Asibong would surmise, "the internalization of her mother's blankness converts her own insides into a zombie-ridden crypt, populated by secrets and foreclosures which linger, spectral and unsymbolizable" (172).

128. Vicki Hearne, *The White German Shepherd* (New York: Atlantic Monthly Press, 1988), 193; my emphasis.

129. NDiaye, "J'aime cette période de vacances," my translation.

130. Deeming the becoming-dog to be the last in a "quasi-psychotic hyper-relational" series of illogical recognitions that Ladivine resorts to in the course of her "vacation," that are "beyond the restrictive codes of identity," and that may not be easily distinguishable from madness, Asibong is rightly "loath to posit the development as a positive one" (*Marie NDiaye*, 172–73). Receiving the lesson of "NDiaye's 'blank fantastic,'" writes Asibong, may take a sort of "mad recognition" on the part of the reader, not to say "a complex process of mourning, transference, dialogue and imagination" of the sort he admits to having experienced himself (174). Arguing persuasively that NDiaye's is an oeuvre that works on levels conscious and unconscious, verbal and nonverbal, Asibong suggests that to read it requires keeping one eye wide open to its light and another wide shut to navigate its darkness.

131. NDiaye, "J'aime cette période de vacances"; my translation.

132. Jacques Rancière, *The Lost Thread: The Democracy of Modern Fiction*, trans. Steven Corcoran (New York: Bloomsbury, 2017), xxix; translation modified.

133. "The spirit of seriousness has two characteristics: It considers values as transcendent 'givens,' independent of human subjectivity, and it transfers the quality of 'desirable' from the ontological structure of things to their simple material constitution" (Sartre, *Being and Nothingness*, 626).

134. I'll confess I find in this moment however the most moving framework for understanding the dogs of *Ladivine*—born of Ladivine Sylla's uneducated, superstitious imaginings whose grounds and "origins" can no more be verified than those of the writer herself. NDiaye is noncommittal when interviewed: "I imagine that it might exist in certain parts of the world, but I do not know this" ("J'aime cette période en vacances").

135. Hearne, *Adam's Task*, 85.

136. To quote Peter Steiner's clever cartoon caption (*New Yorker*, July 5, 1993).

CHAPTER 4

1. Marie Darrieussecq, *Le mal de mer* (Paris: POL, 1999), 39.

2. Marie Darrieussecq, *Undercurrents: A Novel*, trans. Linda Coverdale (New York: New Press, 2001), 28. For the rest of this chapter I refer to this American edition.

3. Marie Darrieussecq, *Breathing Underwater*, trans. Linda Coverdale (London: Faber and Faber, 2001), 29.

4. As Elissa Marder writes compellingly, "bits of language that cannot be assimilated into concepts get spit out as literature" (*The Mother in the Age of Mechanical Reproduction: Psychoanalysis, Photography, Deconstruction*. New York: Fordham University Press, 2012.)

5. Anat Pick, *Creaturely Poetics: Animality and Vulnerability in Literature and Film* (New York: Columbia University Press, 2011), 85. The "crisis of the human form" explored by *Truismes*, writes Pick, inherits from the refusal by

"a long and heterogeneous tradition of antiliberal, antihumanist French writing" (Sade, Bataille, Cendrars) to cover up humans' "incomplete becoming—the struggle of the human to assume and to inhabit a definite form" (83; 94).

6. Marie Darrieussecq, *Naissance des fantômes* (Paris: Gallimard, 1998), 16 / *My Phantom Husband*, trans. Esther Allen (New York: New Press, 1999), 6.

7. On spectrality in Darrieussecq see Sonja Stojanovic's wonderful piece "Marie Darrieussecq's Ghost," *Symposium* 69, no. 4 (Oct–Dec 2015), 190–202, and also chapter 3 of her doctoral thesis *Spectral Preoccupations: Reading Through Post-War French Fiction* (Brown University, 2017). On the sea in Darrieussecq, see among others Catherine Rodgers, "Marie Darrieussecq: écrivaine de l'entre-deux," in *Women in the Middle*, a special issue of *Women in French Studies* 2009, 105–17.

8. Henri Michaux, *Selected Writings: The Space Within*, trans. Richard Ellman (New York: New Directions, 1951), 43. Michaux had also titled a poem "Naissance" [Birth], an account of the successive and frenetic births of a certain Pon. Darrieussecq, when I spoke with her, was not familiar with these writings by Michaux. But in my opinion Michaux had read Darrieussecq. (This chronologically untenable claim will make more sense later in the chapter.)

9. Marie Darrieussecq, *Bref séjour chez les vivants* (Paris: POL, 2001), 24, 153 / *A Brief Stay with the Living*, trans. Ian Monk (London: Faber and Faber, 2003), 12, 109; translation modified.

10. Marie Darrieussecq, *Rapport de police* (Paris: POL, 2010), 87; translations are mine.

11. Stéphanie Posthumus, *French 'Écocritique': Reading Contemporary French Theory and Fiction Ecologically* (Toronto: University of Toronto Press, 2017); see notably chapter 1, "Ecological Subjectivity: Guattari and Darrieussecq."

12. Marie Darrieussecq, *Le pays* [The country] (Paris: POL, 2005), 64; translations are mine.

13. For a beautiful reflection on lessness and other "-nesses" in Beckett, see Robert Harvey, *Witnessness: Beckett, Dante, Levi and the Foundations of Responsibility* (New York: Continuum, 2010), which I turn to briefly and in relation to other questions later in the chapter.

14. We might remember here the very similar image that concludes the madeleine sequence in Proust: "And as in the game wherein the Japanese amuse themselves by filling a porcelain bowl with water and steeping in it little pieces of paper which until then are without character or form, but, the moment they become wet, stretch and twist and take on colour and distinctive shape, become flowers or houses or people, solid and recognisable, so in that moment all the flowers in our garden and in M. Swann's park, and the water-lilies on the Vivonne and the good folk of the village and their little dwellings and the parish church and the whole of Combray and its surroundings, taking shape and solidity, sprang into being, town and gardens alike, from my cup of tea." Marcel Proust, *In Search of Lost Time*, vol. 1: *Swann's Way*, trans. C. K. Scott Moncrieff, Terence Kilmartin, and D. J. Enright (London: Vintage, 1996), 54–55.

15. Marie Darrieussecq, "My Mother Told Me Monsters Do Not Exist," in *Zoo: Nouvelles* (Paris: POL, 2006), 149; translations are mine.

16. See the chapter "C is for Culture": "The surfers say, 'We completely agree. What do we do? We don't cease to insinuate ourselves into the folds of nature. For us, nature is an ensemble of mobile folds. We insinuate ourselves in the fold of the wave.'" Gilles Deleuze (with Claire Parnet), *Gilles Deleuze's ABC Primer*, trans. Andrew Shurtz et al. (credited as "We Have Photoshop"), (New York: The Supplement Number One, 2010), 45–46.

17. In *Difference and Repetition* Deleuze would claim this of the revolution, for instance. (Hard not to prefer the idea of all revolutions to come to that of all flies to come.) Gilles Deleuze, *Difference and Repetition*, trans. Paul Patton (New York: Columbia University Press, 1995).

18. Marie Darrieussecq, *Tom est mort* (Paris: POL, 2007), 108 / *Tom Is Dead*, trans. Lia Hills (Melbourne: Text Publishing, 2009), 75.

19. The phantom limb is a metaphor Darrieussecq favors; see, for instance, *Le pays*, 66; *Tom Is Dead*, 67/45.

20. Darrieussecq, "My Mother Told Me," 143; my translation.

21. Éric Chevillard, *Du hérisson* (Paris: Minuit, 2002), 27. All translations from this work are mine.

22. I am thinking here of Ponge's "Notes prises pour un coquillage" and "Le soleil placé en abyme."

23. Francis Ponge, *La table*, in *Œuvres complètes*, ed. Bernard Beugnot (Paris: Gallimard, 2002), 941 / *The Table*, trans. Colombina Zamponi (Cambridge, Mass.: Wakefield, 2017), 76.

24. Mathieu Larnaudie, "Des crabes, des anges et des monstres" (interview with Éric Chevillard), in *Devenirs du roman*, ed. François Bégaudeau et al. (Paris: Inculte/Naïve, 2007), 97–98; my translation. On Chevillard's *Du hérisson* see my "Un hérisson peut toujours arriver," in "Écopoétique," ed. Alain Romestaing, Pierre Schoentjes, and Anne Simon, special issue, *Revue Critique de Fixxion Française Contemporaine* 11 (Winter 2015): 71–80; on his animals more generally see Tiphaine Samoyault, "Rendre bête," in *Pour Chevillard*, ed. Pierre Bayard et al. (Paris: Minuit, 2014), 37–58.

25. Adam Nicolson, "Where Have All Our Hedgehogs Gone?," *The Guardian*, January 16, 2006, https://www.theguardian.com/environment/2006/jan/17/g2.ruralaffairs.

26. Jacques Derrida, "Che cos'è la poesia?," in *Points . . . Interviews, 1974–1994*, trans. Peggy Kamuf (Stanford, Calif.: Stanford University Press, 1995), 297.

27. This synopsis I delightedly borrow from Michelle Clayton's "Animal-estar: Animal Affections in Vallejo's Poetry," in *Politics, Poetics, Affect: Re-visioning César Vallejo*, ed. Stephen M. Hart (Cambridge: Cambridge Scholars, 2013), 117–33, which very imaginatively works with the Derrida essay; 117 for the quoted phrase.

28. Franz Kafka, *The Complete Stories*, 428.

29. Joseph Lavery, "Deconstruction and Petting: Untamed Animots in Derrida and Kafka," in *Demenageries: Thinking (of) Animals after Derrida*, ed. Anne E. Berger and Marta Segarra (Amsterdam: Rodopi, 2011), 129.

30. In an inspired passage, Lavery puts Odradek in relation with the reel and thread of Hans of Freudian *fort/da* fame, to note that these two "moments of

foundational queerness" in Freud and Kafka are both produced by "the animating of spools" ("Deconstruction and Petting," 134–35).

31. Lavery, "Deconstruction and Petting," 427–28. An excellent Odradek bibliography (including the work of Werner Hamacher and Peter Fenves) is cited at the end of Lavery's essay. Also see Eleanor Helms's "The Difficult Task of Being Real: Odradek, the Kittenlamb, and the Historical Individual," and Esther Bauer's "The Power of the Look: Franz Kafka's 'The Cares of a Family Man,'" both in *Kafka's Creatures: Animals, Hybrids and Other Fantastic Beings*, ed. Marc Lucht and Donna Yarri (Lanham, Md.: Lexington Books, 2010), 81–99, 157–73.

32. Kafka, *The Complete Stories*, 426–27.

33. Bauer, "The Power of the Look," 160.

34. Éric Chevillard, *Palafox* (Paris: Minuit, 2003).

35. Jorge Luis Borges, *Labyrinths: Selected Stories and Other Writings* (New York: New Directions, 1964), 199–200. Borges is quoting the Han Yu apologue from Margouliès's *Anthologie raisonnée de la littérature chinoise* (1948).

36. The Heraclitean idea *Phusis kruptesthai philei* (Nature loves to hide) is crucial to the thinking of Jean-Christophe Bailly; see "Le visible est le caché," in *Le parti pris des animaux* (Paris: Christian Bourgois, 2013), 25–33.

37. Jacques Derrida, "Istrice 2. Ick bünn all hier," in *Points de suspension: Entretiens*, ed. Elisabeth Weber (Paris: Galilée, 1992), 309–36 / "Istrice 2: Ick bünn all hier," in *Points de suspension*, 300–326; see 319–22. I am grateful to Michelle Clayton for alerting me to this lead. See her more cogent summary of the hedgehog sequel in "Animalestar," 122.

38. See chapter 3 in this book.

39. "No interruption," she writes a couple of pages earlier to describe the attempt to achieve a thinking about nothing: "To think about not thinking is to already be thinking: first mental loop, carousels and swings" (37; my translation).

40. See Jeanne Lafont, "Topology and Efficiency," in *Lacan: Topologically Speaking*, ed. Ellie Ragland and Dragan Milovanovic (New York: Other Press, 2004), 3–27.

41. Lafont, "Topology and Efficiency," 6.

42. Gérard Genette, *Mimologics*, trans. Thaïs E. Morgan (Lincoln: University of Nebraska Press, 1995), 300.

43. Émile Benveniste, *Problems in General Linguistics*, trans. Mary Elizabeth Meek (Coral Gables, Fla.: University of Miami Press, 1971), 224.

44. As cited and translated in Genette, *Mimologics*, 297.

45. Jacques Derrida, *Signsponge/Signéponge* (bilingual edition), trans. Richard Rand (New York: Columbia University Press, 1984), 54–55, 92–93.

46. I refer here to the crystalline pages on Ponge in Marder's Ph.D. dissertation, which I hope she will publish one day: "Human, None Too Human: Readings in Literature, Psychoanalysis and Film" (Yale University, 1989); see chapter 4, "What Speaks: Reading Ponge's Smile" (106–28), and chapter 5, "Successive Failures in Ponge" (129–84).

47. See the notes to Ponge, *Œuvres complètes*, 1:906.

48. Francis Ponge, *Selected Poems*, trans. C. K. Williams, John Montague, and Margaret Guiton, ed. Margaret Guiton (Winston-Salem, N.C.: Wake Forest

University Press, 1994), 37. The poems I quote are translated by C. K. Williams unless stated otherwise.

49. Marder, "Human, None Too Human," 125. In *Words of Light: Theses on the Photography of History* (Princeton, N.J.: Princeton University Press, 1997), Eduardo Cadava also calls the mollusk "the perfect autobiographical form" in that "it registers, inscribes and imprints every moment of the process whereby what is living is petrified" and thus "names a kind of rhythm of the transit between life and death" (122). Cadava offers his meditation on the mollusk by way of commentary on Walter Benjamin's account in *Berlin Childhood* of a childhood visit to a photography studio: "I dwelt in the nineteenth century as a mollusk dwells in its shell, and the century now lies hollow before me like an empty shell. I hold it to my ear" (quoted in *Words of Light*, 109). Cadava evocatively unravels the thread that allows the mollusk to serve as a potent analogon for a photographic conception of subjecthood: "Like a slow-motion, time lapse camera [the shell] in fact records every second of the mollusk's life" (121). The poignancy of the relation in both cases is that a likeness (of shell to mollusk, of image to self) at a certain point turns into—or is revealed as—difference, leading to the truth that there is no representation of self without a disappearance (and doubling) of self. "In the exposure of self that is the photograph, the intimacy of being is traversed by exteriority" (115). A note on page 152 makes clear that Cadava has discussed fruitfully with Marder mollusks as well as the Ponge connection.

50. In this closing line of Carroll's "nonsense" poem "The Hunting of the Snark," the Snark (an auspicious prey animal and the intended object of the long chase), once found, turns out to be, unfortunately, the Boojum (for some Snarks are Boojums), a frightful being whose encounter causes the hunter to "softly and suddenly vanish away." Lewis Carroll, *The Complete Illustrated Works* (New York: Gramercy Books, 1995), 206.

51. Marder, "Human, None Too Human," 127.

52. Ponge, *Œuvres complètes*, 1:40 / *Selected Poems*, 67; translation modified.

53. "Speech speaks," writes Marder. "It is not our property but our means of survival. We do not survive as ourselves, but as that unknown race we are yet to become. And if we speak well, we can be spoken by it" (128). And it is true that Ponge in the last lines of "Notes pour un coquillage" writes the most unequivocally about a world that will outlive the human: "Then, after all the animals have died out, air and little grains of sand will slowly penetrate it, while it still shines and erodes upon the ground and gradually disaggregates into sparkles: oh sterile, impalpable dust, oh brilliant residue, though endlessly churned and kneaded between the millstones of air and sea there will come an AT LAST! No one's there any longer [*L'on n'est plus là*] to make anything anything more, even glass, out of sand, and IT'S ALL OVER!" (Ponge, *Œuvres complètes*, 1:40–41 / *Selected Poems*, 67).

54. See Benveniste's well-known analysis of the pronouns "I" and "you": "Language wards off th[e] danger [of intersubjective communication requiring a unique self-identifying word—and by extension a unique language—for every speaker] by insituting a unique but mobile sign, *I*, which can be assumed by each speaker on the condition that he refers each time only to the instance of

his own discourse [*un ensemble de signes 'vides,' non référentiels par rapport à la 'réalité,' toujours disponibles, et qui deviennent 'pleins' dès qu'un locuteur les assume dans chaque instance de son discours*]"; "the indicators *I* and *You* cannot exist as potentialities; they exist only insofar as they are actualized in the instance of discourse, in which, by each of their own instances, they mark the process of appropriation by the speaker." Émile Benveniste, *Problèmes de linguistique générale* (Paris: Gallimard, 1966), 1:254–55 / *Problems in General Linguistics*, 220.

55. Gilles Deleuze, *Logique du sens* (Paris: Minuit, 1969), 44 / *Logic of Sense*, trans. Mark Lester with Charles Stivale (New York: Columbia University Press, 1990), 31.

56. "This form situates the agency of the ego [*l'instance du moi*], before its social determination, in a fictional direction [*dans une ligne de fiction*] that will always remain irreducible for the individual alone, or rather, which will only rejoin the coming-into-being [*le devenir*] of the subject asymptotically, whatever the success of the dialectical syntheses by which he must resolve as *I* his discordance with his own reality." Jacques Lacan, *Écrits* (Paris: Seuil, 1999), 93 / *Écrits: A Selection*, trans. Alan Sheridan (Bristol, U.K.: Tavistock/Routledge, 1989), 2.

57. Darrieussecq cites Lacan in several places in *Rapport de police*, including in these few lines that reveal the extent to which her fascination with the "I" owes something to the psychoanalyst: "I is another [*Je est un autre*]: a scissoring that opens the I, and fills it with this thinking emptiness [*ce vide qui pense*]. Who is thinking when I am thinking? Where is it thinking? [*Où est-ce que ça pense?*] 'I think where I am not, and I am where I think not,' famous formula by Lacan to describe the unconscious" (240; my translation).

58. Jacques Derrida, *Séminaire: La bête et le souverain*, vol. 2: *2002–2003* (Paris: Galilée, 2010), 54–55 / *The Beast and the Sovereign*, vol. 2, trans. Geoffrey Bennington (Chicago: University of Chicago Press, 2011), 26–27.

59. The interview with Maurizio Ferraris (with questions translated from Italian to French by Charles Alunni) was originally published in *Aut aut* 235 (January–February 1990), shortly after the publication of Derrida's response to *Che cos'è la poesia?*

60. If one looks more closely at Heidegger's text, it appears that what Derrida remembers as a mimicked objection is in fact offered as an account in Heidegger's own voice of the perplexing fact that difference is not something that the thinker brings to Being/beings, inserting it between them, but rather that it is precisely by virtue of difference that Being presents itself *as* beings, and can be accessed in no other way, that is, can never *not* present itself in difference. And that therefore thinking would be deluded to think that it contributes something—difference—*to* Being/beings. In other words, far from claiming to himself be making such a contribution (which is how Derrida remembers it), Heidegger is rather telling us that difference is resolutely not of the order of representation but of the order of actualized ontology. Arguably, this does not fundamentally alter the association of the hedgehog with the logic of what can have arrived before it has completed its journey, and in a sense before it has even left—unless it is to say that the Grimm tale is an even more fundamental and sincere "hypotext" for Heidegger than Derrida remembered, and that perhaps

in certain key passages is a continual replay of the effects of a hedgehog "trick": "Being does not leave its own place and go over to beings, as though beings were first without Being and could be approached by Being subsequently. Being transits (that), comes unconcealingly over (that) which arrives as something of itself unconcealed only by that coming-over [*Überkommnis*]. Arrival means: to keep concealed in unconcealedness—to abide present in this keeping—to be a being." Martin Heidegger, *Identity and Difference*, trans. Joan Stambaugh (Chicago: University of Chicago Press, 1969), 64.

61. Catachresis in this sense is central to Derrida's thinking. See his "Mythologie blanche: La métaphore dans le texte philosophique," in *Marges de la philosophie* (Paris: Minuit, 1972) / "White Mythology: Metaphor in the Text of Philosophy," trans. F. C. T. Moore, in *Margins of Philosophy* (Chicago: University of Chicago Press, 1982).

62. Of course, there could be other ways of telling the story of the fate of animals in Western thought—for example, by considering Foucault's account in *Les mots et les choses* (*The Order of Things*) of the passage from the order of natural history to that of biology, where animals go from being living things sharing the space of representation with language (and thus as frankly visible as they were describable) to being grave embodiments of life and death, their essence submerged in the unseen depths of the material realm, as if on the far side of language. And in a deep sense, the two accounts (Foucault's and Ferraris's) might not be incompatible, given that both place the animal on the side of death and provide a telling of how an idea of man emerged in the place of and against the animal. But the question of where the animal stands vis-à-vis the letter (even in the effort to map the points of contact between the two accounts) proves more difficult (and ultimately richer) a question—precisely one that literature stages and responds to over and over again, if never definitively ("For thinking concerning the animal, if there is such a thing, derives from poetry": see below).

63. Carla Freccero, "Chercher la chatte: Derrida's Queer Feminine Animality," in *French Thinking about Animals*, ed. Louisa Mackenzie and Stephanie Posthumus (East Lansing: Michigan State University Press, 2015), 105–20.

64. Lewis Carroll, *Aventures d'Alice au pays des merveilles*, trans. Henri Bué (New York: Dover, 1972), 84. The English translation is mine.

65. Jean-Luc Nancy, *À plus d'un titre: Jacques Derrida. Sur un portrait de Valerio Adami* (Paris: Galilée, 2007), 37; emphasis in original; my translation. Alain David, discussing Levinas in "Cynesthèse," also refers to the cat's grin (as a hypallage—a quality emancipated from the object—and) as a paradigm for thinking the mode of presence of the dead: "Comment sourient les morts? Ce sourire ne peut que s'extraire d'une chaire absente pour apparaître seul, pareil au sourire du chat du Cheshire, dans *Alice au pays des merveilles.*" Alain David, "Cynesthèse: Autoportrait au chien," in *L'animal autobiographique: Autour de Jacques Derrida*, ed. Marie-Louise Mallet (Paris: Galilée, 1999), 307.

66. Marie-Dominique Garnier, "Animal Writes: Derrida's *Que Donc* and Other Tails," in *Demenageries*, ed. Anne-Emmanuelle Berger and Marta Segarra (Amsterdam: Rodopi, 2011), 33–38.

67. Thus I retraced this parasitical element. See Lewis Carroll, *Alice au pays des merveilles et Ce qu'Alice trouva de l'autre côté du miroir*, trans. Jacques

Papy (Paris: Jean-Jacques Pauvert, 1961), 91, 98, 134–38. It remains intriguing that the philosophers would carry it over at all, since Derrida quotes systematically from the English original, and since Denise Paul "Fanny" Granjouan, Deleuze's wife and close cothinker, was an Anglicist.

68. Jacques Derrida, *The Work of Mourning*, ed. Michael Naas and Pascale-Anne Brault (Chicago: University of Chicago Press, 2001), 195. Thanks to David Wills for helping me verify that this was indeed the only other reference to Carroll in Derrida's work.

EPILOGUE

1. The lack of a hermit crab poem per se should be nuanced to some extent, as the hermit crab receives rather glorious mention in Ponge's "Notes toward a Shellfish": "Quand le seigneur sort de sa demeure il fait certes moins d'impression que lorsque le bernard-l'hermite laisse apercevoir sa monstrueuse pince à l'embouchure du superbe cornet qui l'héberge." / "A lord emerging from his manor is a far less impressive sight than the monstrous claw of a hermit crab glimpsed at the mouthpiece of the magnificent corner which shelters him." Ponge, "Notes pour un coquillage," in *Œuvres complètes*, ed. Bernard Beugnot (Paris: Gallimard, 2002), 1:39 / "Notes toward a Shellfish," in *Selected Poems*, trans. C. K. Williams, John Montague, and Margaret Guiton, ed. Margaret Guiton (Winston-Salèm, N.C.: Wake Forest University Press, 1994), 65.

2. For Darrieussecq novels that mention hermit crabs, see *Bref séjour chez les vivants* (Paris: POL, 2001), 30, 52–53, 59–61, 65, 214 / *A Brief Stay with the Living*, trans. Ian Monk (London: Faber and Faber, 2003), 17, 33, 39–40, 43, 155; *Le pays* [The country] (Paris: POL, 2005), 183; *Naissance des fantômes* (Paris: Gallimard, 1998), 80 / *My Phantom Husband*, trans. Esther Allen (New York: New Press, 1999), 71. And there could well be more that when I last checked had retracted momentarily from view.

3. *Le bernard l'ermite, crustacé marin: Un documentaire de Jean Painlevé*, 1930; "experimental[ly]" because, as the voice-over makes clear, "In the sea there are a lot of shells, and many more shells than hermit crabs. This housing crisis is therefore purely experimental." All translations from Painlevé are my own.

4. The most dramatic sequences of *Le bernard l'ermite* feature indeed beautiful symphonic scores composed by Vincenzo Bellini.

5. The Wikipedia entry on the hermit crab (accessed January 3, 2018) in turn cites as its references the following publications: Randi D. Rotjan, Jeffrey R. Chabot, and Sara M. Lewis, "Social Context of Shell Acquisition in *Coenobita clypeatus* Hermit Crabs," *Behavioral Ecology* 21, no. 3 (2010): 639–46, doi:10.1093/beheco/arq027; Ferris Jabr, "On a Tiny Caribbean Island, Hermit Crabs Form Sophisticated Social Networks," *Scientific American*, June 5, 2012; and Robert Sanders, "Hermit Crabs Socialize to Evict Their Neighbors," October 26, 2012, University of California, Berkeley.

6. Wikipedia again (accessed January 3, 2018). Excerpts from the "Vacancy Chain" article quoted here cite Lawrence Pinfield, *The Operation of Internal*

Labor Markets (New York: Plenum Press and Chase, 1995); Ivan D., "Vacancy Chains," *Annual Review of Sociology* 17 (1991): 133–54.

7. Darrieussecq had been determined not to publish her dissertation and in the introduction to *Rapport de police* vows that this is the only nonfictional essay she will ever publish. See *Rapport de police* (Paris: POL, 2010), 27). That a writer so committed to exorbitant expropriating understandings of self, who in *Le pays* had evoked a "thinking without a subject" (35) and even proposed a cleft *j/e* as the truest cipher-pronoun, should have been charged by another with "singerie" (apeing) and with laying her eggs in another bird's nest is highly ironic—indeed, a misrecognition of species as well as a misrecognition of stakes. Shouldn't it have been obvious that Darrieussecq's *j/e* is not a monkey nor a cuckoo but a (radical) *hermit crab*?

8. At this point it should be clear that even if hermit crabs are singularly suited to revealing the structure in question, *every thing* has this obscure, thankless function or fantasy of partly providing a name for "nothing."

9. Jean Baudrillard, *L'échange impossible* (Paris: Galilée, 1999), 16 / *Impossible Exchange*, trans. Chris Turner (London: Verso, 2001), 7.

Index

FLASHPOINTS

1. *On Pain of Speech: Fantasies of the First Order and the Literary Rant,* Dina Al-Kassim
2. *Moses and Multiculturalism,* Barbara Johnson, with a foreword by Barbara Rietveld
3. *The Cosmic Time of Empire: Modern Britain and World Literature,* Adam Barrows
4. *Poetry in Pieces: César Vallejo and Lyric Modernity,* Michelle Clayton
5. *Disarming Words: Empire and the Seductions of Translation in Egypt,* Shaden M. Tageldin
6. *Wings for Our Courage: Gender, Erudition, and Republican Thought,* Stephanie H. Jed
7. *The Cultural Return,* Susan Hegeman
8. *English Heart, Hindi Heartland: The Political Life of Literature in India,* Rashmi Sadana
9. *The Cylinder: Kinematics of the Nineteenth Century,* Helmut Müller-Sievers
10. *Polymorphous Domesticities: Pets, Bodies, and Desire in Four Modern Writers,* Juliana Schiesari
11. *Flesh and Fish Blood: Postcolonialism, Translation, and the Vernacular,* S. Shankar
12. *The Fear of French Negroes: Transcolonial Collaboration in the Revolutionary Americas,* Sara E. Johnson
13. *Figurative Inquisitions: Conversion, Torture, and Truth in the Luso-Hispanic Atlantic,* Erin Graff Zivin
14. *Cosmopolitan Desires: Global Modernity and World Literature in Latin America,* Mariano Siskind
15. *Fiction Beyond Secularism,* Justin Neuman
16. *Periodizing Jameson: Dialectics, the University, and the Desire for Narrative,* Phillip E. Wegner
17. *The Practical Past,* Hayden White
18. *The Powers of the False: Reading, Writing, Thinking Beyond Truth and Fiction,* Doro Wiese
19. *The Object of the Atlantic: Concrete Aesthetics in Cuba, Brazil, and Spain, 1868–1968,* Rachel Price
20. *Epic and Exile: Novels of the German Popular Front 1933–1945,* Hunter Bivens
21. *An Innocent Abroad: Lectures in China,* J. Hillis Miller
22. *Form and Instability: East Europe, Literature, Postimperial Difference,* Anita Starosta
23. *Bombay Modern: Arun Kolatkar and Bilingual Literary Culture,* Anjali Nerlekar
24. *Intimate Relations: Social Reform and the Late Nineteenth-Century South Asian Novel,* Krupa Shandilya
25. *Media Laboratories: Late Modernist Authorship in South America,* Sarah Ann Wells
26. *Acoustic Properties: Radio, Narrative, and the New Neighborhood of the Americas,* Tom McEnaney

27. *The New Woman: Literary Modernism, Queer Theory, and the Trans Feminine Allegory*, Emma Heaney
28. *Civilizing War: Imperial Politics and the Poetics of National Rupture*, Nasser Mufti
29. *Late Colonial Sublime: Neo-Epics and the End of Romanticism*, G. S. Sahota
30. *Globalizing Race: Anti-Semitism, Empire, and the Politics of Scale in Modern French and European Culture*, Dorian Bell
31. *Domestications: American Empire, Literary Culture, and the Postcolonial Lens*, Hosam Mohamed AboulEla
32. *Behold an Animal: Four Exorbitant Readings*, Thangam Ravindranathan